SharePoint® 2007 Collaboration For Dummies®

Typical Elements of a SharePoint Site's Home Page

The typical home page of a SharePoint site uses the Team Site t
elements that enable you and your team members to navigate th
called the Left and Right Web Part zones.

D1298158

Site Logo

Content Navigation Breadcrumbs

Search box

Site Title   Site Tabs   Site Description   Welcome Menu

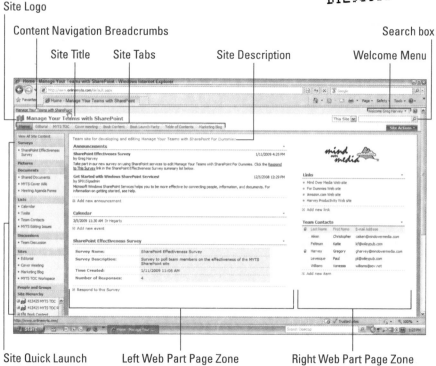

Site Quick Launch   Left Web Part Page Zone   Right Web Part Page Zone

List and Library Page Keyboard Shortcuts

Keys to Press	Result
Alt+N	Selects New menu
Alt+C	Selects Actions menu
Alt+I	Selects Settings menu

For Dummies: Bestselling Book Series for Beginners

SharePoint® 2007 Collaboration For Dummies®

Cheat Sheet

General Site Keyboard Shortcuts

Keys to Press	Result
Alt+1	Selects the Home Site tab
Alt+3	Selects the View All Site Content link
Alt+6	Selects the Help button
Alt+/ (forward slash)	Selects the Actions button
Alt+S	Selects the site's Search box
Alt+L	Selects the site's Welcome menu button

Top Ten Challenges to Successful Collaboration

1. Teams need to clearly understand their responsibilities in order to have any chance of achieving the goals of the collaboration.

2. Behind every successful team there needs to stand an effective team leader.

3. Teams have to have easy access to the information they need to make decisions and get their work done.

4. A team is only as strong as its weakest member.

5. You're never going to respond to a message you never receive.

6. You can't begin to deal with issues until someone tells you that they're there.

7. Issues always come up when people work closely together — it's how they're resolved that counts.

8. The open give and take of ideas is often what sparks real creativity in the group.

9. Tasks that don't get assigned in a timely manner don't have any chance of getting done by their due dates.

10. You can't measure the success of the collaboration if you can't measure your teams' performance.

For Dummies: Bestselling Book Series for Beginners

SharePoint® 2007 Collaboration

FOR DUMMIES®

SharePoint® 2007 Collaboration

FOR

DUMMIES®

by Greg Harvey

WILEY

Wiley Publishing, Inc.

SharePoint® 2007 Collaboration For Dummies®

Published by
Wiley Publishing, Inc.
111 River Street
Hoboken, NJ 07030-5774

www.wiley.com

WILEY

About the Author

Greg Harvey has authored tons of computer books, the most recent being *Manage Your Life with Outlook For Dummies* and the most popular being *Excel 2007 For Dummies* and *Excel 2007 All-In-One Desk Reference For Dummies*. He started out training business users on how to use IBM personal computers and their attendant computer software in the rough and tumble days of DOS, WordStar, and Lotus 1-2-3 in the mid-1980s of the last century. After working for a number of independent training firms, he went on to teach semester-long courses in spreadsheet and database management software at Golden Gate University in San Francisco.

His love of teaching has translated into an equal love of writing. *For Dummies* books are, of course, his all-time favorites to write because they enable him to write to his favorite audience: the beginner. They also enable him to use humor (a key element to success in the training room) and, most delightful of all, to express an opinion or two about the subject matter at hand.

Greg received his doctorate in Humanities in Philosophy and Religion with a concentration in Asian Studies and Comparative Religion last May. Everyone is glad that Greg was finally able to get out of school before he retired.

For the past two years, he has been actively researching productivity in the modern workplace and the various ideas and systems developed for improving work/life balance and improving teamwork and ensuring successful collaboration, using Microsoft's Outlook and SharePoint software, respectively.

Dedication

To all the readers who supported my work over my astonishing and long-lived career in technical publishing

Author's Acknowledgments

Let me take this opportunity to thank all the people, both at Wiley Publishing, Inc., and at Mind over Media, Inc., whose dedication and talent combined to get this book out and into your hands in such great shape.

At Wiley Publishing, Inc., I want to thank Andy Cummings and Katie Feltman for their encouragement and help in getting this project under way and their ongoing support every step of the way. I also want to thank Paul Levesque for his encouragement and for making sure that the project stayed on course and made it into production so that all the talented folks on the production team could create this great final product.

At Mind over Media, I want to thank Christopher Aiken for his review of the manuscript and invaluable input and suggestions on how best to address both the theoretical and more practical concerns of forming successful teams and collaborating using SharePoint.

Publisher's Acknowledgments

We're proud of this book; please send us your comments through our online registration form located at `http://dummies.custhelp.com`. For other comments, please contact our Customer Care Department within the U.S. at 877-762-2974, outside the U.S. at 317-572-3993, or fax 317-572-4002.

Some of the people who helped bring this book to market include the following:

Acquisitions, Editorial

Senior Project Editor: Paul Levesque

Senior Acquisitions Editor: Katie Feltman

Copy Editor: Virginia Sanders

Technical Editor: John Mueller

Editorial Manager: Leah Cameron

Media Development Assistant Producers: Angela Denny, Josh Frank, and Shawn Patrick

Editorial Assistant: Amanda Foxworth

Sr. Editorial Assistant: Cherie Case

Cartoons: Rich Tennant (`www.the5thwave.com`)

Composition Services

Project Coordinator: Katherine Key

Layout and Graphics: Reuben W. Davis, Christine Williams

Proofreader: Laura L. Bowman

Indexer: Cheryl Duksta

Publishing and Editorial for Technology Dummies

  Richard Swadley, Vice President and Executive Group Publisher

  Andy Cummings, Vice President and Publisher

  Mary Bednarek, Executive Acquisitions Director

  Mary C. Corder, Editorial Director

Publishing for Consumer Dummies

  Diane Graves Steele, Vice President and Publisher

Composition Services

  Debbie Stailey, Director of Composition Services

Contents at a Glance

Table of Contents

Introduction

SharePoint has certainly come a long way since the days of SharePoint Team Services, an early attempt by Microsoft to offer the general business user an opportunity to participate directly in online information sharing. I'm happy to say that SharePoint 2007, through the combination of Windows SharePoint Services 3.0 and Microsoft Office SharePoint Server 2007 technologies, now offers you a plethora of collaborative tools. These tools make all sorts of information sharing and collaboration not only possible but easily within the reach of any businessperson with a modicum of computer experience using a Web browser and common Office applications such as Outlook, Word, and Excel.

This book on using SharePoint 2007 for information sharing is very different from the many others published to date. It is *not* intended for the IT professional who wants to know what makes SharePoint tick and how he can get under the hood and rev it up for the enterprise solutions at hand. (Please see Vanessa Williams's excellent book, *Microsoft SharePoint 2007 For Dummies,* from Wiley Publishing, if this happens to be you.)

Rather, this book speaks directly to the business users who have *absolutely* no interest in SharePoint beyond what it can offer them in the way of information sharing and team collaboration. Here, there's no peeking under the hood. In fact, I purposively shy away from discussing the technical underpinnings of SharePoint. I assume that this kind of chatter is of no interest to the typical business user and does little or nothing to answer the essential question of this work; namely, "How do I make this rather strange, Web-oriented space a place where my teams can readily access the information they need and successfully collaborate on the project that brings them together?"

The purpose of this book is to open the door for the typical businessperson to the multifaceted world of information sharing offered by SharePoint 2007. I wholeheartedly believe that this software offers you a great environment for collaboration, and it's my sincere hope that this book helps you make the most of it.

How to Use This Book

This book isn't meant to be read from beginning to end or from cover to cover. Although its chapters are loosely organized in a logical order, each topic covered in a chapter is really meant to stand pretty much on its own. It's really up to you to figure out where you need to go and what information will be of most help.

This book is like a reference in which you start out by looking up the topic you need information about (either in the table of contents or the index), and then you refer directly to the section of interest. I explain most topics conversationally (as though you were in my office). Sometimes, however, my regiment-commander mentality takes over, and I list the steps you need to take to accomplish a particular task in a particular section.

I do recommend that you start, at the very least, by perusing the glossary and the Part of Tens. Starting at the end of the book can help you get a handle on the unavoidable SharePoint jargon and grasp some of the basic steps that you'll need to take to get your SharePoint site ready for collaboration. After that, it's off to the chapters that give you the detailed information you need to shift the collaboration into high gear.

Foolish Assumptions

The only assumption I make about you, dear reader (other than you're highly motivated to find out what exactly SharePoint is and what it can do for you), is that you have access to a new SharePoint site (using at least Windows SharePoint Services 3.0, if not Microsoft Office SharePoint Server 2007 as well). And further, you must customize this new SharePoint site and get it ready for your teams to use in some sort of collaborative project.

I also make one other foolish assumption; namely, that your new SharePoint site has the same basic layout and elements as the one shown in many of the figures throughout this book. Just be aware that although the layout shown in these figures is the one that most new SharePoint sites are based upon, it is by no means the only one that can be used; your IT department may select a different layout for your new site.

Also, be aware that SharePoint comprises a wide variety of different technologies and features, not of all which may be installed and activated by your IT department or SharePoint hosting service on your new SharePoint site. This means that your site may have some additional options that you don't see in the figures shown in this book. Likewise, some of the options shown in a few of the figures may not be available on your SharePoint site. By and large, however, you shouldn't have any trouble following along with the text and figures in this book, because the vast majority of the features and options that I cover here are standard to all SharePoint sites.

As for your experience and skill level with SharePoint, it really doesn't matter whether you've ever had the opportunity to visit a SharePoint site, let alone customize one. The important thing is that you maintain a willingness both to explore aspects of this program that are new to you and to adopt a new perspective towards those aspects with which you're already familiar.

Beyond that, you simply need to be open to developing the skills you need to provide your teams with everything they need to successfully collaborate. Remember that there are no gold stars for knowing more about SharePoint and its hundreds of features. In fact, the only brownie points given are for knowing how to use those SharePoint features to your best advantage in fostering information sharing and collaboration among your teams.

How This Book Is Organized

This book is organized in five parts. Each part contains two or more chapters with related content. Each chapter is further divided into loosely related sections that cover the basics of the topic at hand. You should not, however, get too hung up about following along with the structure of the book; ultimately, it doesn't matter at all if you find out how to manage your SharePoint Tasks lists before you find out how to schedule events for your teams in the SharePoint Calendar list. The important thing is that you find the information — and understand it when you find it — when you need to explore a new aspect of teamwork using SharePoint to achieve it.

In case you're interested, here's a synopsis of what you find in each part that follows.

Part 1: Implementing SharePoint Collaboration

The three chapters in this part set the stage for using SharePoint as your primary collaborative tool. They not only give basic information on what SharePoint is and what it can do for you, but they also give you the basics on customizing the site to suit your teams and giving them access to the new SharePoint site.

Part II: Managing Your SharePoint Data

The two chapters in this part give you an overview of SharePoint's data capabilities. Chapter 4 acquaints you with *data lists,* the fundamental SharePoint component used in information sharing. Chapter 5 then gives you the lowdown on using *libraries,* the basic SharePoint component used to give your teams access to all the supporting documents they need.

Part III: Getting the Most Out of Your SharePoint Site

SharePoint 2007 features many specialized components designed to foster different collaborative experiences. The chapters in this part explore the major ones that you'll typically use in the course of your collaboration.

Chapter 6 shows you how to use meeting workspaces to manage your team meetings. Chapter 7 acquaints you with using surveys and discussion boards to get feedback from your teams. Chapter 8 discusses enhancing interaction among team members using SharePoint blogs (Web logs) and Wiki pages (Web pages that the teams can easily edit and change). Chapter 9 takes up the subject of the team editing of documents that you place in a special document workspace. Finally, Chapter 10 looks at task management by showing you how to create and use various types of task lists and workflows to assign tasks as well as to monitor them.

Part IV: Using Office Programs with SharePoint

SharePoint's tight integration with many of the programs in the Office 2007 suite is the subject of this part. Chapter 11 explores ways you can connect SharePoint to Outlook 2007 so that you can access its information from the comfort of your own Inbox. Chapter 12 looks at ways you can use the two mainstays of Office, Word and Excel, with SharePoint. Chapter 13 introduces you to Office SharePoint Designer 2007 (Microsoft's new Web design software for SharePoint sites) and shows you how you can use its Workflow Designer to create custom workflows for your SharePoint task lists. Chapter 14 investigates the connection between InfoPath 2007 (Microsoft's electronic forms application) and SharePoint and how to use InfoPath to customize form templates that you publish in special SharePoint form libraries.

Part V: The Part of Tens

The two chapters in the final part give you access to two of my top ten lists. Chapter 15 gives you my top ten tips on customizing a new SharePoint site and getting it ready for your teams. Chapter 16 then gives you the rundown of the top ten challenges that you must meet in order to ensure a successful collaborative experience with SharePoint.

Conventions Used in This Book

When it comes to menu commands, this book uses command arrows to lead you from the initial pull-down menu, to any submenus, finally to the command option you ultimately want. For example, if you need to customize the content of a particular Web Part (a special box in which reusable content is displayed) on your SharePoint page using the pull-down menu on its Edit button, that instruction would look like this: Choose Edit⇨Modify Shared Web Part.

Also, if you're really observant, you may notice a slight discrepancy between the capitalization of the names of options in windows and dialog boxes (such as headings, links, option buttons, and check boxes) as they appear in the book and how they actually appear in SharePoint on your computer screen. I intentionally use the convention of capitalizing the initial letters of all the main words of a dialog box option to help you differentiate the name of the option from the rest of the text describing its use. So, for example, you may see the instruction, "type the name of the new site's Web page in the URL Name text box" in the book even though this text box actually appears as "URL name" on the New SharePoint Site page.

Special icons

The following icons are strategically placed in the margins to point out stuff you may or may not want to read.

This icon alerts you to nerdy discussions that you may well want to skip (or read when no one else is around).

This icon alerts you to shortcuts or other valuable hints related to the topic at hand.

This icon alerts you to information to keep in mind if you want to meet with a modicum of success.

This icon alerts you to information to keep in mind if you want to avert some dire future problems.

Where to Go from Here

I have a couple of suggestions for where to go from here (after you get a chuckle from the great Rich Tennant cartoons). You may want to go directly to the glossary to check out the SharePoint jargon and then take a gander at the Part of Tens to check out my top ten lists: Chapter 15 describes ways to customize your SharePoint site, and then Chapter 16 explains the challenges you and your teams need to meet to ensure a happy and productive collaborative experience with SharePoint. Otherwise, I suggest you start by taking a look at the material in Chapter 1 and using its information and suggestions to get a feel for what SharePoint is and what it can do for you.

Part I

Implementing SharePoint Collaboration

The 5th Wave   By Rich Tennant

"We're helping Dave test his new network prototype."

In this part . . .

Getting your SharePoint site ready for your teams to use is the theme of this part, and it's one of the most important tasks you'll undertake. Here, you get a basic overview of what SharePoint is and how you can use it to further collaboration. You also get vital information on how to customize your SharePoint site to fit the needs of your team. Finally, you find out about giving your teams access to the new SharePoint site and inviting them to start using it.

Chapter 1

Collaborating with SharePoint

*W*ebster's dictionary defines collaboration — from the Latin for *laboring together* — first and foremost as "working jointly or together especially in an intellectual endeavor." As you find out in this chapter, SharePoint 2007 makes this kind of "working together" especially easy and efficient. SharePoint makes it possible for your teams to readily access the information they need to make decisions and to share essential ideas and feedback.

This chapter begins by describing what exactly SharePoint 2007 is before moving on to explaining just a wee bit about how it does its magic. (I cover just enough of the magic, mind you, to give you a basic understanding of how you and your teams interface with the software in the process of collaborating and yet hopefully not enough to overwhelm you by drowning you in totally incomprehensible geek speak.) As part and parcel of this general introduction to the wondrous workings of SharePoint 2007, I also introduce you to each of the major components that make up this very versatile software tool.

The chapter then goes on to give you all the information you need on navigating a typical SharePoint site before grounding you in the use of its online help system to which, in addition to this nifty reference, you can turn when you have questions about using a particular SharePoint feature.

Using SharePoint to Collaborate

SharePoint 2007 offers a set of sophisticated Web-based software tools designed to make it easy for you to share essential information with all the members of your teams. SharePoint also can enable team members to freely share their ideas and for you to effortlessly garner their feedback.

To help you understand how SharePoint does all these things, the following sections include a basic introduction to what SharePoint is and how it functions. Following this is a discussion of how your teams can put SharePoint's many features to good use to successfully accomplish a wide array of projects that benefit from good, old-fashioned teamwork coupled with high-tech collaboration.

Discovering what SharePoint is and how it works

Don't feel bad at all if you're not really sure what exactly SharePoint is and what it does. (You are by no means alone in your bewilderment.) The confusion stems mainly from the fact that SharePoint's *not* like the typical Microsoft software programs you find in the Office suite, such as Word, Excel, and PowerPoint.

In fact, rather than any sort of unified application program, SharePoint represents a conglomeration of totally Web-based technologies that have frequently changed names and identities in a rather short period of time. As of the writing of this book, Microsoft markets its SharePoint technology in the following two forms:

- ✔ **Windows SharePoint Services 3.0 (WSS):** The core SharePoint technology available as a free download that runs on Windows Server 2003/2008. WSS provides the basic platform that makes it possible for you and your teams to build the sites that enable information sharing and collaboration.

- ✔ **Microsoft Office SharePoint Server 2007 (MOSS):** An extension of Windows SharePoint Services that expands the capabilities of the basic WSS platform to enable the development of enterprise business solutions. This product is licensed by Microsoft in several different versions, the basic two being the Standard Edition and Enterprise Edition. The Standard Edition gives you enhanced features in the area of content management, search, portal, and collaboration, and the Enterprise Edition extends these enhancements to include extra business forms and intelligence features. (It's also *quite* expensive!)

From a technical standpoint, SharePoint 2007 actually refers to the combination of WSS 3.0 with some version of MOSS 2007. Informally, however, when people refer to SharePoint 2007 (or SharePoint, for short), they are actually not referring just to Windows SharePoint Services 3.0, the Web-based platform that does the bulk of the job in enabling the sharing of all kinds of data and information with your team members. Keep in mind, however, that this book covers only WSS 3.0 features under the generic name "SharePoint." The MOSS 2007 enhancements to the basic SharePoint platform offered by WSS 3.0 are well beyond this book's scope.

Keep in mind that Microsoft considers SharePoint 2007 as the core information sharing and collaboration platform for the entire 2007 Microsoft Office System. As a result, SharePoint 2007 technology is very closely integrated with the major Microsoft Office 2007 applications, such as Outlook, Word, and Excel. This is great news if you're currently a user of the latest version of Microsoft Office, and a great incentive to upgrade to Office 2007 if you're serious about using SharePoint 2007 for team collaboration and still haven't gotten around to upgrading your Office applications.

Because all of SharePoint's information sharing and collaboration services are Web-based, this means that you and your team members are going to access the shared information and collaborate with one another on the Web over the Internet. Normally, you'll do this with a Web browser such as Microsoft Internet Explorer or Mozilla Firefox running on a personal computer under Windows XP or Vista. You can, however, also access SharePoint information on a mobile device such as a cell phone that has Internet access and some form of a Web browser.

Understanding SharePoint as a Web-based technology

The following few practical issues are directly related to the fact that SharePoint is an entirely Web-based technology:

- **Displayed with Special Web Pages:** The information you choose to share with your teams is presented and accessed in the form of Web sites with a special type of Web page (*a la* ASP.NET 3.0) whose content and structure you can modify directly from within your Web browser or by using a special editing program such as Office SharePoint Designer 2007. (See Chapter 13 for more on using this program.)

- **Accessed via Web Browser:** You and your teams can access the information on SharePoint sites from any Internet-ready device. Instead of having to have the right software installed on the device, you only need a valid user ID and password in order to gain access to the SharePoint sites with some sort of Web browser.

Delivered by Web Server: As a Web-based technology, SharePoint requires the use of some sort of Web server to house the WSS and MOSS software along with the SharePoint team sites and the documents and data that you share with your team members. This Web server can either be one maintained by your company in house or one hosted externally by a professional Internet provider that offers SharePoint 2007 technology. (A bunch of service providers host SharePoint sites — to locate one, do a Web search for "SharePoint 2007 hosting.")

Discovering how teams can use SharePoint to successfully collaborate

Assuming that you're an administrator of your SharePoint site, you can use SharePoint 2007 to facilitate the successful collaboration on most any type of business project that requires teams to share information and ideas with one another. SharePoint's many built-in site templates make it quick and easy to create specialized subsites that contain the elements appropriate for the type of information or idea sharing that your particular teams require.

The normal out-of-the-box site templates are organized into four major categories: Collaboration, Meetings, Application Templates, and Custom. If any of these ready-made templates don't give you exactly what you need, SharePoint makes it easy for you to customize almost any of the elements that a particular template happens to use.

Sharing information in SharePoint

A SharePoint team site enables you to make all sorts of information readily available to the members of the teams that need to access it in order to successfully collaborate with one another on a project.

The information you share on a SharePoint site typically is one of two forms:

- **Discrete files** such as Word documents, Excel workbooks, PowerPoint presentations, and even InfoPath electronic forms or graphics stored in a standard graphics file format such as JPEG or GIF
- **Data sets** stored within other Office application files, such as contacts from your Outlook personal data file, financial figures stored in an Excel workbook, or records stored in the tables of an Access database

In SharePoint, you add the discrete files you want to make available to your teams to *libraries* that you create for that particular type of document involved. You add data from other compatible files to a *list* that you create for that particular type of data.

Sharing ideas in SharePoint

In SharePoint 2007, you and your team members can share your ideas and collaborate with one another using any of the following SharePoint 2007 features:

- ✔ **Alerts:** Set alerts on site lists and libraries to automatically inform any or all of your team members by e-mail message of any changes you or other team members make, including changes to the existing content or the addition of new content.

- ✔ **Document workspace:** Set up a document workspace as a special place for housing a particular document or set of documents that requires collaborative input and editing.

- ✔ **Meeting workspace:** Set up a meeting workspace to inform team members of upcoming meetings and to provide them a common space for accessing any information pertinent to the meeting.

- ✔ **Survey:** Set up a survey to garner feedback from your team members about a particular issue of interest to the team or project.

- ✔ **Discussion board:** Set up a discussion board to provide a forum for your team members to discuss a particular issue using a threaded discussion format.

- ✔ **Wiki page:** Set up a wiki page to provide a page of content where any of your team members can freely edit the content and layout of the page as they see fit.

- ✔ **Blog site:** Set up a blog site to provide a discussion blog where your team members can post sequential responses to your thoughts or comments on issues of interest to the team or project.

Exploring the SharePoint Home Page

Figure 1-1 shows the typical home page of a new SharePoint site (the very one used in creating the book you're reading). The home page is the main page of any SharePoint site, the one that appears each time a team member with permission to access the SharePoint site logs on to it.

As you can see in this figure, a home page is divided basically into two unequal rows. The much narrower top row contains the basic global site navigation, command, and search controls. The much thicker bottom row is then divided into two sections. The section on the left contains a bank of controls for navigating the current site — referred to as the Quick Launch group list (Quick Launch, for short). The much larger section on the right side contains a place for listed content. This section, in turn, is divided into a wider left column that contains a place for new announcements and calendar events and a narrower right column with the Windows SharePoint Services logo and a place to add links to other Web sites that may be of interest to the team.

Top Link bar

View All Site Content   Lists   Site Actions

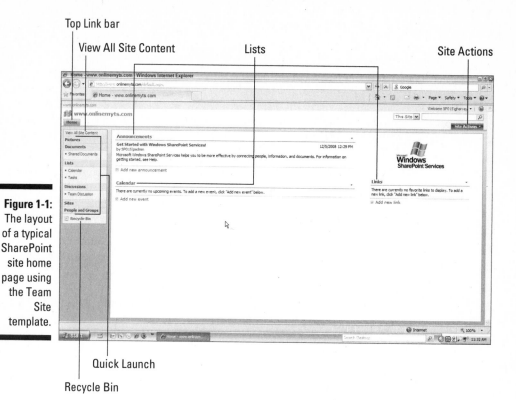

Figure 1-1:
The layout
of a typical
SharePoint
site home
page using
the Team
Site
template.

Quick Launch

Recycle Bin

Checking out the typical components of a SharePoint site

The home page of a new SharePoint site normally uses the Team Site template. This Team Site template introduces you to many of the components you'll typically encounter when creating and using your own SharePoint sites. These common elements include

✔ **Top Link bar:** Click the site tabs that appear in this bar to go to the top-level page of each subsite that you add to your main SharePoint site. When you first start work on a new SharePoint site, this bar contains only a Home site tab that, when clicked, takes you to the main or home page of your SharePoint site.

✔ **Site Actions:** Click this button to access a drop-down list with three options: Create (to add a new element to the current site), Edit Page (to add, delete, or modify elements on the current page), and Site Settings (to display a page showing overall site information and links for displaying pages with lists of particular elements).

✔ **View All Site Content:** Click this link to display a page showing all the SharePoint elements used in the current site, including a description of each and the last time it was modified.

✔ **Quick Launch:** Click the links in the Quick Launch group list to display pages showing filtered lists of various elements used in the site, including such components as picture and document libraries, lists of calendar events, tasks, team discussions, subsites, members permitted to use the site, and the Recycle Bin where you can rescue stuff you deleted but haven't yet permanently removed from the site.

✔ **Announcements, Calendar, and Links:** These areas display a listing of any site announcements, upcoming events, or links to other Web sites of interest that you add by clicking the Add New Announcement, Add New Event, or Add New Link hyperlink that appears at the bottom of each of these sections, respectively.

✔ **Windows SharePoint Service Logo:** This area displays the graphic image of the Windows SharePoint Service logo. You can easily replace this image with that of your own logo. (See Chapter 2 for details.)

✔ **Recycle Bin:** Click this link to display a page showing all the items from the site that you've deleted but haven't yet gotten rid of permanently.

Navigating a SharePoint site

As you'd expect from a totally Web-based application, many, if not most, of the controls on a SharePoint site are links. And just like links in any traditional Web site, when you position the mouse pointer over them, the pointer changes from an arrowhead to a hand pointer (and if the link is attached to some text, that text becomes underlined), indicating that you can click the link to make the jump to its target.

In addition to the many links that you typically encounter on a standard page of a SharePoint site, you'll also run into a few pull-down command menus (clustered in the upper-right corner of the top of the page). These menus are always indicated by the appearance of a standard drop-down button to the right of the command button's text, although most often you can open the drop-down list attached to the button by clicking anywhere on the button.

A tale of a trail of breadcrumbs

SharePoint sites display a couple of navigation controls that you don't find in your usual Office applications. These controls are referred to as *breadcrumbs,* and they're named after the Hansel and Gretel fairy tale in which a brother and sister leave a trail of breadcrumbs in a forest to find their way home only to have the crumbs eaten by wild animals.

In SharePoint 2007, you run into two types of breadcrumb navigation controls (both shown in Figure 1-2):

✔ **Global Navigation Breadcrumb:** This breadcrumb appears in the upper-left corner of a page. Normally, this breadcrumb contains only one link: that of the top-level site in a site collection (including all subsites). However, this breadcrumb does display other related links when you create subsites that aren't directly linked to the top-level site.

✔ **Content Navigation Breadcrumb:** This breadcrumb appears beneath the Home tab in the Top Link bar above the name or description of the current page whenever you follow links to pages on the top-level site or pages on subsites that you add. To jump back to a page that's on a previous or higher level, simply click its link in the breadcrumb trail that's separated by > (greater than) symbols.

You can use breadcrumb controls only to retrace steps that you've taken in a SharePoint site trail. This means that the last or current breadcrumb in the trail is informational only and never carries a live link. Keep in mind that with Web browsers such as Internet Explorer and Firefox you can also retrace your steps in a trail from the keyboard by pressing Alt+← as many times as needed and that you can jump directly to the top-level of a subsite by clicking the name of its tab. You can also quickly get to the home page of the entire SharePoint site by clicking the Home tab.

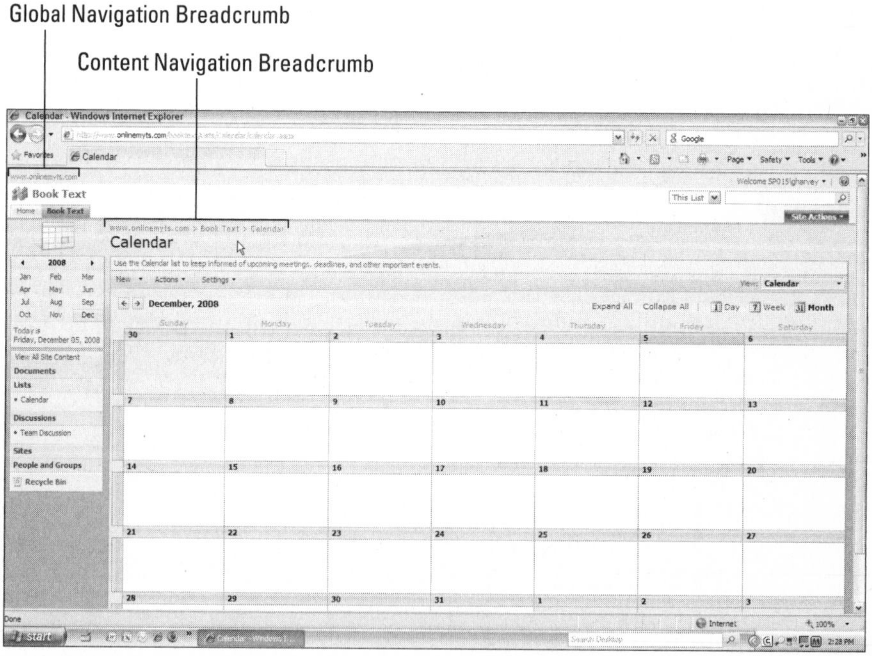

Global Navigation Breadcrumb

Content Navigation Breadcrumb

Figure 1-2: The Content Navigation Breadcrumb shows the path to the Calendar page of a Book Text subsite on the onlineMYTS SharePoint site.

Enabling and using the Tree View

SharePoint offers another nifty way to navigate your SharePoint site: Tree View. In this view, you get an additional hierarchical display of all the components on your SharePoint site, including any and all subcomponents. You can then expand and condense the items with subcomponents in the Tree View as you would a typical folder list in an Office application such as Outlook. You then click any of the components displayed in the Tree View to display its page on the SharePoint site.

Unfortunately, the Tree View is turned off when you first start working in SharePoint, so you have to enable it by following these simple steps:

1. **Log on to your SharePoint site by entering the URL address of your site in your Web browser and then entering your username and password when prompted for it.**

2. **On the home page, click the Site Actions button to open its drop-down menu.**

   The Site Actions drop-down menu on the home page contains three options: Create, Edit, and Site Settings.

3. **Click the Site Settings button.**

   SharePoint opens the Site Settings page.

4. **Click the Tree View link in the Look and Feel column (the second one from the left) of the Site Settings page.**

   SharePoint displays the Tree View page, which contains check boxes for enabling and disabling both the Quick Launch group list and the Tree View. (See Figure 1-3.)

5. **Select the Enable Tree View check box and then click OK.**

   SharePoint returns you to the Site Settings page.

6. **Click the Home tab in the Top Link bar.**

After you return to the home page of your SharePoint site after enabling the Tree View (see Figure 1-4), you'll notice that a new Site Hierarchy group list now appears immediately beneath the Quick Launch in the left panel. This group list shows all the components on your SharePoint site (with Expand buttons for any of them that have subcomponents).

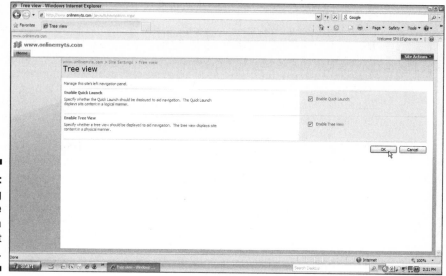

Figure 1-3:
Enabling
the Tree
View on a
SharePoint
site.

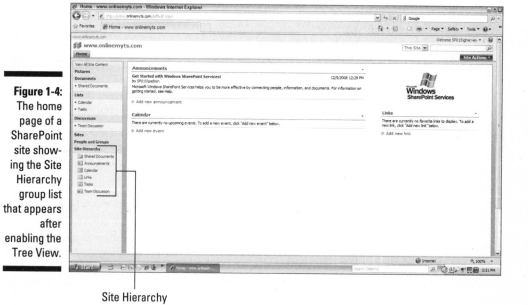

Figure 1-4:
The home
page of a
SharePoint
site show-
ing the Site
Hierarchy
group list
that appears
after
enabling the
Tree View.

Site Hierarchy

Using Quick Launch links

The main SharePoint site and each subsite that you add contains its own set of Quick Launch links (simply called the Quick Launch by the folks at Microsoft). This group of links appears beneath the View All Site Content link (which displays a list of all the content on the current site).

The links in the Quick Launch are arranged in categories that depend upon the type of site you're viewing (which, in turn, usually depends upon the type of template that that site uses). For example, when you view a site based on the Team Site template, the Quick Launch contains Pictures, Documents, Lists, Discussions, Sites, and People and Groups. (Refer to Figure 1-1.) But when you view a subsite based on the Wiki Site template, for instance, only a single Wiki Pages category appears in the Quick Launch of this subsite.

As you add pages to your main site or subsites, SharePoint automatically adds the name of the new page to the appropriate category (although you can override this setting and choose not to have a link to the new page appear in the Quick Launch). This makes it easy to visit a page on the current site or to visit the main page of a subsite because all you have to do is click its name in the appropriate category.

Don't forget that the names of the categories that appear in boldface type in the Quick Launch area of a site (such as Pictures, Documents, Lists, and Sites) are also live hyperlinks. By clicking these category links, you display a page that lists all of the current content in that category and also enables you to add new content as well as edit the existing content.

Taking a quick tour of an out-of-the-box SharePoint site

Now it's time to get some experience with navigating a typical SharePoint site. To do so, follow along with my steps as I take you on a short tour of a brand-new SharePoint site using the links that are available at the starting gate, the moment I first log on to its home page:

1. **Click the link attached to the title, Get Started with Windows SharePoint Services, which appears under the Announcements heading in the main section of the SharePoint home page. (Refer to Figure 1-1.)**

   When you start a new SharePoint site, the program automatically adds this general announcement about SharePoint and its uses in the name of the site administrator. When you click the link that's attached to its title, SharePoint displays its own announcements page (see Figure 1-5) where you edit its contents.

2. Click the Announcements link in the Content Navigation Breadcrumb.

SharePoint jumps back one level to display the general Announcements page. (See Figure 1-6.) This page shows a chronological list of all the announcements added to the site. (Currently, there's only one announcement in this list — the Get Started one.)

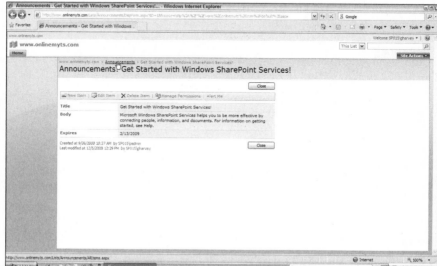

Figure 1-5:
Visiting the automatic Get Started with Windows SharePoint Services announcements page.

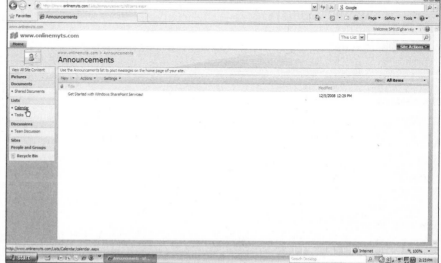

Figure 1-6:
Backing up a level to view the list of all announcements on the Announcements page.

3. **Click the link attached to the Calendar item in the Lists category of the Quick Launch.**

   SharePoint jumps you directly to the Calendar page. (See Figure 1-7.) This page shows you all the meetings, appointments, and deadlines that you've scheduled for the current month, using the very familiar Sunday-to-Saturday weekly layout that you can edit and add to. In addition, you can also view the Date Navigator, which appears immediately above the View All Site Content link and the Quick Launch. The Date Navigator allows you to both review your schedule for past months and add upcoming engagements for future months.

4. **Click the View All Site Content link under the Date Navigator and at the top of the Quick Launch in the left panel of the Calendar page.**

   SharePoint jumps you directly to the All Site Content page for the site. (See Figure 1-8.) This page displays a list by category of all the content on your site. This is a very valuable page because it not only gives an at-a-glance view of your SharePoint site, but also provides you with links to the existing pages (so that you can open them for editing) as well as a Create button (to the immediate right of the View All Site Content link) that you can use to add new pages.

5. **Click the Home tab in the Top Link bar.**

   SharePoint immediately returns you to the home page of the SharePoint site.

Date Navigator

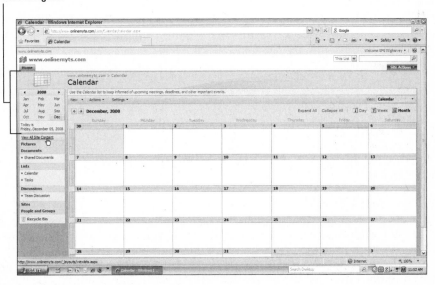

Figure 1-7:
Jumping
directly
to the
Calendar
page of
the main
SharePoint
site.

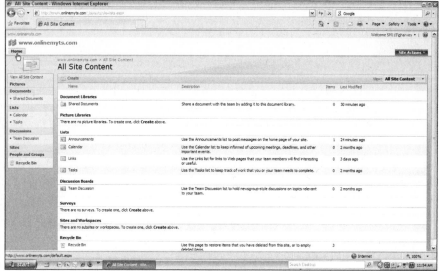

Figure 1-8:
Jumping
directly to
the All Site
Content
page of
the main
SharePoint
site.

As you can see from this brief introductory tour (which I urge you to try on your own SharePoint site), the links on a SharePoint site are plentiful and enable you to quickly navigate any of its pages.

Getting Online SharePoint Help

Don't forget about the extensive online SharePoint help that's available to you at any time while you're working on your site. To access the online help, click the Help button in the top-right corner of the site.

This task is a bit tricky if you're using Internet Explorer 8, however, because for some unknown reason the SharePoint site Help button (with its question mark icon) appears almost directly beneath the Help button for this Web browser. This means that if you use this particular browser to access your SharePoint site, you can all too easily click the wrong Help button and end up with Explorer help when you want SharePoint help.

When you click the SharePoint Help button, the program opens a separate, smaller browser window that typically contains the home page of the Windows SharePoint Services 3.0 Help and How-To window, as shown in Figure 1-9. As you can see in this figure, this page contains a number of topics ranging from the standard "Welcome" to the more specialized "Working in International Environments."

If your SharePoint site is hosted, you may be prompted for your user ID and password the first time you attempt to open the SharePoint Help window during a work session.

To get more information about a particular help topic, click its link. If you have a question about a particular SharePoint feature (such as keyboard shortcuts) or a topic not covered in this initial list (such as spreadsheets in SharePoint), use the search feature by typing the feature or topic in the Help and How-To window's Search text box in its upper-right corner and then pressing Enter.

After you've displayed the help information you need in the Help browser window, you can print it by turning on your printer and then clicking the Print button near the top on the left of the screen. If the help article you want to print contains several subsections, be sure to click the Show All button that appears at the top of the main article before you click the Print button.

If you want to work on something in your SharePoint site after consulting a particular help topic in the Help window, click the SharePoint site's program button on the Windows taskbar or click somewhere directly on the SharePoint site browser window if part of it appears behind the Help browser window. Doing this automatically minimizes the Help window while at the same time activating the SharePoint site browser window and bringing it to the forefront. You can then redisplay the SharePoint Help window at any time to get more online help simply by clicking its program button on the Windows taskbar.

SharePoint Help button

Internet Explorer Help button

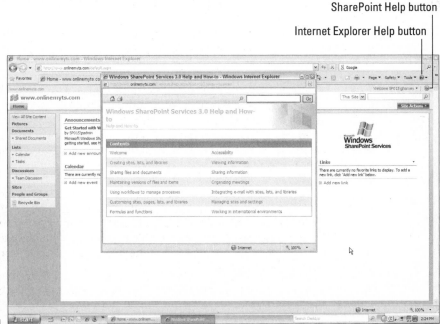

Figure 1-9:
The
Windows
SharePoint
Services
Help
window as
it first opens
in Internet
Explorer.

When you're finished using the online SharePoint help during your work session, you can close the Help browser window by clicking the Close button that appears in the window's upper-right corner. Doing this returns you immediately to the browser window containing your SharePoint site where you can continue working.

Finding Your Way on the SharePoint Site with Search

Your SharePoint site includes a Search box that you can often use to quickly locate and then visit particular components. This can become a particularly efficient way to navigate your SharePoint site, especially as the site grows.

The Search box is located on each SharePoint page directly beneath the Welcome drop-down list and Help buttons and immediately above the Site Actions button. The Search box itself is sandwiched between a Scope drop-down list (which typically contains the value This Site or All Sites) on the left and a Go Search button (with the magnifying glass icon) on the right.

To perform a search for particular content on your SharePoint site, make sure that This Site is displayed in the Scope drop-down list and then enter the search text that SharePoint's search feature will find. This search text normally consists of keywords found on the page or pages of the site you want to locate. For example, to find pages on my SharePoint site where both the terms *book* and *cover* are mentioned, I enter the following search text in the Search box:

```
book cover
```

However, if I want SharePoint to find the pages where the term *book* is mentioned but not the term *cover,* I enter the following search text in the Search box:

```
book -cover
```

When you enter more than one term in the Search box separated by spaces, Windows SharePoint Services 3.0 assumes an implicit AND condition (so that in my first example, SharePoint searches for the terms *book* and *cover*). If you want to explicitly exclude a term from the search, you need to enter the minus sign before the term (as in my second example where SharePoint searches for all occurrences of the term *book* where *cover* is not mentioned).

After you enter the search text in the Search box and designate the scope of the search in the Scope drop-down list, you're ready to have SharePoint conduct the search by clicking the Go Search button (or pressing Enter when the cursor is still in the Search box).

SharePoint then searches for the search text over the range of site components designated by the Scope drop-down list. If the program doesn't find any matches, it displays a Search Results page with the message `No Results Matching Your Search Were Found`. You can then refine your search text and use it to conduct another (hopefully, more successful) search.

If SharePoint does find matches for the search text, the program then lists them — arranged by their weighted significance to the search text — on the first of possibly many Search Results pages. Each match in this list contains a live link that you can then click to jump directly to that page on your SharePoint site.

Above the list of search results, you can find the total number of matches found to your search text and links to individual Search Results pages (if these matches require multiple pages). This area also contains a View by Modified Date link that you can click to sort the matches by the date that their pages were lasted edited (from most to least recent) rather than by their relevance to the search text.

Figure 1-10 shows you the first Search Results page that SharePoint returned after I searched on my site with *book cover* as the search text. This first Search Results page displays the top ten matches (out of close to 120 total) to this search text. And to open the Book Cover meeting page referred to in the first match, all I have to do is click its link.

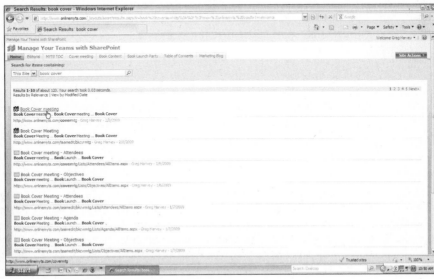

Figure 1-10: The Search Results page gave me several results after I searched the SharePoint site for *book cover.*

Chapter 2

Setting Up the SharePoint Site for Your Teams

In This Chapter

▶ Understanding the basic components and structure of a SharePoint site

▶ Selecting a new theme for your SharePoint site

▶ Adding subsites to your SharePoint site

▶ Looking at the contents and structure of the SharePoint site templates

▶ Editing the content on the home page of your SharePoint site

This chapter covers the basic ways you can customize a brand-new SharePoint site so that your site contains just the right components and presents them just the way your teams need them in order to effectively collaborate. As part of setting up the SharePoint site for your teams, you'll find that you can quickly and easily customize much of the appearance and contents of the site right within your Web browser.

However, before I cover ways to tailor the standard, out-of-the-box SharePoint team site that your company's IT department or SharePoint host company turns over to you, you need to have a basic understanding of the principal parts of a SharePoint site and how SharePoint typically organizes them. Armed with this working knowledge, you'll then be ready to get to work customizing the new site specifically for your teams' use.

Finding out how SharePoint Sites Are Organized

To understand how SharePoint sites are organized, you first need to be familiar with the basic building blocks that SharePoint uses to present the various kinds of information you choose to share. After that, you're ready to see how these blocks relate to one another in the typical SharePoint site hierarchy.

Checking out the basics

The basic building block of any SharePoint site is a special type of Web page referred to as a *Web Part page*. Although the Web Part page isn't the only type of Web page that SharePoint supports, it's by far the most prevalent and the type that you and your teams will probably be using the most.

A Web Part page is so called because it uses a special type of container called a *Web Part* to present its information. This means that all the various kinds of SharePoint information on a page (such as the list of announcements, links, documents, surveys, forms, discussion boards, wikis, and so on) use Web Parts. Even the logo image and the calendar that appear on different pages of a SharePoint site are contained in their own Web Parts.

In fact, about the only elements that appear on a SharePoint page that don't use some sort of Web Part are the specific navigation tools and command menus that a particular page uses — the Site tabs that appear in the Top Link bar, for example, as well as the Quick Launch, Search bar, and Site Actions command button.

Using Web Part zones to format a page's Web Parts

Here's a little SharePoint secret: The various page templates Microsoft makes available to SharePoint users are little more than specialized arrangements of Web Parts designed for particular uses, such as sharing documents, presenting data, listing site users, or soliciting team feedback. Each page template then has its own Web Part(s). This includes even the so-called Blank Site template, which is devoid of all other Web Parts except for a single Image Web Part, the one that contains and displays the Windows SharePoint Services logo that appears on the right side of all the site templates.

Many SharePoint templates, such as the aforementioned site templates, format the default Web Parts that appear on their pages by dividing the page into different *Web Part zones* and then placing particular Web Parts into specific zones. These Web Part zones then create columns of certain widths, and these columns control how the information in their particular Web Parts is displayed.

For example, the Team Site template, normally used to create the home page for a new SharePoint site, contains two zones: Left and Right. And when you put the home page into Edit mode (by choosing the Edit Page command from its Site Actions drop-down menu), you can immediately see that these two zones are unequal in width, with the Left Web Part zone more than twice as wide as the Right Web Part zone, as shown in Figure 2-1.

Left Web Part zone   Right Web Part zone

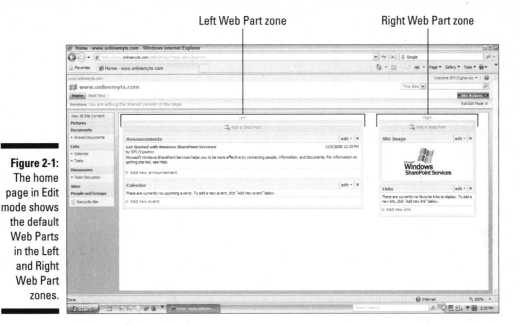

Figure 2-1:
The home
page in Edit
mode shows
the default
Web Parts
in the Left
and Right
Web Part
zones.

When you first start using a new SharePoint home page that's based on the Team Site template, the Left Web Part zone contains the Announcements and Calendar Web Parts, and the Right zone contains the Image and Links Web Parts. There's no law stating that you have to keep these elements where they are, but the default dimensions of the Left and Right Web Part zones *do* determine the formatting of the information that their Web Parts contain.

In Figure 2-2, I switched the default Web Parts so that the Image and Links Web Parts that used to appear in the Right zone now appear in the Left zone, and the Announcements and Calendar Web Parts that started out in the Left zone are now in the Right zone. (You do this kind of switcheroo with a simple drag-and-drop, as you find out later in this chapter.)

As you can see in this figure, the Windows SharePoint Services logo in the Image Web Part is still centered both vertically and horizontally in the Left Web Part zone. In this new configuration, however, there's a great deal more white space this time between the left and right borders of a much wider — although not any higher — Web Part. So too, the parts of the default announcement listed in the Announcements in the Right Web Part zone are still formatted relative to one another as before, although the line breaks in the actual text are very different due to the much narrower nature of the Web Part.

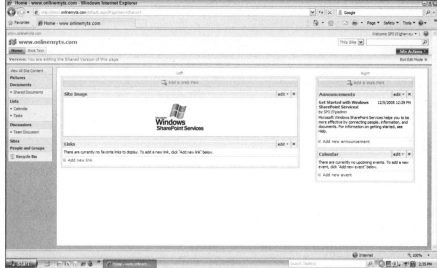

Figure 2-2:
I pulled
the ol'
switcheroo
on the Web
Parts in the
Left and
Right Web
Part zones
of the home
page.

Using different Web Parts for different types of information

Each Web Part that's added to a Web Part page is designed to format and display a distinct type of information. In light of that fact, SharePoint 2007 comes with a bunch of generic Web Parts that you can use when customizing the contents of your SharePoint site.

The generic Web Parts that are most often available to you when customizing your SharePoint site include the following:

✔ **Announcements:** Displays a list of messages pertinent to the project that you want your team members to be aware of.

✔ **Calendar:** Displays a list of scheduled events relevant to the teams such as upcoming meetings, milestones, and the all-important deadlines.

✔ **Content Editor Web Part:** Used to add formatted text, images, tables, and hyperlinks to your SharePoint site. The Content Editor enables you to add HTML source code, plain text, rich text, and links to text files.

✔ **Form Web Part:** Used to customize forms and connect them to other Web Parts as well as to filter lists so that only the information you and your teams need to see is displayed.

✔ **Image Web Part:** Used to add graphics files with photos and other images that your teams need access to. You can save these images in any of the following graphics file formats: BMP (bitmap), EMF (Enhanced Metafile), GIF (Graphics Interchange Format), JPEG (Joint Photographic Experts Group), and PNG (Portable Networks Graphics).

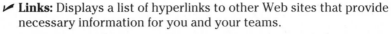

✔ **Links:** Displays a list of hyperlinks to other Web sites that provide necessary information for you and your teams.

✔ **Page Viewer Web Part:** Displays the content of another Web site (such as the corporate Web site or a special intranet site), folder, or files to which your teams have network access. The content of a linked Web page appears within a Web frame, provided that the Web browser used to view the SharePoint site supports the HTML IFRAME code.

Keep in mind that to view folders or files with the Page Viewer Web Part, the SharePoint site must be viewed in Internet Explorer.

✔ **Relevant Documents:** Displays a list of documents that provide your teams with necessary information about the project or the tasks that you assign them.

✔ **Shared Documents:** Displays a list of documents that your teams need to access and potentially edit (provided they have the necessary permission).

✔ **Site Users:** Displays a list of the users and groups that have access to the SharePoint site. You can use this list to contact individual users and/ or groups, edit their personal profiles, and modify their site permissions. (See Chapter 3 for details.)

✔ **Tasks:** Displays a list of project tasks that your teams need to complete. It's also used to edit their status, the particular team members to which said tasks have been assigned, and to include additional tasks.

✔ **Team Discussion:** Displays a discussion list that enables team members to conduct newsgroup type discussions on topics important to the completion of the project.

✔ **User Tasks:** Displays a list of projects for which you're responsible. It's also used to edit them.

✔ **XML Web Part:** Displays documents and forms that rely on XML (Extensible Markup Language) codes and XSLT (Extensible Style sheet Language Transformations) styling to format and display their data.

Understanding the hierarchy of a typical SharePoint site

The various Web Part pages — with all the Web Part lists, discussion boards, site images, and so forth that a typical SharePoint site contains — are related to each other in a rigid hierarchy. This hierarchy is a top-down tree structure like the one shown in Figure 2-3.

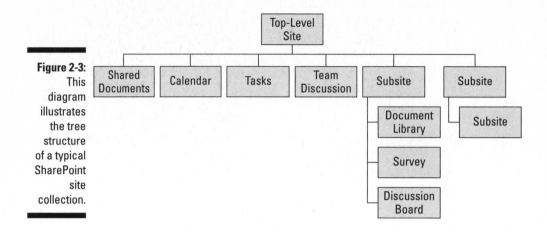

Figure 2-3:
This
diagram
illustrates
the tree
structure
of a typical
SharePoint
site
collection.

The top-level site at the summit of this tree contains the SharePoint home page. This is the Web page that appears whenever you or one of your team members log on to the site. This home page is an ASP.NET type Web page, and for that reason, it's usually named `default.aspx`. This page name is automatically appended to the URL that your IT or SharePoint host assigns to the site when you enter the URL in your Web browser.

This top-level site is also the primary access point for all the other pages that are added to the SharePoint site. When you first start work on a new SharePoint site, these include empty Shared Documents, Calendar, Tasks, and Team Discussion pages, which you access by clicking the appropriate link in the home page Quick Launch section.

Remember that each time you access a page from the SharePoint home page that's lower in the hierarchy, SharePoint notes your path in the Content Navigation Breadcrumb that appears beneath the site tabs in the Top Link bar. You can always move back up a level in a SharePoint hierarchy by clicking a previous link in the Content Navigation Breadcrumb.

Looking at the function of subsites in a SharePoint site

In addition to Web Part pages, you can add subsites to your top-level SharePoint site. (A subsite is also known as a *child site,* making the single top-level site its *parent site.*) Each subsite that you add must then be accessed from the home page on the top-level site by clicking its link in the All Site Content page, in the Top Link bar, or in the Quick Launch Sites category. (I'm assuming, of course, that you chose to add this Quick Launch link for the new subsite, even though it is optional.)

SharePoint subsites function somewhat like file folders do in a traditional hierarchical computer file system such as the one used by your good old Windows XP or Vista operating system. A subsite's primary function is to enable you to set up separate areas for documents, surveys, discussions, and so forth for specific teams or team members that are involved in the project. For example, when using a SharePoint site for new product development, you might create a subsite for your accounting team that contains spreadsheets and other pertinent financial data and yet another for the advertising team that contains publicity photos and other documents related to competing products.

Each subsite that you see fit to add to your SharePoint site can have its own Web Part pages with such things as document libraries, surveys, calendars, discussion boards, and lists as well as its own permissions that grant different team members different levels of access. Moreover, your subsites can even have their own subsites with their own Web Part pages if the need arises for a particular team. (Refer to Figure 2-3.)

When you add a subsite to your SharePoint site, you can save a great deal of design time by selecting a SharePoint template that contains most, if not all, of the Web Parts that you're going to need in order to display the kind of information that's important to the team that needs the subsite. See the "Adding Subsites to Your SharePoint Site" section, later in this chapter, for more on the types of templates you can select when setting up new subsites.

Checking out the common properties of a SharePoint site collection

All the subsites — together with the top-level SharePoint site from which they're accessed — are collectively known as a *site collection.* Each SharePoint site collection shares common properties:

- ✔ **Navigation controls:** Each subsite of the top-level SharePoint site is given its own site tab in the Top Link bar as well as a link in the home page's Quick Launch. However, a subsite of another subsite receives only a link in the parent subsite's Quick Launch (provided that you don't override the default setting of displaying the subsite in the Quick Launch of the parent site).

- ✔ **Design elements:** Each site collection uses a single default site theme that determines the collections of colors and fonts that all its pages and Web Parts use.

- ✔ **Lists:** This includes all the libraries, calendars, links, tasks, and discussions that you add to the top-level site as well as all those that you add to its subsites.

- ✔ **Searches:** All searches that you conduct using a page's Search box span the entire site collection.

In practical terms, all the data (that is, lists) in a single SharePoint site collection reside in the same database that your IT team must back up and — if anything should ever happen to its Web server — restore as a single unit. Again, this is analogous to a master folder that contains all sorts of subfolders whose data are automatically copied whenever you back up the master folder.

Customizing the Appearance of Your SharePoint Site

So far in this chapter, I concentrate on the typical SharePoint components and how they fit together to create an entire site. Now it's time to find out how easily you can customize the "typical" components into something uniquely designed for your own needs — and you can do it while armed with nothing more than the very Web browser you use to access and view the site.

I begin this discussion on customizing the look of a new SharePoint site by pointing out the difference between personal modifications you make to a site's Web Parts as opposed to those customizations you make that automatically are shared with the team members who access the site. Then, I go on to show you how really simple it is to customize the title, description, logo, site theme, Quick Launch, and the Top Link bar that your site uses.

Personalizing a SharePoint page

Most of the time you'll be customizing the Web Parts on various pages of your SharePoint site for the benefit of all the teams who share its information during the period of your collaboration (assuming, of course, that you're a site administrator with full permissions to customize and edit any part of its content — see Chapter 3 for details). Keep in mind, however, that you can also personalize the appearance of the SharePoint pages so they display just the information you — and you alone — want to see when you're logged on to the site.

For example, you may want to add a Site Users Web Part to just *your* version of the SharePoint home page to show you a list of the site users and their online status each time you log on to the site. This information doesn't necessarily have to appear on the shared pages that the rest of the team members see and use.

To make changes to just your version of a SharePoint page without affecting the Web Parts viewed by other users, you need to turn on the Personalize This Page setting before you make your modifications to the Web Parts on that page. To do this, follow these steps:

1. **Open your SharePoint site in your Web browser and, if your system requires it, log on to the SharePoint site using your own user ID and password.**

   SharePoint displays the home page with your SharePoint site username appearing after Welcome on its drop-down menu in the upper-right corner of the screen.

2. **Select the SharePoint page whose view you want to personally customize by one of these methods: by clicking its hyperlink on the Top Link bar, by clicking the link in the home page Quick Launch, or by clicking somewhere in the body of the page.**

   If you want to personally customize the home page of the SharePoint site, skip Step 2. Also, be aware that you can personally customize the view of any page to which you have access in the site collection even if the page is on a subsite of the top-level SharePoint site.

3. **Click the Welcome menu button containing your username in the upper-right corner of the page you want to personally customize to open the Welcome drop-down menu.**

   When the Welcome drop-down menu opens, it typically contains at least the following options: My Settings, Sign In as Different User, Sign Out, and Personalize This Page. (See Figure 2-4.)

4. **Choose the Personalize This Page option from the bottom of the page's Welcome drop-down menu.**

   SharePoint opens the current page in Edit mode, while at the same time displaying a bar at the top of the page with the version message, "You are editing the Personal Version of this page," as shown in Figure 2-5.

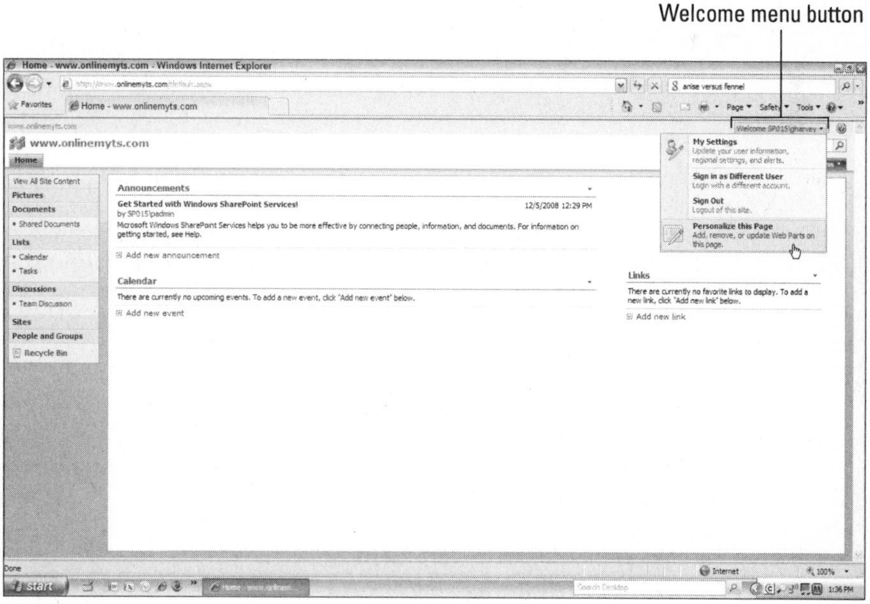

Welcome menu button

Figure 2-4:
Select the Personalize This Page command on the Welcome drop-down menu of the SharePoint site home page.

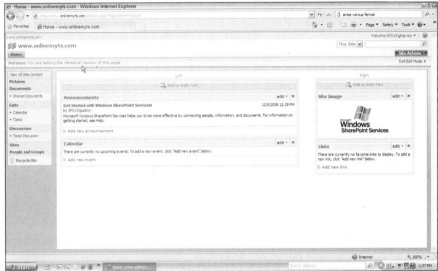

Figure 2-5:
You can edit
the Web
Parts on a
personal
version of
the home
page of the
SharePoint
site.

5. **Make all your personal changes to the Web Parts on the current page and then click the Exit Edit Mode button — the button with the X that appears on the right side of the bar containing the Personal Version message.**

   SharePoint takes the page out of Edit mode, and the bar with the Personal Version message — and its accompanying Exit Edit Mode button — disappears from the top of the page.

As soon as you exit Edit mode after completing your changes to a personal view of a page, the page goes right back into the default shared editing mode. This means that any editing changes that you subsequently make to the page's Web Parts using the regular Edit Page option on the Site Settings drop-down menu once more show up in every team member's view of the page. And if you yet again want to make personal changes for only your view of the page, you need to use the Personalize This Page command on your Welcome drop-down menu to edit the page for a second time.

After you personalize the Web Parts on a particular page on your SharePoint site, these personal changes appear each time you log on to the site and view the page. You can, however, still switch the page to a shared view that shows the Web Parts the way they appear to your other team members. To do this, open your personal Welcome drop-down menu and then choose the Show Shared View option (shown in Figure 2-6) that now appears at the very bottom of the menu as a result of your previous personalization of the page.

Figure 2-6:
Select
the Show
Shared
View option
on your
Welcome
menu to
switch from
a personal
view to a
shared view
of the page.

Modifying the Look and Feel options from the Site Settings page

SharePoint makes it easy to modify various aspects of the look and feel of your site. All you have to do is open the Site Settings page for your site, similar to the one shown in Figure 2-7. You do this by following these two simple steps:

1. **Click the Site Actions button on the far right side of the screen.**

   The Site Actions button is in the same row as the Home and other Site tab buttons.

2. **From the Site Actions drop-down menu, choose the Site Settings option (located at the bottom).**

   SharePoint opens the Site Settings page. This page contains a number of options in five distinct columns, ranging from Users and Permissions through Site Collection Administration. Right now you're interested in the second column — the one with all the Look and Feel options.

The next sections delve a little deeper into each one of the Look and Feel options.

Site Actions button

Figure 2-7:
Select the
Site Settings
page for the
top-level
SharePoint
site.

Changing the SharePoint site's title, description, and logo

When you first begin work on a new SharePoint site, you may have the site's URL address appearing as its title, having a standard SharePoint graphic as its logo, and having no description of the site whatsoever. If you want, you can replace the URL or any other title that's originally assigned to the site with a new title, substitute your company's logo for the default SharePoint version, and add a site description (to appear on the home page of the site immediately above the Announcements Web Part). All you have to do is click the Title, Description, and Icon link in the Look and Feel column of the Site Settings page. (Refer to Figure 2-7.)

When you do this, SharePoint opens a Title, Description, and Icon page similar to the one shown in Figure 2-8. Here you can use its Title and Description text boxes and the Logo URL and Description text boxes to add a bit more instructive and descriptive information about your site.

When entering the URL linking to the graphics file that contains your company's logo image, you don't have to enter the site's entire URL address if a copy of the logo file has already been uploaded to the SharePoint server's default images folder. Rather, you can use the relative address /_layouts/ images/ followed by the name of the graphics file, as in

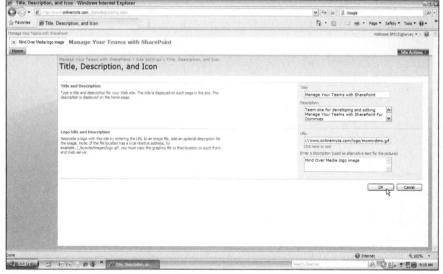

Figure 2-8:
You can
modify the
SharePoint
site's title,
description,
and logo.

```
/_layouts/images/momtrdmk.gif
```

If you need to upload the graphic file, you can do so by creating a special place for it called a Picture library (see Chapter 5) and then copying the image to it before you modify the logo URL setting. Then, specify the URL address of the image in the Picture library, starting with the SharePoint site's Internet address followed by the library name and image filename as in:

```
http://www.onlinemyts.com/logo/momtrdmk.gif
```

Then, after entering the address in the URL text box, to make sure that you've entered the correct URL and that SharePoint can locate the image file you specify, click the Click Here to Test link. If everything's hunky-dory, SharePoint then opens a window showing the logo's image.

Figure 2-9 shows you how the home page of my SharePoint site appears after modifying the site's title and logo and adding a site description. As you can see, modifying just this information on the home page goes a long way towards customizing its appearance and making the site feel much more like your own.

Site Logo   Site Title   Site Description

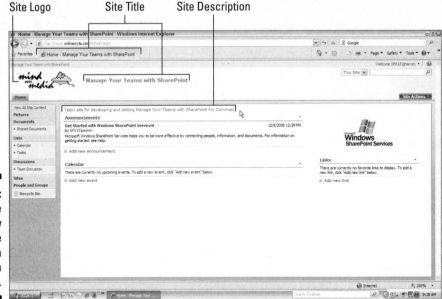

Figure 2-9:
My home
page now
shows the
site's title, a
logo, and a
description.

Selecting a new site theme

When you start a new SharePoint site, the program automatically selects a standard blue-based design theme (aptly named the Default Theme) for the entire site. You can, if you want, easily change this to one of the other 18 or so built-in themes that come standard with the program.

Just be aware that in SharePoint 2007, selecting a new site theme is a completely take-it-or-leave-it proposition because the program doesn't provide any way for you to customize just particular parts of the site theme, such as a custom text or background color.

To select a new theme for your site, click the Site Theme link in the Look and Feel column of the Site Settings page. (Refer to Figure 2-7.) SharePoint then opens a Site Theme page similar to the one shown in Figure 2-10. On this page, click the descriptive name of the theme in the list box on the right and then look at the preview of its design scheme (paying special attention to its use of colors) in the Preview area to the immediate left. When you find a site theme that you want to use, click the Apply button to put it into operation and make it the new official theme.

Keep in mind that all subsites that you subsequently add to the top-level site (see "Adding Subsites to Your SharePoint Site" for details later in this chapter) use the standard, blue-based Default Theme no matter what new site theme you've selected for the top-level site at the time of their creation. I guess this is one instance of a trait that the child site just doesn't inherit directly from its parent!

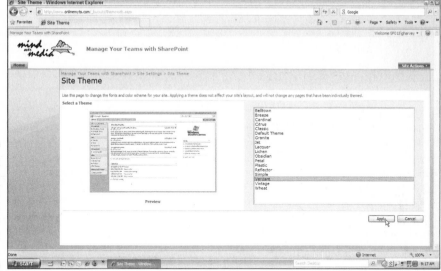

Figure 2-10:
You can
select a
new theme
for the
SharePoint
site.

It's a very good idea to select different site themes for the various subsites that you create for individual team use. Assigning a subsite a site theme with a unique (without being garish) color scheme makes the site stand out a lot more. This makes the subsite much more distinctive and easier to pick out in the bunch, thus minimizing user confusion and making the overall SharePoint site a lot easier for your teams to navigate.

Modifying the Quick Launch

The Quick Launch links appear in a panel on the left side of most Web Part pages, right between the View All Site Content link at the top and the Recycle Bin link at the bottom. Quick Launch links are arranged by category and enable you and your team members to jump directly to pages of interest.

As you go about adding Web Part pages to your SharePoint site, the program is set to automatically add links to these pages in the appropriate category of the Quick Launch. You can, however, easily override this default setting at the time of the page's creation and choose not to have any link to the page appear in the Quick Launch area.

If a tab for a page doesn't appear in the Top Link bar or a link doesn't appear in the Quick Launch area, remember that you can always access the page from the All Site Content page, which you can open by clicking the View All Site Content link immediately above the Quick Launch links themselves. Links to all the pages added to the SharePoint site show up in the appropriate category on the All Site Content page regardless of whether they're listed in the Top Link bar or Quick Launch.

SharePoint makes it easy to edit the contents of the Quick Launch area. When editing the Quick Launch, you add or remove links to existing pages, add new category headings, and change the order in which the categories of links appear as well as individual pages within a category. To edit the Quick Launch links for your top-level site or one of its subsites, follow these few steps:

1. **Navigate to the subsite whose Quick Launch you want to customize.**

   If you want to customize the Quick Launch on the home page of your site, all you have to do is log on to the SharePoint site before proceeding to Step 2.

2. **Choose Site Settings from the Site Actions drop-down menu.**

   SharePoint opens the Site Settings page similar to the one shown earlier in Figure 2-7.

3. **Click the Quick Launch link in the Look and Feel column of the Site Settings page.**

   SharePoint opens a Quick Launch page for the current site with a row of three option buttons — New Link, New Heading, and Change Order — above a list of its categories and pages. (The page will look a lot like what you see in Figure 2-11.)

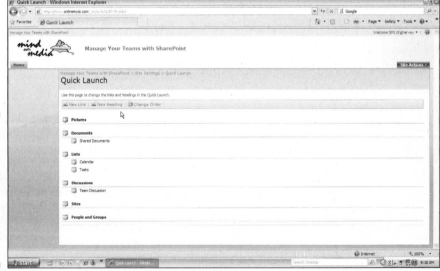

Figure 2-11:
You can modify the Quick Launch on the home page of the SharePoint site.

Adding Quick Launch links and changing their order

You can use any of the three options that appear at the top of the Quick Launch page to add links to the Quick Launch or to customize the order in which they appear:

- ✔ **New Link:** Enables you to add a link to an existing SharePoint page that doesn't currently appear on the Quick Launch. When you click New Link, SharePoint opens a New Link page with URL and Heading options that you use to type the URL address for the SharePoint page, to enter a description for the link, and to select its category heading.

- ✔ **New Heading:** Enables you to add a category heading by creating a link to an existing page that lists all the pages of a certain type (such as default document libraries, lists, discussion boards, surveys, and so forth) on the SharePoint site. When you click the New Heading link, SharePoint opens a New Heading page with URL options that you use to specify the URL address for the SharePoint page and to enter a description for the heading.

- ✔ **Change Order:** Enables you to modify the order in which the categories appear in the Quick Launch list as well as the order in which individual page links appear in particular categories. When you click Change Order, SharePoint opens a Quick Launch page that shows the headings and pages on the Quick Launch with drop-down lists immediately to the left of each heading. You also see a page link next to each heading, displaying a number that designates its current order (1, 2, 3, and so on) either within the entire sequence of category headings or within the pages in a particular category. To change the order of headings in the Quick Launch, use the page's drop-down lists to select new numbers that create the desired sequence of category headings. Likewise, to change the order of pages within a particular category, select new numbers that determine their sequencing.

When specifying the URL address for a new link, the Type the Web Address text box already contains `http://` to which you add the complete path starting with the Web address (as in `www.onlinemyts`) followed by the list of subsites in the path and finally the filename of the page (minus any filename extension such as `.asp` or `.html`). So, for example, to add a new link to a page named Finances located in the Accounting subsite of a SharePoint site named AcmeSharePoint.com, you'd enter the following URL address in the Type the Web Address text box after the `http://`:

```
www.acmesharepoint.com/accounting/finances
```

Editing Quick Launch links

You can also edit any of the links to particular categories or individual pages that appear on the Quick Launch page. To do this, click the link's icon (the one with the picture of a tiny datasheet with a pencil lying on top of it) that appears immediately to the left of the category or individual page name. SharePoint then opens either an Edit Heading or Edit Link page (depending upon whether you clicked a category link or a page link).

You can use the options on the Edit Heading page to modify the Web address of the heading page or its category or to remove the heading from the Quick Launch (along with any page links it contains). You can use the options on the Edit Link page to modify the Web address, description, or category heading for the page or to remove it from the Quick Launch entirely.

To edit the Web address or description for a heading or link, just modify the URL address or descriptive text in the appropriate text box. To modify the heading for a page, simply select it from the Heading drop-down list box. To delete the heading or page, click the Delete button and then click OK in the alert dialog box that appears to warn you that deleting the link also deletes all links that exist beneath it.

Don't forget that removing a category heading and links to particular pages deletes them only from the Quick Launch. It does not, however, remove their pages from the SharePoint Web site. This means that you can still access their pages either through links in the Top Link bar or on the All Site Content page.

If your intention is to delete the page itself as well as the Quick Launch link to it, you need to view the page in SharePoint. Then, choose the Site Settings option from the Site Actions drop-down menu, navigate to the Site Administration column (the second column from the right), and then click the Delete This Site link located there. Just be aware that if you then go ahead and click the Delete button in the Delete This Site page as well as the OK button in the alert dialog box that then appears, the page will be gone and you'll have no choice but to re-create it if you deleted the page in error.

Customizing the Top Link bar

The Top Link bar contains site tabs with links that you and your team members can click to jump directly to particular subsites of interest. Normally, as you create your SharePoint subsites (see the section, "Adding Subsites to Your SharePoint Site" that immediately follows for details), the program automatically adds site tabs with links to them in the Top Link bar in the order in which the subsites are added to the SharePoint site. You can, however, easily override this default setting at the time of the subsite's creation and choose not to have any tab for its page appear in the Top Link bar.

If a tab to a subsite doesn't appear in the Top Link bar or Quick Launch area, you can always access the subsite from the All Site Content page, which you can open from the SharePoint site's home page by clicking the View All Site Content link above the Quick Launch. The names of your subsites (with live links to them) then appear under the Sites and Workspaces heading on this All Site Content page.

As is the case with the Quick Launch links, you can also customize and edit the Top Link bar. When editing the Top Link bar, you can add or remove tabs with links to existing subsites, add new tabs, as well as change the order in which the tabs appear. To edit the Top Link bar, click the Top Link bar link in the Look and Feel column of the Site Settings page.

SharePoint then opens a Top Link Bar page similar to the one shown in Figure 2-12. This page contains a list of all the links that currently appear in the Top Link bar as well as a New Link and Change Order button. (Note that the Change Order button doesn't appear on the Top Link Bar page when your site's Top Link bar has only the Home tab in it, as is the case when you first start customizing your SharePoint site.)

When the Top Link Bar page is open, you can make any of the following modifications to the bar:

✔ **Add a tab:** To add a new tab with a link to an existing page on your SharePoint site (or even to a Web page external to the SharePoint site), click the New Link option to open the New Link page and then enter the page's URL address as well as a description in the appropriate text box. (Note that the description you enter in the Type the Description text box then becomes the name of the tab on the Top Link bar — you probably want to keep the description brief.)

✔ **Rearrange tabs:** To change the order in which the tabs appear on the Top Link bar, click the Change Order link to open a version of the Top Link Bar page that contains drop-down list boxes showing the number of each tab's current order in a Link Order column. Then, use these drop-down lists to select new numbers that create the desired sequence of tabs on the Top Link bar.

✔ **Edit tabs and their links:** To edit the URL address of a link or the description (name) of its tab, click its icon to open its Edit Link page where you can then modify the Web address and/or description before clicking OK.

✔ **Remove tabs:** To delete a tab and its link from the Top Link bar, open its Edit Link page (by clicking its icon), click the Delete button, and then click OK in the alert dialog box that appears.

Although most of the links in the Top Link bar are to subsites that you add to your SharePoint site, they don't have to be. Remember that if you feel you need them, you can add links to any Web page, whether inside or outside the SharePoint site. All you have to do is specify a legitimate Web address in the text box called Type the Web Address when adding the link.

Figure 2-12:
Customizing
the Top Link
bar for the
SharePoint
site.

Adding Subsites to Your SharePoint Site

You can create any number of subsites for your top-level SharePoint site — subsites that are then directly accessed from the top-level site via some sort of link. As I mention earlier in this chapter, some SharePoint designers create a subsite for each of the specialized teams (accounting, advertising, administration, and so on) to suit their unique informational needs.

Although a great many of the subsites you'll add are directly beneath the top-level site in the hierarchy, nothing prevents you from adding a subsite to another subsite, thus creating yet another branch down in the tree structure. (Refer to the hierarchy diagram shown earlier in Figure 2-3.)

Creating a subsite is a rather straightforward process:

1. **Go to the SharePoint page that you want to be directly above the new subsite.**

   If you want to add a subsite to the top-level site, you can do this by clicking the Home tab on the Top Link bar.

2. **Choose Create from the Site Actions drop-down menu.**

   SharePoint opens a Create page similar to the one shown in Figure 2-13.

3. **Click the Sites and Workspaces link in the Web Pages column on the far right of the Create page.**

SharePoint opens a New SharePoint Site page similar to the one shown in Figures 2-14 and 2-15. You use the options on this page to name the new site; give it a URL; select a template for it; and specify its user permission, navigation, and navigation inheritance settings.

4. Enter a name for the subsite in the Title text box and then press Tab.

The name you enter here shows up on all navigation links as well as on all pages that you add to this subsite.

Figure 2-13: You can add a new SharePoint subsite from the Create page.

Figure 2-14: The top part of the New SharePoint Site page shows Title, Description, URL, and Template options.

Figure 2-15:
The bottom part of
the New
SharePoint
Site page
shows the
Permissions,
Navigation,
and
Navigation
Inheritance
options.

5. **(Optional) Enter a description for the new subsite in the Description text box and then press the Tab key.**

   The description you enter here appears only on the subsite's main page.

6. **Enter a filename for the new site in the URL Name text box and then press the Tab key.**

   SharePoint creates a new subsite with the filename you designate here. Therefore, don't use any spaces or any punctuation characters when designating this name and make sure that the name you enter is unique and not one you've used before when adding pages. Also, try to keep the name as short as possible while still making it as descriptive as you need it to be.

7. **Click the name of the template to use in creating the site in the Select a Template list box. (See the "Selecting the right template for the audience of your subsite" section that follows for details.)**

   If you don't choose a template in this list box, SharePoint creates the new subsite from its Team Site template — the same one used to generate the home page of your SharePoint site.

8. **Modify any of the Permissions, Navigation, and Navigation Inheritance default settings that you want to change. (See the "Setting permission and navigation settings" section later in this chapter for details.)**

   If you don't modify any of these default settings, your team members have the same permissions in the new subsite as they do in its parent site, and a link to the new subsite appears in the Top Link bar as well as under the Sites heading in the parent site's Quick Launch.

9. **Click the Create button either at the very top**
   New SharePoint Site page.

   SharePoint then spends a few moments generating
   page using the settings you designate in the New Si

After SharePoint finishes creating your new subsite, Share
page in your Web browser. This page is blank except for th
for by the template you selected and the navigation control
You can then go about customizing the Web Parts and theme
information and data as needed.

Selecting the right template for the audience of your subsite

When selecting a template for a new subsite, you need to keep in mind
the intended audience as well as the types of information that the members
of this audience will expect to find there. You also need to take into
consideration the types of interactions, if any, you expect individual
members of this team to have with you and with one another.

Then, you can select a template that meets your informational and collaborative requirements from among the following two categories (knowing that
you can further customize the Web Parts of the template you select if still
needed):

- ✔ **Collaboration:** SharePoint 2007 contains four distinct Collaboration
  templates: Team Site (like the SharePoint home page), Blank Site
  (lacking all Web Parts except for the standard logo), Document
  Workspace (for collaborative document editing — see Chapter 9),
  Wiki Site (for group editing). and Blog (for brainstorming and sharing
  ideas). Chapter 8 discusses wikis and blogs.

- ✔ **Meetings:** All the templates in this category create Meeting Workspaces
  (see Chapter 6) that facilitate the planning and execution of various
  types of meetings, from the simple Basic Meeting Workspace template to
  the much more complex Multipage Meeting Space template.

Your IT department or SharePoint host may also add other categories of site
templates that then show up as extra tabs at the top of the Select a Template
list box on your New SharePoint Site page. For example, my SharePoint host
installed two additional groups of site templates, Application Templates and
Custom, and their tabs appear on this list box on my New SharePoint Site page
(shown earlier in Figures 2-14 and 2-15). The templates in these nonstandard
categories offer additional, specialized site templates that I can use and easily

customize. For example, the Application Templates category contains an Expense Reimbursement and Approval Site template designed to set up a site that helps you and your teams track their expense reports. Likewise, the Custom category contains a Book Text site template for creating a site where authors and editors can collaborate on the manuscript of a new book. (This template would have come in handy in creating this *For Dummies* masterpiece!)

After you've created a new subsite using one of these ready-made templates, you can still customize its standard contents and layout if needed. (See the section "Editing Web Parts on the Pages of Your SharePoint Site" later in this chapter for details.) Keep in mind that SharePoint then enables you to save your customized subsite as its own template that you can, in turn, use to generate other subsites that still need to be added to your SharePoint site.

To save your changes to a subsite as a template, follow these steps:

1. **Navigate to the customized subsite that you want to save as a template and then choose Site Settings from the Site Actions drop-down menu.**

   SharePoint opens the Site Settings page for your subsite.

2. **Click the Save Site as Template link in the Look and Feel column of the Site Settings page.**

   SharePoint opens a Save Site as Template page similar to the one shown in Figure 2-16.

Figure 2-16: Save a customized subsite as a SharePoint site template.

3. **Type a filename for the new template in the File Name text box and then press the Tab key.**

   When entering the filename, don't use spaces and make the name succinct. Also note that SharePoint automatically appends the filename extension .stp (SharePoint Template) to the main filename you create.

4. **Enter a descriptive name for the template in the Template Name text box and then press the Tab key.**

   The name you give your custom template is added to the Custom category of the Select a Template list box in the Template Selection section of the New SharePoint Site page.

5. **Enter a description of the template in the Template Description list box.**

   The idea here is to give an overview of the template's purpose and scope. The description you enter here appears in the Template Selection area of the New SharePoint Site.

6. **(Optional) Select the Include Content check box to have SharePoint make the content that you've added in the process of customizing the site a part of the new template.**

   You can use this option to save content such as a corporate logo or other graphic or text file that needs to be part of every site generated from the template.

   Just be aware, however, that including content in a template can significantly increase its file size and that the content in a template isn't protected in the same way as other standard elements, so you don't want to use this option if the template contains sensitive information.

7. **Click OK to create the custom template.**

   SharePoint saves a copy of the subsite as a template file and displays the Operation Completed Successfully page informing you that you can now create new sites based on it and that you can manage the template from the Site Template Gallery.

8. **Click OK in the Operation Completed Successfully page.**

   SharePoint returns you to the Site Settings page for the subsite that you saved as a custom template.

Keep in mind when creating new subsites that the templates that you save from other customized subsites are appended to the bottom of the Custom list in the Select a Template list box in the Template Selection section of the New SharePoint Site page. (Refer to Figure 2-14.)

Setting permission and navigation settings

When you use the New SharePoint Site page (refer to Figure 2-15) to create a new subsite, SharePoint applies the following default permission and navigation settings:

- ✔ **Permissions:** User permissions in effect on the parent site are automatically transferred to the subsite. If you want to set different user permissions for the subsite you're creating, you need to click the Use Unique Permission option button under the User Permissions heading. (See Chapter 3 for details.)

- ✔ **Navigation:** A link to the new subsite automatically appears on the Quick Launch in the Sites category. If you don't want a link to the new subsite to appear on the Quick Launch, click the No radio button under the question, "Display This Site on the Quick Launch of the Parent Site?" which appears as its heading. Also, if you don't want the site to appear in a tab on the Top Link bar, select the No radio button under the question, "Display This Site on the Top Link Bar of the Parent Site?" which appears as its heading.

- ✔ **Navigation Inheritance:** The Top Link bar used by the parent site is automatically generated for the new subsite. If you don't want a tab for the new site to appear in the Top Link bar and you want to manually manage this bar in the new subsite, click the No option button under the question, "Use the Top Link Bar from the Parent Site?" which appears as its heading.

Adding Individual Web Pages to a Site's Document Library

The subsites you add to your SharePoint site function primarily as hubs or centers for individual teams with specific informational and collaborative needs. (Subsites are always directly accessible from the top-level site.)

Many times, the subsites you set up for particular teams merely require the addition of individual Web pages rather than a full-blown subsite of their own. SharePoint makes it easy to add individual Web pages to any site within the entire SharePoint site collection.

The only trick to adding individual Web pages to a SharePoint site is that these pages must be saved as part of a particular document library that already exists on the site. (When you first start working on a new SharePoint site based on the Team site template, Shared Documents is the sole existing

document library.) This means that links to these individual Web page
show up in the list of documents when that library is displayed in Shar\
(See Chapter 5 for specific information on creating and using document
libraries in SharePoint.)

When adding an individual Web page to a document library, you have a
choice between the following two types of pages:

- **Basic page:** A blank Web page with no Web Part zones to which you can
  add standard Web page content, including pictures and text.
- **Web Part page:** A blank Web page with Web Part zones to which you
  can add your own Web Parts. (See the section "Editing Web Parts on the
  Pages of Your SharePoint Site" that immediately follows.)

When you add a new Basic page or Web Part page, you must specify the
page's filename as well as the document library to which it's being saved. In
addition, when adding a Web Part page, you must select a particular Layout
Template that determines the number and arrangement of Web Part zones to
which you can add custom Web Parts.

After adding a new Basic page to a document library, you can add and edit its
Web content by opening the page in SharePoint and then clicking the Edit
Content link. (The Edit Content link shows up where the Site Actions button
normally appears in the upper-right corner of a Web Part page.) To add Web
Parts to the zones in a new Web Part page, open the page and then choose
Edit Page from the Site Actions drop-down menu.

Editing Web Parts on the Pages of Your SharePoint Site

The easiest way to customize a subsite or an individual Web Part page
that you've added to your SharePoint site is to edit its Web Parts. To do
this, put the Web Part into Edit mode by choosing the Edit Page option
from the Site Actions drop-down menu. (You know you're in Edit mode
when you see the Exit Edit Mode button immediately below the Site
Actions button.)

As soon as you enter Edit mode, SharePoint identifies the Web Part zones
on the page while at the same time displaying an Add a Web Part button
at the top of each zone as well as a title bar at the top of each existing Web
Part. (See Figure 2-17.)

Web Part Title bars   Add a Web Part button   Web Part Zones

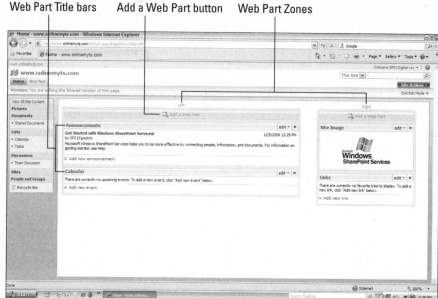

Figure 2-17:
I'm ready
to edit the
Web Parts
on the home
page of my
SharePoint
site.

Adding Web Parts

To add a Web Part to a Web Part page in Edit mode, click the Add a Web Part button that appears at the top of a Web Part zone. When you do this, SharePoint opens an Add Web Parts dialog box bearing the name of the zone to which the Web Part will be added, as shown in Figure 2-18.

This Add Web Parts dialog box contains a list of all the available Web Parts, and they're usually divided into two types: Lists and Libraries and All Web Parts. You then click one or more check boxes next to the Web Parts you want to add. (See the section "Using different Web Parts for different types of information" earlier in this chapter for an explanation of their function.)

After selecting the Web Part(s) to add to your page in this manner, click the Add button to close the Add Web Parts dialog box. The selected Web Part(s) are then inserted at the top of the designated Web Part Zone.

When editing a Web Part page, you can also add Web Parts to any zone from a static Add Web Parts pane displayed on the right side of the screen. Click the Advanced Web Parts Gallery and Options link at the bottom of the Add Web Parts dialog box to display this Add Web Parts pane. Then, select the Web Part zone in the Add To drop-down list before clicking the Web Part in the Web Part List box and clicking the Add button.

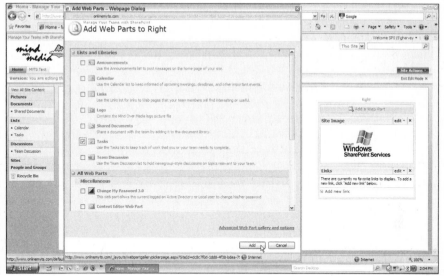

Figure 2-18:
Hm, which
Web Part
should I add
to the Right
Web Part
zone of the
home page?

Rearranging Web Parts

You can rearrange Web Parts on a Web Part page in Edit mode using the standard Windows drag-and-drop method. When repositioning Web Parts, you can move them to new locations within their current Web Part zone as well as between existing Web Part zones.

Position the mouse pointer somewhere on the Web Part's title bar and then — when the pointer changes to a cross with four arrowheads — drag the outline of the Web Part to a new position on the page. SharePoint uses an I-beam pointer to indicate where your Web Part will be inserted when you release the mouse button. When you release the mouse button, the Web Part appears in the new placement, and existing Web Parts in the same zone are adjusted accordingly.

Deleting Web Parts

To remove a Web Part that you no longer need from a Web Part page, click the Web Part's Edit button when the page is in Edit mode and then choose Delete from the Edit button's drop-down menu. SharePoint then displays an alert dialog box indicating that you're about to permanently delete a Web Part. When you click OK, SharePoint deletes the Web Part from the page. Should you later discover that you deleted the Web Part in error, you'll have to go through the trouble of adding it to the desired zone on the Web Part page all over again.

Choose the Close option rather than Delete from the Edit menu (or simply click the Close button — the one with the X to the immediate right of Edit) when you want to temporarily remove the display of a custom Web Part from a particular zone without actually deleting it. That way, you can add the Web Part right back to the page in the same zone or in a new Web Part zone should you later decide its content needs to be shown.

Replacing the Windows SharePoint Services logo with a more pertinent Web Part

If you add your own logo image to the header of your SharePoint site (as I show you how to do earlier in this chapter in the section entitled, "Changing the SharePoint site's title, description, and logo"), you'll probably want to remove the Site Image Web Part with the Windows SharePoint Services logo from the top of the Right Web Part zone on your home page. You can then use the screen real estate formerly taken up by this logo to house a Web Part displaying information that's a little more pertinent to your teams than a Microsoft trademark.

Replacing the Windows SharePoint Services logo with your own logo image

If you don't add your logo to the SharePoint site header, you may want to replace the Windows SharePoint Services image in its Web Part on the home page with your own company's logo. To do this, you must first have uploaded this logo image to the SharePoint site, either to SharePoint's default /_layouts/ images folder (if you have permission) or to a picture library that you've created for the site. (See Chapter 5 for details.)

Then follow these few steps:

1. **Put the home page into Edit mode by choosing Edit Page from the Site Actions drop-down menu.**

2. **Choose Modified Shared Web Part from the Site Image's Edit button drop-down menu.**

    SharePoint opens the Image Web Part pane on the right side of the screen.

3. **In the Image Link text box, replace the relative address /_layouts/ images/homepage.gif with the URL address of your own logo image on the SharePoint site.**

4. **(Optional, but highly recommended) Click the Test Link hyperlink.**

    Assuming that you've entered the right path to the image file and that SharePoint can read this file, your logo should be displayed in the browser window that appears. If this isn't the case, click the window's Close button, edit the address in the Image Link text box, and try the Test Link hyperlink again (until you get it right).

5. **Click the Close button in the browser window displaying your logo image and then click OK in the Image Web Part pane.**

   SharePoint closes the Image Web Part pane and displays your logo in the Site Image Web part.

6. **If you have no further edits to make to the Web Parts on the home page, click the Exit Edit Mode button immediately below the Site Actions button.**

Chapter 3

Giving Your Teams Access to the SharePoint Site

. . . .

In This Chapter

▶ Adding team members to your SharePoint site

▶ Understanding SharePoint groups and permissions

▶ Assigning team members to various SharePoint groups

▶ Modifying group settings and user information for your team members

. . . .

*W*hen you have your SharePoint site organized the way you want (see Chapter 2) and you've added the content your teams initially need in order to start collaborating on a project (see Chapters 4 and 5), you're ready to grant the team members access to your site. This chapter covers the basic process for giving your team members access to the SharePoint site. You do this by enrolling your team members into groups that grant them the permissions for accessing their information and, in certain situations, editing their contents as well.

Adding Team Members as Authenticated SharePoint Site Users

The hallmark of SharePoint 2007 is its ability to give you the highest online security for the information you publish there. To maintain this security, it's *your* responsibility to grant access to each of the individual team members you want as part of your SharePoint site for the purposes of information sharing and collaboration.

Granting access to a team member is typically a twofold process. First, you or a member of your company's IT department (as a site administrator) designates the team member as an *authenticated* user of the SharePoint site by assigning him an initial username and password. Next, you log on to the SharePoint site (again, as an administrator) and then designate this team

?w user of the SharePoint site by assigning him or her to a
:ain site permissions. As part of this process, you can send any
bers an e-mail inviting them to tour the site and then begin
a earnest.

int server is administered internally by your own IT depart-
vant to give the person in charge of setting up your site
members you want added as authenticated users of the
If permitted by your IT department, you can choose initial
usernames and passwords for each of the team members. If this isn't permitted by the IT department in your company, be sure that the IT SharePoint
site administrator provides you with a list of the usernames assigned to each
of your team members (because you'll need this information to assign them
to SharePoint groups).

If your SharePoint site is hosted by an external Internet provider or Web
service, you need to check with its particular procedures for adding users
to your SharePoint site. Many times, the SharePoint service provider
supplies you with a Web address for a User Management page that you use
to authenticate the users of your SharePoint site.

Then, all you have to do is to log on to this page using your administrator
user's name and password and there assign each team member his or her
own unique site username and password. Figure 3-1 shows a typical Web
page for creating a new user for a hosted SharePoint site.

Figure 3-1:
Create a
new user
for a hosted
SharePoint
site.

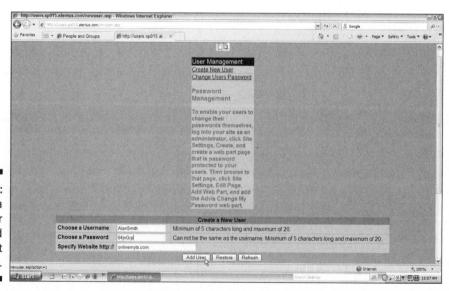

As you can see in this figure, to add a new team member using this particular SharePoint provider's Web page, you assign a unique username and password of between 5 and 20 characters in the Choose a Username and Choose a Password text boxes, respectively (with no spaces or punctuation symbols). Then you specify the Web address of the SharePoint user site to which the user is added in the Specify Website text box. (Conveniently enough, the text box already contains the `http://` URL address prefix.)

Understanding SharePoint Groups and Permissions

SharePoint 2007 maintains online security of your SharePoint site on many different levels. Site-level permissions (the top level) determine the overall level of viewing and editing access that each authenticated user has to all the components in the entire site collection.

Because all the subsites you add to your SharePoint site (see Chapter 2) inherit their site permissions directly from the top-level site, if you give your team members top-level site access, they retain that access in all the subsites you create — unless you specifically modify a particular member's permissions.

The common site permissions that you can bestow upon authenticated users include the following levels:

- ✔ **Full Control:** Gives the SharePoint user complete site management, including all capabilities bestowed by the other site-permission levels (see the following bullets) as well as the ability to modify the user permissions of authenticated SharePoint users.

- ✔ **Design:** Enables the SharePoint user to modify the layout of the SharePoint site — either by using a Web browser or through the use of Office SharePoint Designer 2007 (see Chapter 13) — as well as to edit items and browse the site content.

- ✔ **Contribute:** Enables the SharePoint user to add to and edit items added to the pages of the SharePoint site, including data stored in various lists (see Chapter 4) and files stored in various libraries (see Chapter 5).

- ✔ **Read:** Enables the SharePoint user to browse the information on the site, including downloading files such as Word documents, Excel workbooks, and PowerPoint presentations stored in site libraries for viewing and printing in their native application programs.

Adding or removing site collection administrators

The administrator or administrators of a SharePoint site, by definition, have Full Control permissions for the entire site collection. Moreover, administrators are permitted to designate other authenticated users as administrators as well as to change the site-level (and individual) permission levels of any SharePoint user.

To see who the administrator(s) of the SharePoint site actually are — and then view and edit their user profiles, if you so desire — just follow these steps:

1. **Log on to the SharePoint site and then choose Site Settings from the Site Actions drop-down menu on the home page.**

   SharePoint opens the Site Settings page for the SharePoint site.

2. **Click the Site Collection Administrators link located in the initial Users and Permissions column of the Site Settings page.**

   SharePoint displays a Site Collection Administrators page similar to the one shown in Figure 3-2. If you've logged on to the SharePoint site as an administrator (in which case, your username appears in the list of names displayed in the Site Collection Administrators list box), you can add names of administrators in this list box as well as delete names from it.

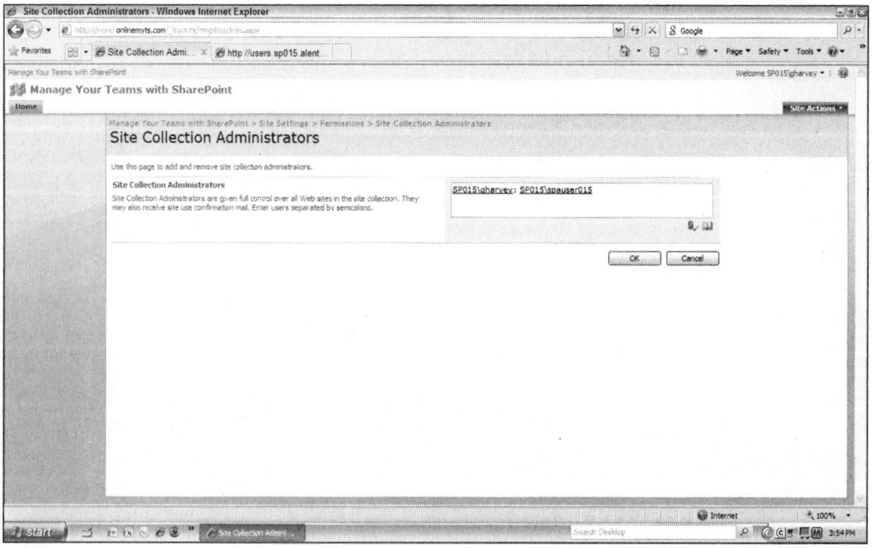

Figure 3-2:
You can add administrators to a SharePoint site.

3. **To add an administrator, enter his or her username in the Site Collection Administrators list box. To remove an administrator, click his or her username and then press the Delete key.**

   When adding usernames to this list box, you can click the Browse button (the one with the open book icon) to select authenticated usernames in the Select People dialog box. If you type the username, click the Check Names button (the one with the check mark under a person's bust) to verify that you've entered the username correctly and that SharePoint recognizes the team member as an authenticated user. Note that if SharePoint can find a match, it underlines the names, and you can then click them for recommended replacements.

   You can add multiple names to the list box in one fell swoop, as long as each username is separated by a semicolon (;).

4. **Click OK to put your administrator changes into effect or click Cancel if you were just browsing the list.**

   SharePoint makes your changes and then returns you to the Site Settings page.

Adding a Site Users Web Part to your SharePoint home page

As I mention in Chapter 2 when discussing personalizing your SharePoint site, SharePoint 2007 includes a Site Users Web Part that you can add to a page. This Web Part lists the name of the site administrator followed by the names of all the site's user groups. This Web Part also contains an Add a New User link that you can use to open an Add Users page, where you add new users as well as set the permissions and assign groups to any new authenticated users you've added to your site.

The greatest feature of this Web Part is the Presence icon that appears next to the username when a team member is online. You can use this icon to communicate with the team member via instant messaging as well as to send him an e-mail or schedule a meeting with him.

The Administrator and Site groups listed in the Site Users list each contain a live link. You can follow the administrator's link to view and/or modify his or her user information, and you can follow the user group links to view and/or modify the teams assigned to each group. (See the "Assigning Individual Team Members to SharePoint Groups" section that immediately follows for details.)

If the thought of adding a Site Users Web Part to your home page seems appealing, follow these steps:

1. **Log on to your SharePoint site.**

2. **Click the Personalize This Page option on the Welcome button's drop-down menu.**

   SharePoint displays an Edit Mode panel on the home page with the message that you're editing a Personal Version of the page.

   I assume here that you don't want this Web Part to be a part of the home page when other team members log on to the site, so you'll want to specify it as a Personal Version of the home page. Also, I chose the Right Web Part zone because the information displayed in the Site Users Web Part doesn't require the width of the Left zone and is a better fit in the Right zone.

3. **Click the Add a Web Part button at the top of the Right Web Part zone.**

   SharePoint opens the Add Web Parts to Right dialog box.

4. **Select the check box in front of the Site Users Web Part option and then click the Add button.**

   SharePoint closes the Add Web Parts to Right dialog box and then adds the Site Users Web Part to the top of the Right Web Part zone.

5. **Position the mouse pointer on the title bar of the Site Users Web Part and then drag its outline down until the I-beam appears beneath the final Web Part in the Right zone (the Links Web Part if you haven't yet customized this zone) and then release the mouse button to drop it into place.**

   The Site Users Web Part now appears at the bottom of the Right Web Part zone.

6. **Click the Exit Edit Mode button on the far-right side of the Version bar.**

   SharePoint exits Edit mode, and the Site Users Web Part at the bottom of the Right zone appears with links for the site administrator and site users groups listed. Your page should look similar to Figure 3-3.

Keep in mind that after you add the Site Users Web Part to a Personal Version of the SharePoint home page, that Web Part no longer appears on the page if you switch to Shared view by selecting the Show Shared View option that now appears on the Welcome button's drop-down menu. To then make the Site Users Web Part again available on your home page, you have to click the Show Personal View option that replaces Show Shared View on the Welcome button's drop-down menu.

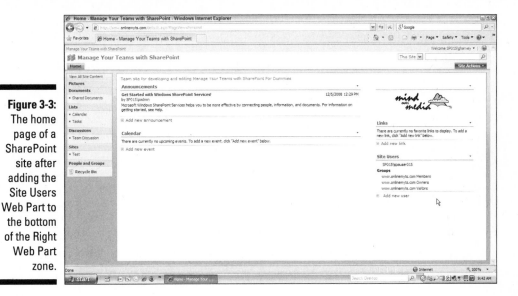

Figure 3-3:
The home
page of a
SharePoint
site after
adding the
Site Users
Web Part to
the bottom
of the Right
Web Part
zone.

Assigning Individual Team Members to SharePoint Groups

To help you manage site permissions for your team members, Windows SharePoint Services enables you to assign any team members you've added as authenticated users to different SharePoint user groups. Each group is assigned its own site permissions level as follows:

- ✓ **Owners [Full Control]:** Team members you add to the Owner's group become administrators who can change the content and layout of the site as well as modify permissions for authenticated users.

- ✓ **Visitors [Read]:** Team members you add to this group are restricted to browsing the contents of the site, although they can download files stored in libraries for editing and printing in their native application programs.

- ✓ **Members [Contribute]:** Team members you add to this group can modify the contents of the site as well as browse it.

If you want to give a particular team member Design permissions — permissions that enable him or her to modify the layout of the site as well as to edit and browse its contents — you either need to assign this level directly to that team member (see "Adding authenticated users to a SharePoint group" later in the chapter for details) or you need to create a new SharePoint Design group where you can then place that team member (as outlined in the

"Creating a new SharePoint group" section that immediately follows). You have to engage in this workaround because Windows SharePoint Services 3.0 doesn't have a ready-made user group with Design permissions.

Creating a new SharePoint group

If none of the ready-made SharePoint user groups have quite the required group settings you want — or don't bestow the desired permissions level you need — you can (as a site administrator with Full Control permissions) create a custom group to do the job. You can then add authenticated users who merit its group settings and permissions level to your newly customized group.

To see how this works, follow the steps in the procedure for creating a new Design user group that bestows the Design permissions on all authenticated users assigned to the group:

1. **Log on to your SharePoint site and then choose Site Settings from the Site Actions drop-down menu.**

   SharePoint opens the Site Settings page.

2. **Click the People and Groups link at the top of the Users and Permissions column.**

   SharePoint opens the Peoples and Groups page for your SharePoint site.

3. **Choose New Group from the New drop-down menu.**

   SharePoint opens the New Group page, similar to the one shown in Figure 3-4.

4. **Type the name of the new user group in the Name text box and then press Tab.**

   SharePoint advances the insertion point to the About Me list box.

5. **Type a description of the new group in the About Me list box.**

   This explanation should describe the type of users, settings, and/or permission levels that you assign to the group.

6. **(Optional) Select a new user who's responsible for making any modifications to the new group's settings in the Group Owner text box.**

   SharePoint automatically displays the name of the primary administrator of the SharePoint site in the Group Owner text box. If you decide to designate another user as the group owner who is solely responsible for making changes to its setting, this person must have Full Control permissions on the SharePoint site.

Figure 3-4:
Use the
New Group
page to
create a
new user
group for
site users.

7. **(Optional) Modify any of the Group Settings options that you want to change for the new group.**

   By default, only users who you assign to the new group can view its membership list, and only the group owner can edit this list. However, you can modify the following settings:

   - *Who can view the membership of the group?* To enable any SharePoint user to view this membership list, select the Everyone option.

   - *Who can edit the membership of the group?* To enable any group member (not generally recommended) to edit the membership list, select the Group Members option.

8. **(Optional) Enable Membership Requests and modify its settings if you want to enable users to send you requests opting for being added to the group or for being removed from it.**

   - *Allow requests to join/leave this group?* To allow requests for membership in the group (as well as removal from it), select the Yes option.

   - *Auto-accept requests?* To have all requests to join and leave the group automatically accepted, select the Yes option.

   By default, SharePoint sends requests to join or leave the group to your primary e-mail address. To have all requests e-mailed to another e-mail address, you need to enter that address in the Send Membership Requests to the Following E-Mail Address text box.

9. **In the Give Group Permissions to This Site area at the bottom of the page, select the check box of the permission level (Full Control, Design, Contribute, or Read) that users you assign to the new group should have.**

10. **Click the Create button.**

    SharePoint creates the new group using the settings you selected.

When the program finishes creating the new user group, SharePoint automatically opens a People and Group page. This page displays the name of the new group and shows it selected (with highlighting) in the Groups links in the left panel. In addition, your name appears listed as the sole user in this group (unless you changed the group owner back in Step 6).

You can then use the Add Users option on the New drop-down menu of this People and Groups page to add all the authenticated users you want to the new custom group you just created. (See the "Adding authenticated users to a SharePoint group" section that follows immediately for details.)

Adding authenticated users to a SharePoint group

The procedure for adding users to a SharePoint group is very straightforward. Just be aware that SharePoint gives you a couple of ways to open the People and Groups page, which lists all current users in the Members group and from which you can add authenticated users to your site.

The most direct way to open this page is to click the People and Groups link at the bottom of the Quick Launch for the site's home page. You can also open this People and Groups page for the site by clicking the People and Groups link that appears in the Users and Permissions column of the Site Settings page (opened by choosing Site Settings from the Site Actions drop-down menu).

Then, with a People and Groups page open, you can follow these steps to add team members (who are authenticated users) to any of the available user groups:

1. **Choose Add Users from the New drop-down menu.**

    SharePoint opens an Add Users page for your site, similar to the one shown in Figure 3-5.

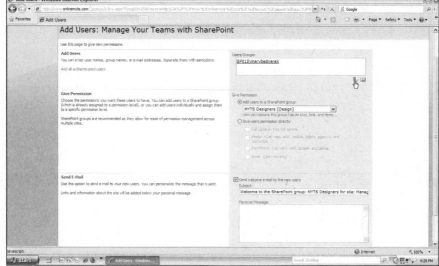

Figure 3-5:
You might
need to add
authenti-
cated
users to a
particular
group
on your
SharePoint
site.

2. **Enter the usernames, separated with semicolons (;), of all the team members you want to add to a particular user group in the Users/ Groups list box.**

   When adding usernames to this list box, you can click the Browse button (the one with the open book icon) to open the Select People dialog box, where you can search for authenticated users by typing part of their usernames into the Find text box and then pressing Enter. SharePoint then finds the username and displays and selects it in the list box below. You can then add it by clicking the Add button before you click OK.

   If you type the usernames, click the Check Names button (the one with the check mark under a person's bust) to verify that you've entered the names correctly and that SharePoint recognizes them as authenticated users.

3. **On the Add Users to a SharePoint Group drop-down list, select the name of the user group with the site permissions you want to assign the user(s) listed above in the Users/Groups list box (if that group's name isn't already displayed in this drop-down list box).**

   Note that if none of the ready-made user groups bestow the level of permissions that you want to grant, you need to click the Give Users Permission Directly option button and then click the check box of the permission level (Full Control, Design, Contribute, or Read) that you want to assign.

4. **(Optional) To add a personal message to the welcome e-mails that SharePoint automatically sends to the users you're adding, click the Personal Message list box and then type the text of your message.**

If you don't need to send welcome e-mail messages to the team members you're adding to the SharePoint site, deselect the Send Welcome E-Mail to the New User check box.

5. **Click OK at the bottom of the Add Users page.**

SharePoint adds the users you specified to the group you designated. The program then opens the People and Groups page for that user group, where all the usernames of all team members you added are now listed.

Managing SharePoint Users and Groups

SharePoint makes it easy to manage both the team members you add as users to your site and the SharePoint groups to which you assign them. Simply click the People and Groups link at the bottom of the Quick Launch (immediately above the Recycle Bin) on your SharePoint site's home page.

The program then typically displays a People and Groups page (similar to the one shown in Figure 3-6), which shows a list of the users you've added to the Members SharePoint group. To view users that you've added to another user group, simply click its link in the Groups area on the left, which appears immediately above the View All Site Content link and the Quick Launch. To view all the users that have access to the SharePoint site, click the All People link that appears in the Groups area above the page's Quick Launch.

Figure 3-6:
Managing users and groups from the People and Groups page in a SharePoint site.

Groups area

Modifying a SharePoint group's site permissions

You can easily view (as well as edit) the settings and permissions for any of the SharePoint groups that your particular site uses (assuming, of course, that you're logged on as an administrator). Simply click the Site Permissions link above the View All Site Content link to open a Permissions page for your site (similar to the one shown in Figure 3-7).

This Permissions page contains a list of all the SharePoint groups used on your site as well as the usernames of any team members you've added to the site without assigning them to a particular group (by directly assigning their permissions level).

To edit the permissions level for a particular group in the list on the Permissions page, follow these steps:

1. **Click the link attached to the name of the group whose permissions need changing (such as Members, Owners, Visitors, and so forth) in the Users/Groups column of the Permissions page.**

   SharePoint opens an Edit Permissions page for the selected group, showing its current permissions level.

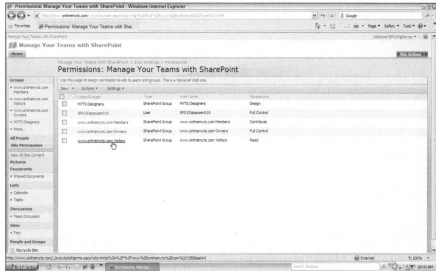

Figure 3-7: On the Permissions page, you can manage the permissions for the SharePoint groups and for users not assigned to any group.

2. **(Optional) Deselect the check box in front of the permissions level currently assigned to the selected group (Full Control, Design, Contribute, or Read).**

    You *always* want to remove the currently assigned permissions level before assigning a new level to a group when that new permissions level is less inclusive than the current one (as in going from Full Control down to Contribute). Otherwise, SharePoint still grants the users in this group the rights associated with the more inclusive level even after you finish editing the group's permissions.

3. **Select the check box in front of the new permissions level you want to assign to the selected group (Full Control, Design, Contribute, or Read).**

    Verify that the check box for the new permissions level — the one you now want the group members to have — is the one selected in the Choose Permissions area.

    Note that if you happen to remove the current permissions level without setting a new one (by clicking OK when all the permissions level check boxes are deselected), the members of the group in question then have no rights to any part of the SharePoint site!

4. **Click OK.**

    SharePoint closes the Edit Permissions page for the selected group and returns you once again to the general Permissions page showing all the groups and the users not assigned to groups.

Modifying a particular team member's site permissions by reassigning his group

Instead of modifying the permissions for an entire SharePoint user group, you may just need to change the level for particular team members. You do this by removing the team member from his or her current SharePoint group and then assigning that member to a new user group with the appropriate permissions.

To change a team member's permissions level when you're logged on to the SharePoint site's home page, follow these steps:

1. **Click the People and Groups link beneath the home page Quick Launch.**

    SharePoint typically opens the People and Groups page for the Members group where you start by selecting the user group from which the team member in question currently derives his permissions.

2. **If the team member isn't part of the Members group, click the link to the SharePoint group to which he's currently assigned in the Groups area of the left panel.**

   When you've displayed the group to which the team member is currently assigned, you ready to select that member.

3. **Select the team member in the group list whose permissions you want to modify by clicking the check box in front of his or her name.**

   Now you're ready to remove the selected team member from the current group and assign him or her to a new group.

4. **Choose Remove Users from Group from the Actions drop-down menu and then click OK in the alert dialog box to confirm the person's removal.**

   Having removed the team member in question from his or her previous SharePoint group, you're now ready to assign the team member to the user group that has the permissions level you now want him or her to have.

5. **In the Groups area of the left panel, click the link to the SharePoint group with the permissions you now want the team member to have.**

   Now all you have to do is add the team member to the new group with the new permissions.

6. **Choose Add Users from the New drop-down menu and then follow the procedure for adding the team member in question to this group.**

   Refer to the section, "Adding authenticated users to a SharePoint group" earlier in this chapter if you need help adding a user.

Editing a team member's user information

After adding your authenticated users to a SharePoint site, you typically can view and edit their user information. You can modify the username, e-mail address, description, department, and job title. In addition, you can also add a photo that visually identifies the user on the SharePoint site in any user list.

To edit the information stored in a team member's user profile, follow these steps:

1. **Click the People and Groups link beneath the home page Quick Launch.**

   SharePoint opens the People and Groups page for the Members group.

2. **Click the All People link in the Groups area on the People and Groups page.**

   SharePoint opens an All People page, which lists all the authenticated users that have been added to the site.

3. **Click the link attached to the name of the team member whose user profile you want to edit.**

   SharePoint opens a User Information page for the selected team member, showing his current user profile information.

4. **Click the Edit Item button at the top of the rows of user information.**

   SharePoint opens an Edit Personal Settings page for the team member with editable fields containing the user profile information, similar to the one shown in Figure 3-8.

5. **Edit any of the information in the individual fields (Account through SIP Address) that need updating.**

   To add the team member's photo to his profile, you must specify the URL address of a SharePoint folder that already contains the uploaded graphics file. (See Chapter 5 for details on uploading graphics to a picture library.)

6. **Click OK.**

   SharePoint closes the Edit Personal Settings page that you just edited and returns you to the All People page, where the updated information now appears for that team member.

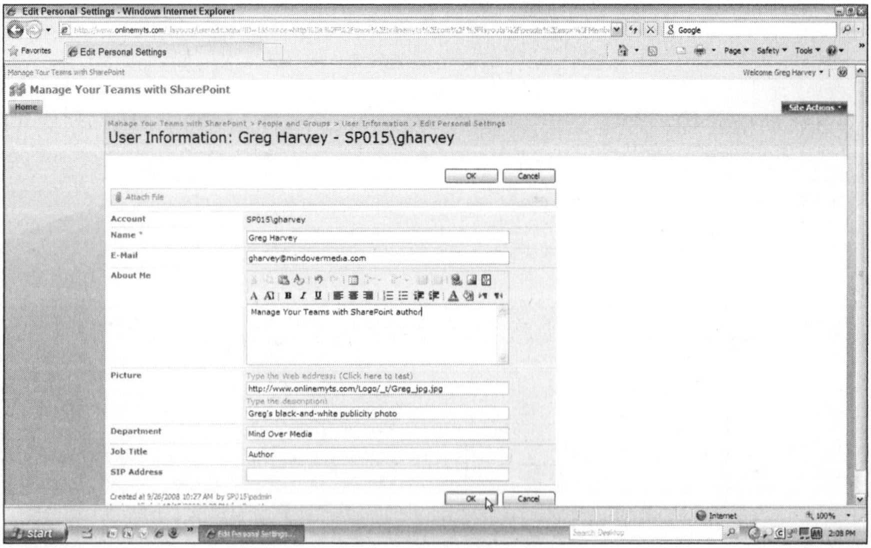

Figure 3-8:
You can edit
the contents
of a user's
profile.

Removing a team member from the SharePoint site

If there comes a time when a particular team member is no longer actively working on the project and therefore no longer needs access to the SharePoint site, you can remove him or her.

To remove a team member from the SharePoint site, follow these steps:

1. **Click the People and Groups link beneath the home page Quick Launch.**

   SharePoint typically opens the People and Groups page for the Members group.

2. **Click the All People link in the Groups area on the People and Groups page.**

   SharePoint opens an All People page that lists all the authenticated users that have been added to the site.

3. **Select the check box in front of the name of the team member you want to remove from the SharePoint site.**

   Now you're ready to remove the team member whose username you selected.

4. **Choose Delete Users from Site Collection from the Actions drop-down menu and then click OK in the alert dialog box to confirm the user's removal.**

   SharePoint removes the name of the selected team member from the All People page, along with his or her permissions to use its contents.

Should you ever find that you need to reinstate a team member that you've removed from your SharePoint site, you can do so by following the procedure for adding the user to the site. (See "Adding authenticated users to a SharePoint group" earlier in this chapter for details.)

Modifying Site Permission Levels

SharePoint enables you, as an administrator, to modify a site's permission levels. You can change particular settings for existing permission levels (such as Members, Contributors, and so on). You can add new site permission levels (such as Visitor or Partial Access) and even delete an existing permission level (which, of course, you'd want to do only after reassigning the site permissions for all team members currently granted that level).

To modify the permission levels for a site, take these steps:

1. **Open the site whose permission levels you want to modify.**

   If you want to modify the permission levels for the top-level site and all subsites below it, open the home page of your SharePoint site.

2. **Choose Site Settings from the Site Actions drop-down menu.**

   SharePoint opens the Site Settings page.

3. **Click the Advanced Permissions link in the Users and Permissions column.**

   SharePoint opens the Permissions page for the selected site.

4. **Choose the Permission Levels option from the Settings drop-down menu.**

   SharePoint opens the Permission Levels page for your site, similar to the one shown in Figure 3-9.

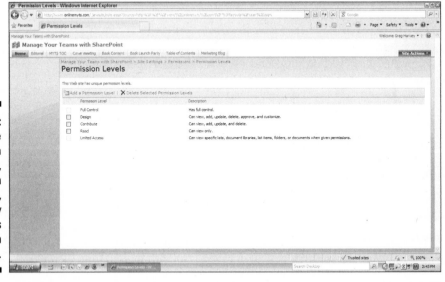

Figure 3-9:
On the Permission Levels page, you can add, delete, or modify your site's permission levels.

On the Permission Levels page, you can then make any of the following changes to the site's particular levels:

- **Add a level:** Click the Add a Permission Level button at the top of the Permission Levels page. Then, on the Add a Permission Level page, enter a name and description for the new level and select each of the check boxes for the individual permission settings you want to enable. When you're ready, click the Create button. To enable all the permission settings for the new level, select the Select All check box immediately beneath the Description list box.

- **Delete a level:** Select the check box(es) for each of the permission levels you want to delete on the Permission Levels page and then click the Delete Selected Permission Levels button. You then need to click the OK button in the alert dialog box asking you to confirm the deletion.

Before you click OK to delete the permission level, be absolutely certain that you've reassigned all the users and groups in that level to another level that you're retaining. If you haven't reassigned them, those folks will get locked out of accessing the site!

- **Modify the settings of an existing level:** Click the name of the permission level whose individual settings you want to tweak in the Permission Level column on the Permission Levels page. SharePoint then opens an Edit Permission Level page for the particular level you selected. You can then modify particular permission settings for this level by selecting individual check boxes to enable new settings and/or by deselecting check boxes to disable them before you click the Submit button.

Perhaps you want to create a new permissions level for the site that's based on the settings of the level currently open in the Edit Permission Level page. If so, click the Copy Permission Level button at the bottom of the page, name the level "copy," and then make any necessary changes to its individual settings before clicking the Create button.

Part II
Managing Your SharePoint Data

The 5th Wave   By Rich Tennant

"I'm not saying I believe in anything. All I know is since it's been there our server is running 50% faster."

In this part . . .

SharePoint is all about sharing information in one form or another. In this part, you find out all about SharePoint lists and libraries, the two principal ways to store vital data on your SharePoint site. With lists, you can give your teams access to all the facts and figures they need to collaborate. With libraries, you can give them access to all the supporting documents they need.

Chapter 4

Creating and Maintaining SharePoint Lists

In This Chapter

▶ Understanding the vital role that lists play in SharePoint 2007

▶ Reviewing the major types of lists you can have in SharePoint sites

▶ Adding lists to your SharePoint site

▶ Adding and importing data into the lists you use

▶ Customizing your SharePoint lists to suit your site's data needs

*L*ists form the very core of a SharePoint 2007 site. Almost all the information that you share with your fellow team members is in the form of some sort of SharePoint list. Even SharePoint libraries (the subject of the next chapter), although routinely considered a separate SharePoint component, are in fact SharePoint lists that give you information and links to various documents and graphics files you share with your team members.

This chapter gives you an overview of SharePoint lists by introducing you to their general types and functions. The chapter also gives you a rundown on the basic care and handling of SharePoint lists. This coverage includes how to create new lists, edit existing ones, customize their layout, and do fundamental sorting and filtering of their contents. You can then use this information to create custom lists for your teams and present them with all the information they need to work with.

SharePoint Lists 101

Lists are everywhere in SharePoint. For example, in the main part of the home page of a new SharePoint site, you find three different empty lists — Announcements, Calendar, and Links — that you can immediately start adding data to. And in the left pane of the home page, all the links (including every single one in the Quick Launch) take you to pages that contain their own lists. In fact, clicking the first link in the left pane, View All Site

Content, takes you to the All Site Content page, which contains the grand-daddy of all SharePoint lists: a list of all the lists that exist in the top-level SharePoint site!

The first thing to know about SharePoint lists is that, rather than being simple laundry lists that catalog a bunch of items, they're more often than not bona fide data lists whose individual items are made up of several different types of data that the lists track.

For example, in the case of the Calendar list on the SharePoint home page, its items consist of the upcoming events that you want to publicize to your team members. And the standard types of data recorded for each of these items include such pieces of information as the event's title, location, starting and ending times, and general description.

The standard types of data that a data list catalogs are known as its *fields* (title, location, starting time, and so on in the Calendar list), and the individual items made up from the actual data entered into these fields are known as its *records* (the individual events that the Calendar list chronicles).

As with other applications that work primarily with data (such as Microsoft Excel and Access), the information in data lists is routinely presented in a table layout. In the table, each column contains a different field from the data list, and the individual rows of the table make up its records.

It's important, however, to remember that tabular presentation of a data list is only that. The data in the fields that make up the list's items are stored independently of the table itself. And it's this independence that makes it easy to customize the table by changing the order in which the fields appear within it as well as the number and type of fields that the table displays. In addition, this independence makes it easy to sort the items in the table by various fields of the data list as well as to apply criteria to certain fields that filter the data list so that only the records you want to see remain displayed.

In a typical SharePoint site, you make great use of this ability to quickly set up custom views of data in particular lists so that only the fields and records currently of interest to the team are displayed on a particular Web page.

Adding Lists to Your SharePoint Site

Normally, the procedure for adding a new list to your SharePoint site is twofold. First, you create a new list for the top-level site or a particular subsite. Then, you add the data you want to the new list you've created.

Keep in mind that this twofold process collapses down to a single step when you create a new list directly from a spreadsheet table of data stored in the worksheet of an Excel 2003 or 2007 workbook file. In that case, when you create a new list in SharePoint, the program creates two things:

- ✔ A Web page for the list where you can begin adding data.

- ✔ A Web Part specifically for the list you create that you can use to place the same list on another page of the SharePoint site. Note that this list shows up in the Lists and Libraries section of the Add Web Parts dialog box. (See Chapter 2 for details on using Web Parts.)

Not only can you reuse this new Web Part on a different page within the same subsite, but you can also modify its appearance (officially known as a *view*) without changing how the information is displayed in the original list. For example, you can use the Web Part created for a particular team contacts list to add a view of the list to the Right Web Part zone of the home page of your SharePoint site. There, you can modify the appearance of the Web Part so that only the columns with the team member names and e-mail addresses are displayed. That way, you still have all the contact information on the Web page created for the original list while the Right Web Part zone of the home page just contains e-mail links that make it easy for you and other team members to send each other messages.

The different types of standard lists

SharePoint offers a whole array of different list templates that you can use for your new lists. SharePoint organizes its standard list templates into the following three groups:

- ✔ **Communication:** This group contains SharePoint's standard tools for keeping your team members informed and in contact with each other. It includes **Announcements, Contacts,** and **Discussion Board.**

- ✔ **Tracking:** This group makes it easy to track people, places, and things of interest to you and your team members. It includes **Links, Calendar, Tasks, Project Tasks, Issue Tracking,** and **Survey.**

- ✔ **Custom Lists:** This group enables you to create made-to-order lists that don't fit any of the other patterns and that contain only the fields (columns) you want and need. It includes **Custom List, Custom List in Datasheet View,** and **Import Spreadsheet.**

The following bullet list examines each of the individual templates a bit more closely. Just keep in mind that, when you add a list to a SharePoint site, you can make use of the following templates:

- ✔ **Announcements:** Provides a place to publish brief messages, updating team members on some upcoming aspect of the project and/or its current status.

- ✔ **Contacts:** Provides a place to publish contact information of all different types (team, vendor, client, you name it) that your team members need during the project.

- ✔ **Discussion Board:** Provides a place to get feedback from your team members on some aspect of the project using the familiar threaded discussion format.

- ✔ **Links:** Provides a place to share links to other Web sites that contain information of general or specific interest to the team.

- ✔ **Calendar:** Provides a place to publicize upcoming events (meetings, project milestones, deadlines, and so forth) that are either of general interest or directly involve members of the team. The calendar list presents this information in the very familiar and graphical layout of a paper version of a daily, weekly, or monthly day planner.

- ✔ **Tasks:** Provides a place to publicize a listing of all the tasks that you and your fellow team members need to complete as part of the project.

- ✔ **Project Tasks:** Provides a place to publicize the tasks that you and your teams need to complete as part of a Gantt chart — a type of bar chart that illustrates the start and finish dates of the specific components of a project. Note that you can open and edit a Project Tasks list in Microsoft Office Project 2007 (if you use that application in your work) as well as in the Web browser you use to browse the SharePoint site.

- ✔ **Issue Tracking:** Provides a place to track issues or problems that need to be resolved in the course of the project. You can use this type of list to prioritize issues, assign their resolution to particular team members, and track their settlement.

- ✔ **Survey:** Provides a way to poll individual team members on some aspect of the project and then publicize the group results in the SharePoint site.

- ✔ **Custom List:** Provides a way to create a completely customized list that contains only the fields (columns) you need to use.

- ✔ **Custom List in Datasheet View:** Provides a way to create a customized list whose data is entered in the familiar datasheet format (very similar to entering data in an Excel worksheet with its column and row format). The great thing about entering data for a list in Datasheet view is that it enables you to quickly make mass edits for the list.

- ✔ **Import Spreadsheet:** Provides a way to create a custom list directly from a table of data stored in an Excel 2003 or 2007 worksheet. When SharePoint creates the list from a range of cells in a spreadsheet table, it uses the table's column headings to create the fields.

Creating a new list for the site

The procedure for creating a new list for a SharePoint site is very straight-forward, although it does differ slightly depending upon the template you select for the list you're creating:

1. **Select the site where you want the list to be.**

   If you want to add the list to a top-level SharePoint site, select the home page by clicking the name of the site in the Content Navigation Breadcrumb above the name of the current page. If you want to add a list to a particular subsite, select the main page of that subsite by clicking its tab on the Top Link bar below the name of the current page.

2. **Click the Lists link in the Quick Launch of the site you've selected.**

   SharePoint opens the All Site Content page for the selected site, showing all the lists currently added to the site.

3. **Click the Create button at the top of the listing of all the lists on the All Site Content page.**

   SharePoint opens a Create page similar to the one shown in Figure 4-1. This page contains links to the many different types of lists you can create. (See the section "The different types of standard lists" immediately preceding this one for details.)

4. **Click the link attached to the type of list you want to create in the Communications, Tracking, or Custom Lists columns of the Create page.**

   SharePoint opens a New page corresponding to the type of list you've chosen. (You'll use this page to enter a name for the list as well as a description of its function.)

5. **Enter a name for the new list in the Name text box and then press Tab and enter a description of the list in the Description text box. If you're creating a list from a spreadsheet, you also need to specify the work-book file that contains the table in the File Location text box and then specify the range of cells to use in the Import to Windows SharePoint Services dialog box.**

   For all lists (except those created by importing a spreadsheet), SharePoint automatically displays a link to the page with the new list on the site's Quick Launch. If you don't want the new list to show up on the site's Quick Launch, click the No radio button in the Navigation area of the New page.

   Several types of lists (Tasks, Project Tasks, and Issue Tracking) have an option that you can select for automatically sending e-mail notification when ownership of the list is assigned.

Figure 4-1:
Select the
type of list to
add to your
SharePoint
site.

When creating a survey, the New page contains Survey Options that you can change when you don't want usernames to appear in the survey results and/or don't want to allow users to answer the survey more than once.

6. **(Optional) Make any desired changes to the default settings of the other options that the particular type of list you're creating offers.**

   Now you're ready to create the new list.

7. **Click the Create button (or the Import button, in the case of a list created using the Import Spreadsheet link).**

   SharePoint creates the new list and displays its page so that you can begin customizing its columns or entering its data.

Keep in mind that you can also create a new list by clicking the Create option on the Site Actions drop-down menu to open the Create page. You have to use this method when you're dealing with a subsite that doesn't have a Quick Launch links area.

Entering data into a new list

After creating a list using one of the standard list templates, you can begin adding data to it. To manually enter data for a new record, choose New Item from the New drop-down menu. SharePoint then opens a New Item page containing the series of fields (as either single-line text boxes or multi-line list boxes) for the type of list you created.

For example, Figure 4-2 shows the top part of a New Item page for a new Team Contacts list created from the Contacts list template. This New Item page contains a whole series of fields, starting with Last Name and extending all the way down to Notes (not visible in the figure).

Note, however, that for a Contacts list, the Last Name field at the very top is the only mandatory field (indicated by the red asterisk immediately following this field name at the top of the form). This means that all the other fields in this form are optional and don't have to be filled in if you either don't have data for the fields or don't need to track the information in the particular list you're building.

Also note that the data entry for this type of list contains an Attach File link at the top that you can use to upload particular files and attach them to the record you're creating. So, for example, in the case of the Team Contacts list, I can use this link to mark both a team member's resume (saved as a Word document) and his publicity photo (saved as JPEG graphics file) as a part of his contact record in this list.

When entering information into the fields of a list's data form, keep in mind that a SharePoint data form supports the standard editing keystrokes that you use in Word to move the insertion point/cursor and to edit text. In addition, you can press the Tab key to advance from one field to the next down the data form and press Shift+Tab to move back up to a previous field.

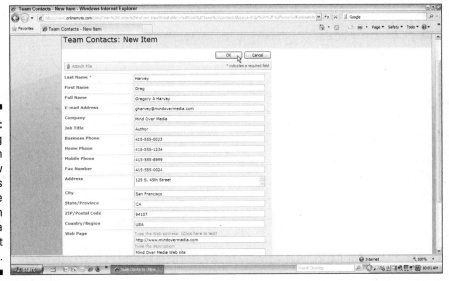

Figure 4-2:
Entering
an item
for a new
Contacts
list on the
New Item
page of a
SharePoint
site.

When you finish entering all your information into the various fields of the list's data form, you then click OK to save the record. SharePoint automatically returns you to the list page where entries for the fields in the default view — the All Contacts view, in the example of the Team Contacts list shown in Figure 4-3 — appear at the top, immediately beneath the column (field) names.

Remember that a list typically contains many more fields than are displayed in the columns of the list's default view. For example, in the case of the Team Contacts list, each record may contain up to a total of 18 fields of information (when you include the Attachments field by adding supporting files to any of its records). Contrast this to the mere six fields of information (seven if you count the paperclip icon for the Attachment field) that appear in the columns of the list's default All Contacts view on the Teams Contacts Web page (see Figure 4-3).

Figure 4-3:
Here's the Team Contacts list after entering the first record showing the entries for the six fields displayed in its default All Contacts view.

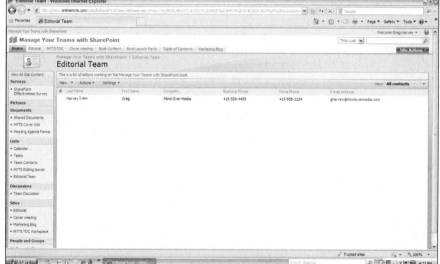

Entering and editing data in a list in Datasheet view

If you have the Microsoft Office 2003 or 2007 Professional version installed on your computer and use a Web browser such as Internet Explorer 7 or 8 with

Active X controls installed, SharePoint 2007 supports a Datasheet view for most of the lists that you create from standard templates (Calendar, Survey, and Discussion Board being the big exceptions).

Datasheet view enables you to add and edit the contents of your list in a familiar spreadsheet-like environment of columns and rows, which facilitates editing the contents of more than one list item at a time. This Datasheet view also enables you to quickly sort and filter the contents of your list on different columns as well as modify the layout of its current list view.

To turn on Datasheet view (for a type of list that supports it), open the Web page containing the list and then choose Edit in Datasheet from the Actions drop-down menu. (Note that if the Edit in Datasheet option doesn't appear on your Actions menu, this is a clear sign that your computer/browser isn't currently set up to support the Access Web Datasheet view.)

The moment you choose Edit in Datasheet, SharePoint redisplays the contents of the list in a row-and-column grid that sets the list in a table of cells very similar to that used by an Excel worksheet. In addition to the row-and-column grid, Datasheet view adds drop-down buttons to the right of the field names in the top row of the list, and you can use those drop-down buttons to sort and filter the list. This view also adds an Access icon in the upper-left corner of the list, which you can use to select the entire list. The view also adds a row of blank cells beneath that last record of the list into which you can add the entries for the next record. (See Figure 4-4, which shows you the new Team Contacts list with a single record after turning on Datasheet view.)

To add data to a list in Datasheet view, follow these steps:

1. **Use the arrow keys to move the cell cursor to the cell in the first column of the list's final blank row that needs data — or simply click that cell with the white-cross mouse pointer.**

   SharePoint shows that the cell is selected by outlining the cell's borders with a heavy, dark blue line.

2. **Enter data for the first field of the new record and then press Tab or the → key.**

   SharePoint advances the cell cursor to the cell in the column to the immediate right and adds a new blank row to the bottom of the list's datasheet.

3. **Enter the data for this field in the current cell and then press Tab or → again to advance to the next field to the right.**

Access icon   Fields   Last Record

New Record

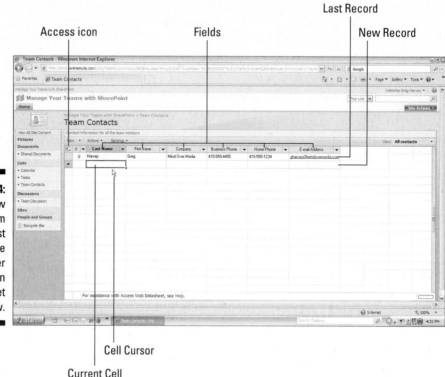

Figure 4-4:
The new
Team
Contacts list
looks like
this after
you turn on
Datasheet
view.

Cell Cursor

Current Cell

Continue entering data for the new record in this manner by repeating Step 3 until you've entered data in the cell located in the final column of that row.

4. Press the Tab or → key.

SharePoint enters the data you've typed into the last cell of the current row and then automatically moves the cell cursor to the first column in the blank row below, setting you up for adding a new record in that row.

If, when making a cell entry in a new row, you type the same initial letters as a previous data entry made in rows above in that column, SharePoint displays a pop-up menu containing the entry or entries that share the same beginning letters. You can then make a duplicate entry in the new cell (assuming that duplicates are appropriate, as in the case of a field such as the Department, Company, City, State, or Country) simply by clicking that entry in the pop-up menu.

When you finish adding all the records to the list in this manner, you can then take the list out of Datasheet view by performing the next step.

5. **Click the Show in Standard View option on the Actions button's drop-down menu.**

SharePoint takes the list out of Datasheet view and back into its Standard view.

Note that you don't have to enter the data for a new record across successive columns of the final blank row of its datasheet (as outlined in the previous procedure). If you prefer, you can enter the data down the rows of each successive column in the list instead. All you have to do is remember to press the Enter key after you finish each cell entry. When you finish entering the last entry for the first field, simply press the Enter key without making any entry in the final blank row and SharePoint will then advance the cell cursor to the top of the very next column. You can then press the ↓ key to move the cell cursor down to the first blank cell in that new column, where you can begin making the entries for that field.

Remember that when you enter data into a list using its Datasheet view, you are entering data only in those fields whose columns are displayed in the current list view. To enter data for fields in the list whose columns aren't displayed, you either have to add their columns to the list view (see "Modifying the columns in a list in Datasheet View," later in this chapter) or you have to enter that data for those fields in the item's data form (which you can easily open from the datasheet by clicking the item's link in the first column of its record).

Selecting and editing cells in Datasheet view

In Datasheet view, you can use a number of keystrokes to make selections and perform commands in the datasheet. (See Table 4-1 for details.) For example, to select a range of cells in the list for editing, hold down the Shift key as you press the appropriate arrow keys.

As long as you hold down the Shift key as you press an arrow key, SharePoint increases the cell selection to include all the cells that the cursor moves through (indicated by light blue highlighting of the individual cells and the heavy dark blue line of the cell cursor outlining the borders of the entire selection). Keep in mind, however, that if you forget to hold down Shift as you press an arrow key, SharePoint merely moves the cell cursor to the next cell without extending the size of the cell selection.

Table 4-1	Keystroke Shortcuts for Editing a SharePoint List in Datasheet View
Press This . . .	*. . . To Do This*
Arrow key	Advance the cell cursor to the next cell in the direction of the arrow (if there is no cell in the direction of the arrow, pressing the key does nothing).
Tab	Advance the cell cursor to the next cell to the right in the current row.
Shift+Tab	Advance the cell cursor to the previous cell to the left in the current row.
Enter	Advance the cell cursor to the next cell down in the current column. (If the cursor is in the last blank cell of a column, it then advances to the top of the next column.)
Home	Advance the cell cursor to the first cell in the current row of the datasheet.
End	Advance the cell cursor to the last cell in the current row of the datasheet.
Ctrl+Home	Advance the cell cursor to the first cell of the datasheet.
Ctrl+End	Advance the cell cursor to the last cell of the datasheet.
Page Down	Scroll to the next list page.
Page Up	Scroll to the previous list page.
Shift+arrow key	Extend the cell selection in the direction of the arrow.
Shift+spacebar	Select all the cells in the current row of the datasheet.
Ctrl+spacebar	Select all the cells in the current column of the datasheet.
Ctrl+A	Select all the cells in the datasheet.
Ctrl+Shift+Home	Extend the cell selection from the current cell to the first cell of the datasheet.
Ctrl+Shift+End	Extend the cell selection from the current cell to the last cell of the datasheet.
Esc	Restore the previous entry to the current cell before the current cell edit has been completed (by pressing Enter or a navigation key).
F1	Open a browser window with Help on using the Access Web Datasheet.
F2	Put the current cell into Edit mode by displaying the insertion point cursor in that cell at the end of the cell's current entry.
Delete	Delete the contents of the current cell selection.

Press This . . .	. . . To Do This
F8	Display the Datasheet task pane with buttons for performing common editing tasks and links for using the list with Microsoft Access and Excel. (See the section "Using the task pane in Datasheet view" immediately following for details.)
Shift+F8	Hide the Datasheet task pane.
Ctrl+C	Copy the contents of the current cell selection to the Windows Clipboard.
Ctrl+V	Paste the contents of the Windows Clipboard into the datasheet.
Ctrl+X	Cut the contents of the current cell selection to the Windows Clipboard.
Ctrl+Z	Undo the last edit in the datasheet.
Shift+F10	Open the context menu with common editing commands for the current cell selection in the datasheet.

Keep in mind that you can make some cell selections in a datasheet with the mouse. To select the entire column containing the cell cursor, position the mouse pointer somewhere in the cell with the field name at the top of the column and then click when the mouse pointer changes to a black arrow pointing down. To select the entire row with the cell cursor, position the mouse pointer in the shaded cell at the very beginning of the datasheet row and then click when the mouse pointer changes to a black arrow pointing to the right. To select all the cells in the entire datasheet, position the mouse pointer in the cell with the Access icon in the very upper-left corner of the table and then click when the mouse pointer changes to a black arrow pointing diagonally downward and to the right.

Using the task pane in Datasheet view

Datasheet view sports a task pane that you can easily display or hide as you enter and edit data in a new list. To open the task pane in Datasheet view, you can either choose Task Pane from the Actions drop-down menu or press F8. To close the task pane, you then either choose Task Pane from the Actions drop-down menu again or press Shift+F8.

Figure 4-5 shows this task pane open in the sample Team Contacts list in Datasheet view. As you can see, the top row of this task pane contains a bunch of buttons that are very useful when you're editing data in the cells of the datasheet.

Immediately below this row of buttons, you find a bunch of links that you can use to work with this list either in Microsoft Access or Excel. (See Chapter 12 for more on using SharePoint data in Office applications such as Access and Excel.)

Remove Filter/Sort

Custom Sort

Undo

Paste

Copy

Cut

Help

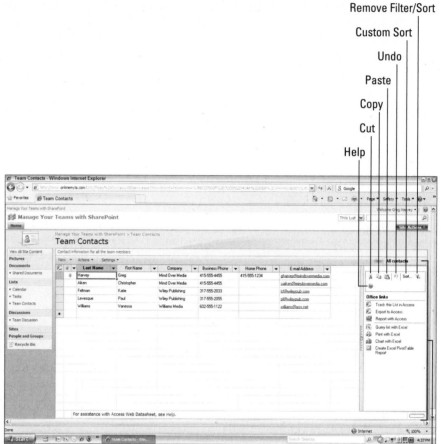

Datasheet Task Pane

Figure 4-5:
This Team Contacts list displays the task pane in Datasheet view.

Modifying the columns in a list in Datasheet view

One of the great features of editing a list in Datasheet view is that this view makes it really easy to modify its columns. All you have to do is select the column by right-clicking its heading and then select one of the following options on its drop-down menu:

✔ **Add Column:** Select this option to add a new field to the list and display its column immediately after the column currently selected in the current list view. See the section "Adding a new column to the list," later in this chapter for details.

✔ **Edit/Delete Column:** Select this option to change some settings for the field (including its field type) in the selected column or to permanently remove it from both the current list view and the list's data form.

✔ **Column Width:** Select this option to widen or narrow the width of the currently selected column. If you select this option, a Column Width dialog box appears, and in it is a dialog box of the same name where you can replace the current column width with a new value. Note that if you narrow a column and then make a data entry in the column that is longer than its new width can display, SharePoint automatically wraps the leftover text to a new line in the row (provided that you haven't selected the Turn Wrap Text Off option on the column's context menu).

✔ **Hide:** Select this option to temporarily remove the display of the selected column from the list. You can then redisplay all hidden columns by selecting the entire list (by pressing Ctrl+A or clicking the first cell with the Access key icon), right-clicking, and then selecting Unhide from the context menu that appears.

You can also open this context menu and access these options for a particular column in the list by clicking to select the column and then pressing Shift+F10.

Adding a new column to the list

When you select the Add Column option on a column's context menu, SharePoint opens a Create Column page for the list, similar to the top part of the page shown in Figure 4-6.

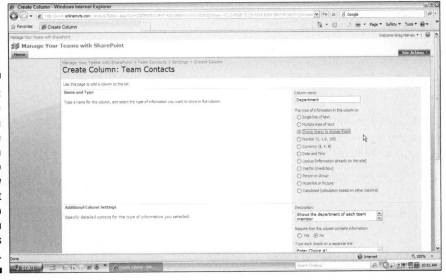

Figure 4-6: I used the options on the Create Column page to add a new Department column to the Team Contacts list.

When adding a new column using the options on the Create Column page, you always specify the following settings:

- ✔ **Column Name:** Enter the name of the field in the Column Name text box.

- ✔ **Type of Information in This Column:** SharePoint automatically makes all new columns you create a Text field with a single line of text. The program, however, offers a wide variety of different field types from which to choose. To change the field type, click the radio button for that type under this heading. Afterward, select the appropriate options specific to the type of field you choose that then appear in the Additional Column Settings section of the Create Column page.

- ✔ **Description:** Enter a description of the new column in the Description text box, indicating the type of information this field is to contain.

- ✔ **Require That This Column Contains Information:** SharePoint automatically makes data entry in the new column you're creating optional. If you want to make data entry mandatory, click the Yes radio button under this heading.

- ✔ **Add to Default View:** SharePoint automatically adds the new column you're creating to the list when it's displayed in that list's default view. If you'd rather that the new column appear only in a custom list view you create later (as described in "Modifying or creating a new view for a standard list," later in this chapter), deselect the Add to Default View check box.

Different options appear in the Additional Column Settings section near the bottom of the Create Column page, depending upon the type of field you select under the Type of Information in This Column heading. For example, if you leave the default Single Line of Text radio button selected, the page contains a Maximum Number of Characters text box option (with a default value of 255 characters), a Default Value radio button (with the Text button selected), and an empty text box option (where you can enter the most likely data entry for that field).

However, when you select another type of field besides text with single or multiple lines, the column options in this section of the page will be much different. For example, Figure 4-7 shows you the types of options that appear in this section of the Create Column page when you select the Choice (Menu to Choose From) radio button in the Name and Type section shown earlier in Figure 4-6. However, even here in Figure 4-7, I deleted the original three generic choices (Enter Choice #1, Enter Choice #2, and Enter Choice #3) in the list box entitled Type Each Choice on a Separate Line, and I replaced them with my own particular departmental choices (Editorial, Marketing, Sales, and Accounting).

Figure 4-7:
Specifying the additional column settings for the new Department column after designating it a Choice field.

Note that these Choice type-specific options not only enable you to specify the user's choices but also let you determine whether these choices appear on a drop-down menu or as radio buttons or check boxes. And when the default Drop-Down Menu option is selected, you can specify whether the user can type his own entry that's not on the drop-down menu and which one of the choices is to appear in the field by default.

Selecting the right field type for a new column

SharePoint gives you a wide choice of field types for the new columns you add to a list. Use the following descriptions to help you decide which field type works best for the column you're adding:

- ✔ **Single Line of Text:** Use this default field type when the new column requires only a short text entry that normally fits on a single line.

- ✔ **Multiple Lines of Text:** Use this field type when the new column requires more text than normally fits on a single line, as would be the case for a field soliciting comments from team members.

- ✔ **Choice (Menu to Choose From):** Use this field type when the entry for the new column is to be selected from a predetermined number of choices as might be the case for a custom Vendor field that gives the user a choice of vendors on a short, preapproved list.

- ✔ **Number (1, 1.0, 100):** Use this field type when the new column requires a numeric entry, such as a custom Units Ordered field that asks the user to enter the number of items he or she has ordered. When creating a Number field, as well as the default value, you can specify the range of numbers allowed, the number of decimal places to display, and whether or not to display numbers as a percentage.

✔ **Currency ($, ¥, €):** Use this field type when the new column requires a financial entry, such as a custom Travel Expense field that asks the user to enter travel expenses associated with completing the project. When creating a Currency field, as well as the default value, you can specify the range of values allowed, the number of decimal places to display, and what country's currency format to use in displaying the value.

✔ **Date and Time:** Use this field type when the new column requires a date or time entry, such as a custom Start Date field that asks the user to specify the date he started work on a particular project or task. When creating a Date and Time field, you can specify whether to include Date Only or Date and Time as well as whether the default date is based on the current date or is calculated.

✔ **Lookup (Information Already on This Site):** Use this field type when the entry returned to the new column depends upon data looked up in another existing list, as in a custom SSN field that returns a particular team member's Social Security number from an SSN field in another custom list on the SharePoint site called Personnel.

✔ **Yes/No (Check Box):** Use this logical field type when the new column requires only that a true or false answer be recorded, as in the case of a custom Active Status field that records whether a particular task or issue you're tracking in the list is still active.

✔ **Person or Group:** Use this field type when the new column requires the entry of an authenticated user on the SharePoint site. When creating a Person or Group field, you can specify whether multiple people or group selections are allowed, whether people only or people and their groups can be selected, whether people can be selected from all authenticated users on the site or only from particular SharePoint groups, and what personal information is displayed in the field when you select the column in the list with the Presence icon (the circle that changes color to reflect a user's current online status).

✔ **Hyperlink or Picture:** Use this field type when the new column requires a URL link to another Web address or an address containing a graphic file that you want displayed in that field when the list is displayed in Standard view. (Only the URLs and not the pictures themselves show up in this field in a list when the list is in Datasheet view.)

✔ **Calculated (Calculation Based on Other Columns):** Use this field type when the new column's entry needs to be returned as the result of a formula calculation between values entered into other fields in the same list, as in the case of a custom Extended Price field that multiplies the quantities entered into a Numeric Units field by the value entered in a Currency Price field in the same record. When creating a Calculated field, you specify the formula that determines what operation (addition, subtraction, multiplication, division, or concatenation [for joining text]) is performed between which columns in the list as well as the type of data that the formula returns (text, number, currency, date and time, or logical, Yes or No).

When creating the formula, start by typing an = (equal) sign and then select the first column by clicking it in the Insert Column list box, click the Add to Formula link, and then type the operator (+ for addition, – for subtraction, * for multiplication, / for division, and & for concatenation). Finally, select the second field to use in the calculation from the Insert Column list box. (For details on how to build formulas using simple operators, see my book *Excel 2007 For Dummies,* from Wiley Publishing).

Sorting records in a list in Datasheet view

The records for a new list are automatically sorted in ascending order (A to Z for text fields and lowest-to-highest value for numeric fields) by the primary required field for its type of list (which just happens to be the column displayed in the first column in the list's default view). Datasheet view makes it easy for you to change this default sort order to any order that better represents your data. You simply click the drop-down button to the right of the field name at the top of the column by which you want the list sorted and then click either the Sort Ascending or Sort Descending option at the top of the drop-down menu.

To sort your list based on more than one field, display the Datasheet task pane to the immediate right of the datasheet view of the list (by choosing Task Pane from the Actions drop-down menu). Then, click its Custom Sort button (called Sort) on this task pane to open the Custom Sort dialog box (shown in Figure 4-8). Here, you select the fields from the drop-down menu to sort the list by more than one column in the order from the most general to specific, each time indicating whether to sort the items in each column using the (default) ascending sort order or descending order. After you've selected the fields to sort the list on, click OK to perform the sort.

Figure 4-8: I've sorted the Team Contacts list by Company, Department, and Last Name in ascending order.

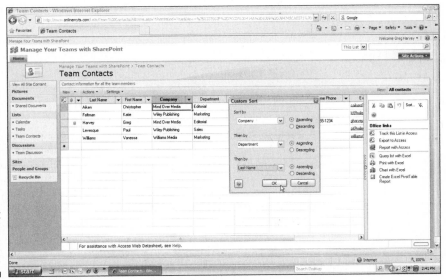

To restore a list to its original sort order, simply click the Remove Filter/Sort button (the one with the funnel icon with a red x on it) that appears in the top row of the Datasheet task pane. To remove the Datasheet task pane from the list, choose the Task Pane option from the Actions drop-down menu.

Filtering records in a list in Datasheet view

Filtering refers to the process of selecting a particular entry in one or more columns of a list to determine what records are then temporarily displayed in the list. Filtering provides an excellent way to quickly display only those records that you need to work with at a particular time.

To filter a list, open a column's drop-down menu and then click the field entry in the list that you then want to use as the criterion for any filtering. For example, to filter the sample Team Contacts list so that only records for folks who work at Wiley Publishing are currently displayed, click the Company column's drop-down button and then choose Wiley Publishing from the menu. SharePoint then hides all the records where the entry in the Company field is any business other than Wiley Publishing.

As with sorting, when filtering a list you can filter the records using more than one column. For example, perhaps you want to further filter the Team Contacts so that only records for team members who work in the Editorial department at Wiley Publishing are displayed. In that case, click the Department column's drop-down button and then click Editorial. SharePoint then hides all the records for the team members working at Wiley Publishing except for those working in the Editorial department.

SharePoint provides a Custom Filter feature that enables you to filter the list on more than a particular entry in the field. This feature enables you to filter the list on a range of values, the exclusion of values, or text that entries begin with. To open the Custom Filter dialog box for a column, choose the Custom Filter option from the column's drop-down menu.

SharePoint then opens the Custom Filter dialog box, similar to the one shown in Figure 4-9. This dialog box contains a series of three drop-down list boxes in the left column, enabling you to select the conditional operators for filtering, and a series of three combo boxes (where you can enter a value or select one from the drop-down list) directly opposite in the right column, enabling you to specify the values or text entries that the conditions use. In between the three rows of drop-down list box/combo box combinations, you find a pair of And and Or radio buttons. You can use these buttons to make the conditions you set up additive (meaning that all the conditions in the series must be met in order for the filtering to take place) or selective (meaning that the filtering takes place when any of the series of conditions are met).

Figure 4-9 illustrates how you can use the Custom Filter dialog box to set a range of values on which a list is filtered. In this case, you're dealing with a Personnel list that contains a Salary field that you want use in the filtering. To filter the list so that only the records for employees who make between $33,000 and $47,500 a year will display, first select the Is Greater Than or Equal To operator from the first drop-down list and then type **33000** in the corresponding text box. Then select the Is Less Than or Equal To operator in the drop-down list in the second row of the Custom Filter dialog box and type **47500** in its corresponding text box, without changing the default selection of the And radio button between the two rows.

Figure 4-10 shows you the filtered list after you click OK in the Custom Filter dialog box. As you can see, now only records where the annual salary is between $33,000 and $47,500 are displayed in the Personnel list.

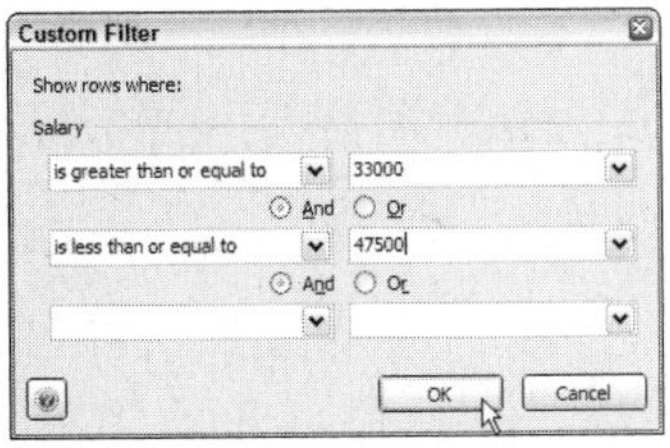

Figure 4-9:
I've created a custom filter to display records in a Personnel list for a range of salaries.

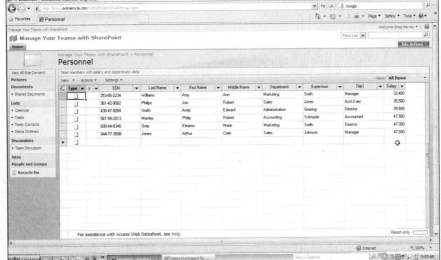

Figure 4-10:
The Personnel list records are filtered for a range of salaries.

To remove the filters from a list so that all of its records are once more displayed, choose Show All from the filtered column's drop-down menu. If you've filtered the list based on entries in several columns, you can remove all the filters at one time by clicking the Remove Filter/Sort button in the top row of the Datasheet task pane. Also, be aware that SharePoint automatically removes any filtering on a list the moment you switch it out of Datasheet view and back into Standard view.

Importing data from another compatible application program

Windows SharePoint Services 3.0 no longer supports a command for importing data directly from another file into a list's datasheet on your SharePoint site. However, you can still do it by using the good old copy-and-paste-through-the-Clipboard trick to get data stored in a compatible format into the list's Datasheet view.

The key to copying and pasting data is that the layout of the data in the source document must be identical to that of the SharePoint list you're importing it into. This means not only that the fields must contain the same type of data (text for a text field and numbers for a numeric field), but that the fields must be arranged in the same order in the source document as they are in the SharePoint list.

In other words, if you've created a table in Word or Excel with four fields in the column order of Item Name, Date Ordered, Units, and Price, your SharePoint list must have these same four fields in the same column order. Furthermore, the initial Item Name column must be a text field (usually with a Single Line of Text), the Date Ordered field must be a Date and Time field, and the Units and Price columns must be numeric. (Units can be a Number field, and Price can be a Currency field.)

Figures 4-11 and 4-12 illustrate how easy it is to copy and paste information in this manner. Figure 4-11 shows a simple table kept in a Word 2007 document whose data you want to copy to the custom SharePoint list shown in Figure 4-12. To make this kind of copy, all you do is open the Word document with the source data table in a program window and then open the page with the destination SharePoint list (in Datasheet view) in a browser window. Then follow these simple steps:

1. **Switch to the Word 2007 window and then select the cells of the table in the Word document that you want copied to the SharePoint list.**

   When selecting the cells, you don't need to select the column headings in the Word table, as these already exist in the custom SharePoint list. You do, however, need to select entire rows (records) of the Word table because you want all the data copied to their corresponding fields in the SharePoint list.

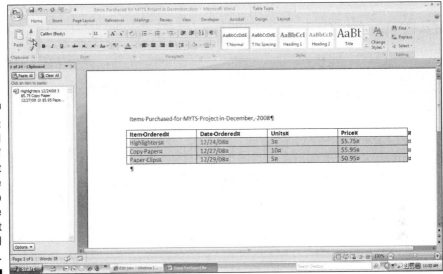

Figure 4-11:
This Word
2007
document
has the
items to
copy to the
SharePoint
list selected
in the table.

2. **Copy the selected data to the Windows Clipboard by clicking the Copy button on the Ribbon (or by pressing Ctrl+C).**

   Word copies the selected table data to the Clipboard.

3. **Switch to the browser window displaying the SharePoint list and then locate the first blank cell in the first row of the list.**

   In the example of the Items Ordered list, the first blank cell in the datasheet is the one directly beneath the one with the Item Name column heading.

4. **Paste the table data copied to the Clipboard into the SharePoint list by right-clicking the first blank cell you located in Step 3 and then choosing Paste from the drop-down menu (or by just pressing Ctrl+V).**

   SharePoint copies all of the table data that was copied to the Clipboard into the SharePoint list, creating new rows as needed, as shown in Figure 4-12.

If you use Outlook 2007, you can easily copy records into a SharePoint list created from the Contacts list template by connecting the list to Outlook. (If you're not up to speed on connecting lists, don't worry; Chapter 11 has all the details you'll need for connecting SharePoint lists with Outlook and doing this sort of neat stuff.) You can then drag the contacts stored in your Contacts folder (or some other subfolder in the Contacts module) into the Outlook folder created for your SharePoint Contacts list either by dragging and dropping or copying and pasting. When you then open the list in the SharePoint site (or refresh the page containing the list), voila! The contact records you copied locally in Outlook are now displayed in the list on the SharePoint site.

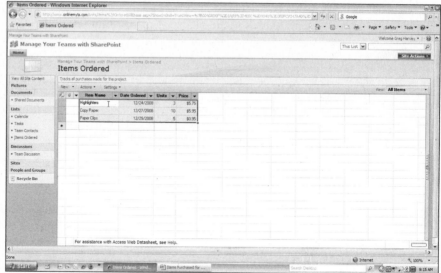

Figure 4-12:
The Items
Ordered
list as it
appears
after
copying the
data from
the Word
document
into its
rows.

Adding columns to a custom list

Whenever you create a new SharePoint list using the Custom List or Custom List in Datasheet View template, the program gives you a list with only two columns:

- ✔ **Attachments:** This field shows a paperclip icon when you attach a document to the record and is one whose field type and other settings you can't edit.

- ✔ **Title:** This field is a Single Line of Text field whose field type and other settings you can edit.

In almost all cases, you'll want to add to (or at the very least customize) the default Title field a bit. To add other fields to the custom list and/or edit the Title field that SharePoint automatically adds to it, click the Settings button at the top of the list and then choose one of the following options from its drop-down menu:

- ✔ **Create Column:** Choose this option to add a new field to the default Title field in the list. SharePoint opens the Create Column page where you specify the column name, type, description, and other settings. (See the section "Adding a new column to the list" earlier in this chapter for details.)

✔ **List Settings:** Choose this option if you want to edit the Title field, add additional fields to the list, or modify other list settings. SharePoint opens a Customize page, similar to the one shown in Figure 4-13. To edit the default Title field, click the Title link to open a Change Column page where you make your modifications. To define a new field, click the Create Column link to open the Create Column page. (See the section "Adding a new column to the list" earlier in this chapter for details.) To add a field to the list from the many predefined fields available to you, click the Add from Existing Site Columns link to open the Add Columns from Site Columns page. Use that page to add columns to the list by clicking their names in the Available Site Columns list box on the left and then clicking the Add button to copy them to the Columns to Add list box on the right.

After adding fields to the list, you can click the Column Ordering link on the list's Customize page to modify the order in which the fields appear in the data form your team members use to add items to the list. Simply indicate its new field position from the top of the data form by selecting its number with the drop-down list boxes attached to each Field Name on the Change Field Order page that appears.

Keep in mind, however, that changing the column ordering in the data form in this manner has no effect whatsoever on the order in which the columns appear in the list's default view. To change this ordering, you must modify the default view or create a new view that uses a different column ordering.

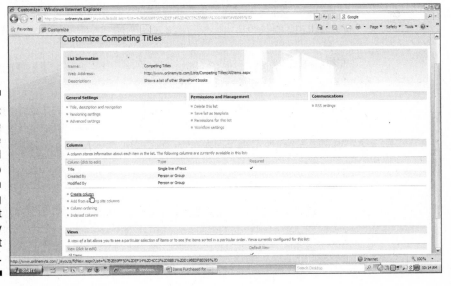

Figure 4-13: I'm using the Customize page to add columns to a custom Competing Titles list on my SharePoint site.

Modifying or creating a new view for a SharePoint list

Regardless of what type of list you create in SharePoint, the program creates a default view for the list. This default view determines what information is displayed in the list as well as how it's displayed.

If the default view doesn't include all the information (fields) that you want your team members to see or includes information that your team doesn't use, you can modify its settings. Better yet, you can create additional views for the same list customized to include just the information your teams need. You can then select any of these new views to display the data in the original SharePoint list on its Web page or in the custom Web Parts list that you subsequently add to other pages in the same site.

Modifying a list view

To modify the settings for the existing list view, follow these steps:

1. **Open the Web page for the list whose view you want to modify.**

   If the list is displayed in the site's Quick Launch, you do this by clicking its link in the Lists category. If the list isn't displayed there, first click the Lists link in the Quick Launch to open the All Site Content page and then click the list's link in the List section.

2. **If the view you want to modify isn't already displayed on the list's Web page (indicated by the view name displayed in the View button), choose the name of the list view you want to change from the View drop-down menu.**

   If you haven't yet created any additional views for the list (see the "Creating a list view" section that follows), the name of the sole default list appears in the View drop-down menu. (Most often, this view is called All *Something or Other* as in All Contacts or All Items.) There won't be any others you can choose from the drop-down menu.

3. **Choose Modify This View from the View drop-down menu.**

   SharePoint opens the Edit View page for the selected view (similar to the top of the page shown in Figure 4-14).

4. **Make all necessary changes to the settings in the various categories on the Edit View page and then click OK.**

   SharePoint then saves your updates as part of the selected list view and returns you to the list's Web page, where the list now reflects the modifications you made to the view.

A list's Edit View page contains a fair number of settings, arranged in the following categories:

- **Name:** The Name settings enable you to rename the list and/or change the address of the Web page that contains the list.

- **Columns:** The Columns settings enable you to determine which columns are displayed in the view you're modifying and the order in which they appear in the list (from left to right). You add columns to the list by selecting their check boxes, and you remove them by deselecting their check boxes. Use the Position from Left drop-down list boxes to fix their sequential numbering that then determines the order in which they appear in the list.

- **Sort:** The Sort settings determine which field or fields are automatically used to sort the list items in that view. To change a view's default sort order, select new columns in the First Sort by Column and/or the Then Sort By Column drop-down list boxes. To have SharePoint use descending order when sorting on a particular column, you then select its Show Items in Descending Order radio button as well.

- **Filter:** The Filter settings determine whether all the items added to a list are automatically displayed in that view. To modify the view so that SharePoint automatically filters the list, select the Show Items Only When the Following Is True radio button and then use the drop-down list box and text box settings to set up the condition for a column or columns. The condition determines which rows of the list are displayed.

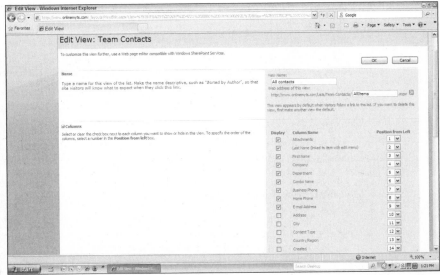

Figure 4-14:
The top part of the Edit View page for the default All Contacts view automatically created for the Team Contacts list.

✔ **Group By:** The Group By settings determine whether SharePoint arranges the items in a list in groups and subgroups complete with Expand/Collapse buttons that your users can then click to show and hide the groups' items. Here's what you can do with the Group By settings:

- To modify the view so that SharePoint automatically groups the list items (and then sorts them within each group and subgroup in either ascending or descending order), click the column to be used first in grouping in the First Group By the Column drop-down list box. If you then want SharePoint to further arrange the items in the list by a subgroup found within the first group (such as Teams within Departments), select its column in the Then Group By the Column drop-down list.

- To have SharePoint use the descending sort order for either or both columns used to create the main group and subgroup, click the appropriate Show Groups in Descending Order radio button.

- To have these groupings expanded in the list view, click the Expanded radio button.

- To change the maximum 100 groups displayed on each page, enter the new higher or lower value in the Number of Groups Per Page text box.

✔ **Totals:** The Total settings determine which field or fields in the list are used in creating arithmetic calculations — usually totals in the case of numeric fields and counts in the case of text fields. To have SharePoint perform a calculation on the entries in a particular field, select the type of calculation to perform on that field from the Total drop-down list. In the case of text fields, you're limited to the Count function. However, in the case of Date and Time fields, you can also choose between Average, Maximum, and Minimum functions. And in the case of Number and Currency fields, you can also choose between the Sum, Std Deviation, and Variance functions.

✔ **Style:** The Style settings determine what basic layout the view uses. To select a new style for the view, click its name in the View Style list box.

✔ **Folders:** The Folders settings determine whether a list that uses folders shows the items inside their folders in the view or creates what SharePoint calls a *flat view* of the items, that is a straight listing of the items without the normal folder hierarchy you see in a folder list.

✔ **Item Limit:** The Item Limit settings determine how many list items are displayed on each Web page. To change the maximum number of items displayed on each Web page, enter a new higher or lower value in the Number of Items to Display text box. To make the new value you enter into this text box the maximum number of items the list returns (rather than simply the maximum number of items displayed per page), click the Limit the Total Number of Items Returned to the Specific Amount radio button. Keep in mind that limiting the number of items returned in your view can really make the pages load faster, especially when you're dealing with a list with lots and lots of data.

✓ **Mobile:** The Mobile settings determine whether the list view is available on a mobile device, such as a cell phone that has Internet access and that uses a SharePoint-compatible Web browser. To make the view you're modifying available on such a mobile device, select the Make This a Mobile View check box. To further make the view the default view for the list on the mobile device, also select the Make This the Default Mobile View check box as well.

Note that both these Mobile view settings apply only to views that were created as Public views rather than Personal views, meaning that they can be used by any team member who has access to the SharePoint site (rather than just by the user who created the view). Note also that all default views that SharePoint creates for the new list are automatically Public views. The only way to designate a view as a Personal view is to do so when you first create a new view. (See the "Creating a list view" section that follows for details.)

Creating a list view

Creating a new view for a list is a two-step procedure: First, you select a View format to use as a general guide for the view, and then you specify the view's settings (using many of the same options as when editing a view).

To start this process, you display the Web page with the list for which you want to create a new view (either by clicking the list's name in the Quick Launch or by clicking the Lists link in the Quick Launch followed by clicking the list's name in the Lists section of the All Site Content page). Then, choose Create View from the View drop-down list.

SharePoint then opens a Create View page for the list, showing the various formats you can use as a guide in creating the new view (similar to the page shown in Figure 4-15). The View formats that you can select from the Create View page include:

✓ **Standard view:** This format displays the items in the list on a Web page in some sort of tabular layout.

✓ **Datasheet view:** This format displays the items in the list in a datasheet similar to an Excel worksheet, with columns and rows that you can quickly edit.

✔ **Calendar view:** This format displays the items in a list visually as a daily, weekly, or monthly calendar like you see in a standard paper day planner (and used by the default Calendar list that SharePoint automatically adds to the top-level site).

✔ **Gantt view:** This format displays the items in a list visually using a Gantt bar chart that tracks the progress of certain items over time. Reserve this format for lists that track tasks that you or your teams must accomplish and that have fields that record important milestones and deadlines.

Note that if your computer has Microsoft Access 2007 installed on it, the Choose a View Format section of your Create View page also contains an Access View link that you can click to launch Microsoft Access 2007 and then use this database application to create an Access form from the list's data. You can use this Access form to edit the list's data or to create a report within Access. (See Chapter 12 for more on using SharePoint with Access 2007.)

The Create View page also displays a Start from an Existing View section that contains a list of all the existing views for the selected list. If you know that the new view you're creating for a list is very similar to one that already exists, you can save time by basing the new view on an existing one. Simply click the name of the existing view in this section and then edit and modify its original settings as needed for the new view.

Figure 4-15:
Select a
View
format for a
new
view being
created
for the
Personnel
list on a
SharePoint
site.

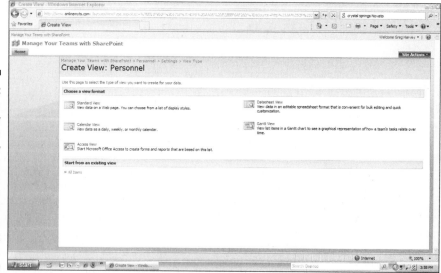

After you select the View format to use for a new view, SharePoint opens a Create View page for the list, using the default settings for the particular format you select. You can then modify these settings as needed (see the section "Modifying a list view" earlier in this chapter for details) before you click OK to have SharePoint create the new view and apply it to the list for which you created it.

Applying a custom view to a list

After creating multiple views for a particular list, you can then apply any one of them to the list when the list is displayed in the SharePoint site.

Simply click the View button that appears on the right side of the command bar at the top of the page and then choose the name of the view you want to apply to the list from the View button's drop-down menu. SharePoint then immediately redisplays the items in the list using whatever settings you've defined for that view.

Creating a copy of a list using a Web Part with a custom view

Whenever you create a new list for your SharePoint site, the program automatically creates a Web Part for that list. You can then use this new Web Part to display the list on any page of the same SharePoint subsite that requires the list information. Not only that, but you can then apply one of the custom views that you've created to the list data displayed in the Web Part without affecting the view used to display the original list on its Web page.

You can put this technique to good use whenever you find the need to create a condensed version of a much larger, original list. This condensed version then presents the full list's information in some way that's much easier for your team members to digest and use. You can sometimes do this by reducing the number fields used in the custom view. Other times, you can accomplish this with a custom view that filters the full list so that only records vital to a specific task or activity are displayed. You can even sometimes make this happen by selecting a more graphic format for the custom view (such as the Calendar view or Gantt view) that presents the list's full information in a more visual way.

To visualize how this technique might work for you, follow along with the steps for creating a condensed version of the Team Contacts list on the SharePoint site home page that team members can use to send e-mail messages to one another without having to access the complete Team Contacts list on its own Web page.

To create this "condensed" Team Contacts list for the home page, start out with the Web Part that SharePoint automatically generates when the original Team Contacts list is created. Then customize the Web Part with the help of a custom E-Mail view fashioned for the list that displays only 3 of its 18 possible fields: Last Name, First Name, and E-Mail Address (because this is all the information needed for one team member to e-mail another). And it just so happens that when the Team Contacts list is displayed using only the three fields in the E-Mail list view, the list fits perfectly in the width of the Right Web Part zone on the home page.

To add this handy form of the Contacts List to the Right Web Part zone of the SharePoint home page, follow these steps:

1. **Click the Home tab on the Top Link bar.**

   SharePoint displays the home page of the SharePoint site.

2. **Choose Edit Page from the Site Actions drop-down menu.**

   SharePoint puts the home page into Edit mode, which shows the location of the Left and Right Web Part zones.

3. **Click the Add a Web Part button at the top of the Right zone.**

   SharePoint opens the Add Web Parts to Right dialog box shown in Figure 4-16.

4. **Select the Team Contacts check box in the Lists and Libraries section and then click the Add button.**

   SharePoint closes the dialog box and redraws the screen, displaying a copy of the Team Contacts list at the top of the Right Web Part zone.

5. **Click the Edit button on the Team Contacts Web Part's title bar and then choose Modify Shared Web Part from its drop-down menu.**

   SharePoint opens the Team Contacts task pane with the List Views section displayed at the top, as shown in Figure 4-17.

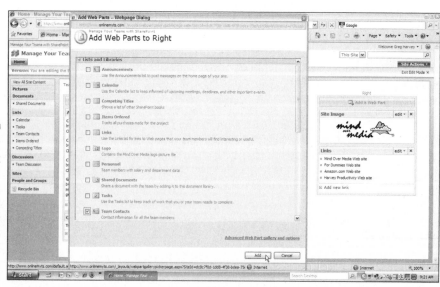

Figure 4-16: Select the Team Contacts Web Part in the Add Web Parts to Right dialog box.

6. **Choose E-mail View from the Selected View drop-down menu.**

   SharePoint displays an alert dialog box warning that switching views removes changes made to the view and can disable Web Part connections.

7. **Click OK in the alert dialog box and then click OK in the Team Contacts task pane.**

   SharePoint closes the task pane and redisplays the Team Contacts list using E-mail view.

8. **Drag the Team Contacts list down in the Right Web Part zone and drop it so that the list is repositioned immediately below the Site Image Web Part with the company logo and then click the Exit Edit Mode button.**

   SharePoint takes the home page out of Edit mode and redraws the page with the condensed form of the Team Contacts list displayed immediately below the company logo, as shown in Figure 4-18.

Now, team members can e-mail one another simply by clicking the e-mail address link next to the names in the copy of the list on the home page. And should they need more information on a team member, such as their business telephone number or department, they can still look that information up in the original form of the Team Contacts list accessed by clicking the Team Contacts link in the Quick Launch.

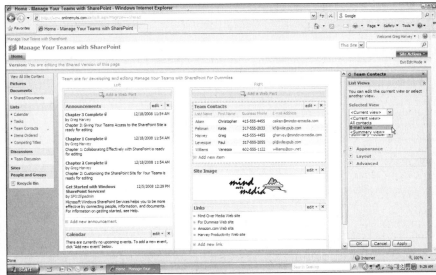

Figure 4-17:
Select the E-mail View for the copy of the Team Contacts list in the Right Web Part zone.

Figure 4-18:
Here's the home of the SharePoint site after repositioning the condensed version of the Team Contacts list and exiting Edit mode.

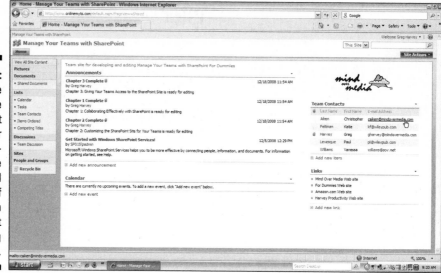

Chapter 5

The Care and Feeding of SharePoint Libraries

In This Chapter

▶ Understanding what SharePoint document libraries are and what they do

▶ Customizing the settings for the default Shared Documents library

▶ Exploring the various ways to upload files to a document library

▶ Adding new documents and picture libraries to your SharePoint site

▶ Filtering document libraries

*L*ists may form the core of SharePoint, but the SharePoint document libraries, the subject of this chapter, are surely its most used feature. No matter what else your SharePoint site does or does not contain, the site is bound to include some type of documents meant to provide essential background material to your teams — material that can be quickly updated and immediately accessed. And that's exactly where SharePoint document libraries come in, by providing you and your teams with a central location for files that are indispensable to the collaboration.

To that end, this chapter covers how to organize and create document libraries for your essential text and data files as well as create picture libraries for your important graphic files. The chapter then shows you how to upload documents to these libraries and make them available to your team members.

The chapter also covers how to connect document libraries with Outlook 2007 so that team members with the appropriate permissions can access the files in a document library right from within Outlook on their local computers (making it possible to use and work with local copies of the document even when they can't get connected to the Internet and access the document on the SharePoint site). Finally, you find out how to filter the contents of a library and use a document library's Check In/Out and Versioning features to monitor the use of documents and automatically keep your team members informed when new versions with important updates are available for their use.

Understanding What Makes SharePoint Libraries Tick

On one level, document libraries represent just a specialized type of SharePoint list. (If you've read Chapter 4 on lists or are presently familiar with the basics of SharePoint lists, you already have a leg up on how they work.) Document libraries present themselves as lists expressly designed to monitor and keep track of the documents you and your team members need to use during the period of your collaboration. As such, they tend to track information such as the document name and type, the date last modified, and who did the editing.

In addition to tracking the usage of essential documents and versions, however, document libraries provide another important element not associated with other standard type of lists: They provide central locations for locating the files they contain and for actually accessing their content.

As with other SharePoint lists, SharePoint automatically adds the document libraries you create to the Quick Launch area of the SharePoint site that contains them (unless you specifically prevent their links from being added there). This means that each document library you add is no more than a single click away, thus making it — and all the documents it houses — readily accessible to you and other authorized users. Moreover, given the file-oriented nature of document libraries, you can easily set them up to mimic the familiar Windows folder/subfolder hierarchy file structure that your teams work with on the company's local network.

Document libraries versus document workspaces

In addition to document libraries, SharePoint 2007 supports special pages called *document workspaces* (the subject of Chapter 9), and you may not be sure why you would use one instead of the other. Think of document libraries as repositories for the text and data files you and your team members need to reference over the entire course of the project. Think of document workspaces as repositories for the text and data files that you and your team members need to edit collaboratively at some point during the course of the project.

After you and your teams complete the editing of the files you store in your document workspaces, more often than not you'll want to move them over to the appropriate document libraries on the SharePoint site and then delete their workspaces. This makes document workspaces usually much more short-lived than document libraries, existing on the site only while the editing's going on. Another major difference is that document workspaces always contain only the single file that you and your teams are currently editing together, whereas document libraries most frequently contain multiple related documents that the team needs to refer to.

Using the Default Shared Documents Library

Typically, when you first start working with a new SharePoint 2007 site created from the Team Site template, the site already contains a new document library called Shared Documents. You can then start working with this default library by customizing it and adding files to it, or you can add your own document libraries to the site to use along with this default library or in place of it.

To open the Shared Documents library, follow these simple steps:

1. **Log on to the home page of your SharePoint site.**

   From the home page, you can open the default document library directly by clicking its Shared Documents link, or you can open it indirectly from the All Site Content page in Document Libraries view. In this example, I open the Shared Documents library indirectly from the All Site Content page.

2. **Click the Documents link attached to the Documents category in the Quick Launch.**

   SharePoint opens the All Site Content page using the Document Libraries view, as shown in Figure 5-1. In this view, all of the document libraries added to the top-level SharePoint site are listed. Because a new SharePoint site has only the single Shared Documents library, this is the only one that currently appears on this page.

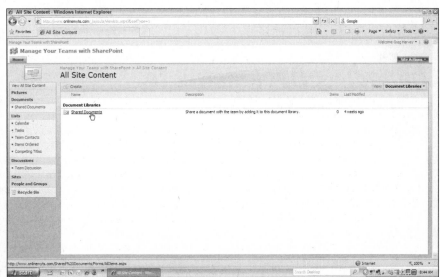

Figure 5-1:
You can
open the
default
Shared
Documents
library from
the All Site
Content
page of a
SharePoint
site.

3. **Click the Shared Documents link in the Name column of the list of document libraries displayed on the All Site Content page.**

   SharePoint opens the Shared Documents page shown in Figure 5-2. This Shared Documents page contains an empty list in four columns: Type, Name, Modified, and Modified By. This list also has four command buttons above its column names: New, Upload, Actions, and Settings.

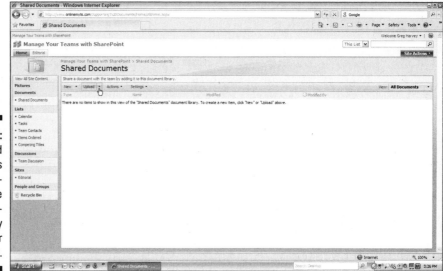

Figure 5-2:
The Shared Documents page showing the empty document library list in four columns.

After you open your Shared Documents library (or create a new document on the site), you're ready to copy the documents it needs from your local computer to the SharePoint site, as I discuss in the following section.

Uploading Documents to a Documents Library

SharePoint gives you a choice of methods for uploading documents into any document library on your SharePoint site. When uploading documents, be aware that typically SharePoint supports a wide range of different application file types. The exceptions generally include a wide range of Windows-related computer files, most notably

✔ **EXE files:** Executable program files can't be opened on a SharePoint site.

✔ **PST files:** Outlook personal data files can't be opened on a SharePoint site.

Just be aware that if one of your team members attempts to open an application-type file for which he or she doesn't have the client program used to create the file or an application that supports its usage, the team member's Web browser will very nicely attempt to automatically open and display its content.

Creating folders for the documents you upload to a library

SharePoint document libraries make it easy for you to create folders for storing the various text and data files you upload to them. Creating folders for the documents that you upload to a particular document library can often make it much easier for you and your team members to peruse the library's contents and locate the file you need to work with.

To create a new folder in a library, choose New Folder from the library's New drop-down menu. SharePoint then opens a New Folder page for the selected document library where you enter a folder name and click OK. SharePoint then adds the name of the folder (indicated by the Folder icon in the initial Type column) to the list of documents in the current document library.

All folders that you create in a document library are technically subfolders of the library, as evidenced by the Content Navigation Breadcrumb at the top of the library's Web page, where you see a folder you've selected in a library as just another breadcrumb in the trail. That breadcrumb trail offers you a direct way back to the library through the live link attached to its name.

After creating a folder in which to upload documents (and remember that the folders that you create in a library can have their own subfolders), you need to open the folders by clicking the link attached to their name in the library's Name column before you can access their files.

Uploading your documents

The main method for uploading documents to a library or one of its folders is to use the Upload Document or Upload Multiple Documents option on the Upload button's drop-down menu.

To upload a single document file to the current document library or the current folder within a library, follow these few steps:

1. **Choose Upload Document from the Upload button's drop-down menu.**

   SharePoint opens a Web page similar to the one shown in Figure 5-3. This Web page contains a Name text box which you can then use to designate a file on your computer's hard drive or on a network drive to which you have access.

Figure 5-3:
I'm uploading a single document to a folder in the Shared Documents library.

2. **Click the Browse button to the immediate right of the Name text box, select the document to upload in the Choose File dialog box, and then click Open.**

   SharePoint inserts the path and filename of the document you select in the Choose File dialog box (called Choose File to Upload if your computer is running Windows XP rather than Vista) into the Name dialog box.

3. **Click OK on the Upload Document Web page.**

   SharePoint then copies the designated file into the current library or folder on your SharePoint site. After SharePoint finishes uploading the file, it returns you to the current library or folder Web page. The newly uploaded file now appears in the document list on this page (in alphabetical order by its filename) with an exclamation point and the word *New* in green immediately following its name.

Note that the Overwrite Existing Files check box is automatically selected on the Upload Document Web page. This means that if you're uploading a file that's already in the library, SharePoint won't stop and ask you to confirm overwriting its contents — which also means that you could conceivably replace a newer version of the document on the SharePoint site with an older, out-of-date version from your local computer. To give you an opportunity to prevent this, deselect the Overwrite Existing Files check box before you click OK to commence the uploading of the selected file. That way, if you're about to upload an older version of a file to a document library, SharePoint will alert you to this fact and give you a chance to abandon the operation.

When you have more than one file you want to copy over from a single folder on a local or network drive on your computer into the same document library on the SharePoint site and you have Microsoft Office installed on your computer, you can vary the uploading steps just a bit.

Instead of choosing Upload Document from the Upload button's drop-down menu, choose Upload Multiple Documents. SharePoint then opens a version of the Upload Document Web page similar to the one shown in Figure 5-4, which splits the main part of the page into two panes: a File pane on the left (where you select the drive and folder containing the files to copy) and a main pane on the right (which displays the files contained in the folder you've selected in the left pane).

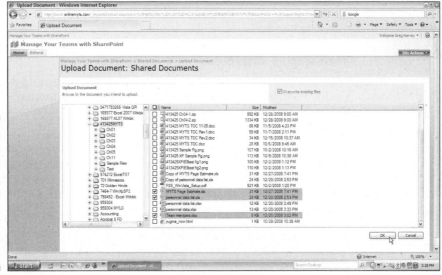

Figure 5-4:
I need to upload multiple documents to a folder in the Shared Documents library.

After you've selected the folder containing the files you want to upload in the pane on the left, you can then refine your selection in the main pane on the right by clicking the check boxes of just those files you want to upload.

After you've selected all the files to copy over to your current document library, simply click OK on the Upload Document page. SharePoint displays an alert dialog box asking you to confirm this operation. You must then click Yes in this dialog box to begin uploading the files to the library on your SharePoint site (indicated in the Uploading Progress dialog box that then appears).

After the selected files are all uploaded, the program returns you to the current library's or folder's Web page, where each of the files now appears in its document list (in alphabetical order by their filenames) with exclamation points and the word *New* in green immediately following their names.

Uploading and copying files via an Internet Explorer window

Using the Upload button on a document library page is not the only way to get files on your local computer copied over to one of your SharePoint document libraries. Provided that your computer has Internet Explorer (version 7 or higher) installed on it, you can also do file uploading via an Explorer window, using the following steps:

1. **Open the library or folder page to which you want to upload local documents in SharePoint.**

2. **Choose Open with Windows Explorer from the Actions drop-down menu.**

   SharePoint opens a Windows Explorer window that displays the contents of the current document library, including all the files and subfolders that it contains (similar to the one shown in Figure 5-5). Note that if your SharePoint site is hosted by a third-party provider, you may be required to enter your username and password in a Connect dialog box and click OK before SharePoint will open this browser window.

3. **In the Windows Explorer window, open the folder on your computer or local network that contains the files you want to upload to your SharePoint document library.**

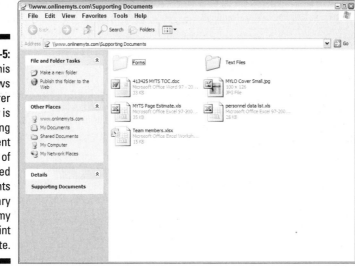

Figure 5-5:
This
Windows
Explorer
window is
displaying
the current
contents of
the Shared
Documents
library
on my
SharePoint
site.

After both the Internet Explorer window with the document library and the Windows Explorer window with the files to be uploaded are open on your computer's desktop, you're ready to make the copies. You can do this either by selecting the local files in the Windows Explorer window (source) and then dragging and dropping them into the SharePoint Internet Explorer window destination, or you can copy the files from the Windows Explorer window and then paste them into the Internet Explorer window.

- If you use the drag-and-drop method to upload the files, resize and position the Windows Explorer and Internet Explorer windows on the desktop so that you can see both of them side by side, so that you can easily select the file icons in the Windows Explorer window for copying, and so that you have sufficient room to drop them into place in the Internet Explorer window.

Use Figure 5-6 as a guide when sizing and positioning the Windows Explorer and Internet Explorer windows on your computer's desktop. You need to make the Windows Explorer window large enough to be able to comfortably select the files to upload and the Internet Explorer window sufficiently large to have some space on which to drop them.

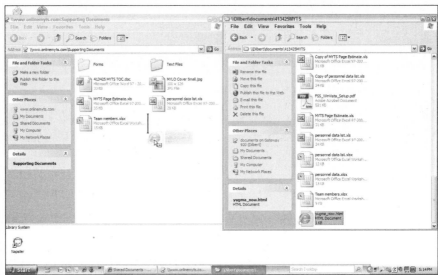

Figure 5-6:
Figure 5-6:
You can use
the drag-
and-drop
method
to upload
local files to
the Shared
Documents
library.

Click the Windows Explorer window and then select the files to
upload by selecting their file icons — you can do this by drawing
an outline around them, dragging through them, or individually
clicking them as you hold down the Ctrl key.

Drag the selected files to the Internet Explorer window and then,
as soon as you see a plus sign on the pointer or it changes to a ver-
tical I-beam pointer, drop the files by releasing the mouse button.

The moment you release the mouse button, SharePoint starts
copying the selected files to the SharePoint library open in the
Internet Explorer window. After the program finishes copying, the
file icons for the copied documents appear in the Internet Explorer
window.

- To use the copy-and-paste method rather than drag-and-drop,
  you press Ctrl+C after selecting to copy the files into the Windows
  Clipboard.

Click the Internet Explorer window on the desktop to make it
active and then press Ctrl+V to start copying the selected files into
the window.

4. **Click the Close buttons on the Windows Explorer and Internet
   Explorer windows you recently opened to return to the library or
   folder page to which you wanted to upload the local documents in the
   first place.**

5. **Click Internet Explorer's Refresh button or press F5.**

The files that you copy via an Internet Explorer window don't show up in the SharePoint library's document list until after you refresh the Internet Explorer browser window to bring its contents up to date.

You don't have to restrict the Windows Explorer windows method outlined in the previous steps to uploading files from a local computer system to your SharePoint site. You can put it to use when you need to move or copy files from one SharePoint document library to another. However, when using drag-and-drop to copy files between two libraries open in different Windows Explorer windows, you need to hold down the Ctrl key as you drag the selected files from the source window and drop them into the destination window. Otherwise, SharePoint moves the selected files instead of copying them.

Uploading files by creating a document library as a Network Place

The last method for uploading files to a document library on your SharePoint site is to create a network folder that points to the SharePoint site and then copy the files (either with the drag-and-drop method or by copying and pasting) to the appropriate document library subfolder within that network folder. If your computer runs Windows XP, you do this by creating a Network Place that's accessible from Windows Explorer. If your computer runs a version of Windows Vista, you do this by mapping the SharePoint site as a network drive accessible from Windows Explorer.

Adding your SharePoint site as a Network Place in Windows XP

If your computer is still running on that good, old, tried-and-true Windows XP, follow these steps to map your SharePoint site as a Network Place available from Windows XP's My Computer window:

1. **Click the Start button on the Windows taskbar and then choose My Network Places from the Start menu.**

Windows opens the My Network Places dialog box.

2. **Click the Add a Network Place link in the Network Tasks section of the Navigation pane.**

Windows opens the Welcome dialog box in the Add a New Place Wizard.

3. **Click the Next button.**

Windows opens the Where Do You Want to Create This Network Place? dialog box in the Add a New Place Wizard. Here, the option with the long name, "Choose Another Network Location: Specify the Address of a Web Site, Network Location, or FTP Site," is selected by default.

4. **Click the Next button.**

   Windows opens the What Is the Address of This Network Place? dialog box in the Add a New Place Wizard.

5. **Type the complete URL address (including the `http://` prefix) of your SharePoint site and then click Next.**

   Windows may display a Connect To dialog box for logging you in to your SharePoint site.

6. **If the Connect To dialog box appears, enter your username (if it's not already displayed) in the User Name text box and enter your SharePoint site password in the Password text box. If you want Windows to be able to automatically log you in each time you open the Network Place you're creating, also select the Remember My Password check box before you click OK.**

   Windows logs you in to your SharePoint site and then adds a Type a Name for This Network Place text box containing the URL of your site in the What Is the Address of This Network Place dialog box in the Add a New Place Wizard.

7. **If you want to replace the URL of your SharePoint site with a more descriptive name, type the new name for the Network Place in the Type a Name for This Network Place text box before you click Next.**

   Windows opens the Completing the Add Network Place dialog box in the Add a New Place Wizard. The Open This Network Place When I Click Finish check box is selected by default.

8. **Click the Finish button.**

   Windows closes the Add a New Place Wizard, returning you to the My Network Places dialog box, where the Network Place folder icon with the name of your SharePoint Network Place now appears.

9. **Double-click the Network Place folder icon representing your SharePoint site.**

   Windows opens the Network Place pointing to your SharePoint site in a Windows Explorer window, similar to the one shown in Figure 5-7. This window shows all of the site's folders (including ones for all the document libraries you've added to the site).

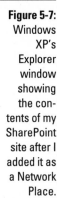

Figure 5-7:
Windows
XP's
Explorer
window
showing
the con-
tents of my
SharePoint
site after I
added it as
a Network
Place.

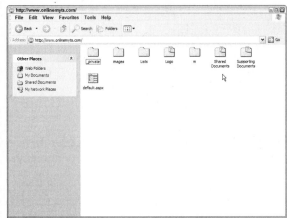

Uploading files to a document library via an XP Network Place

After adding your SharePoint site to a Network Place on your Windows XP computer, you can upload files to your document libraries by following these steps:

1. **Click the Start button on the Windows taskbar and then choose My Network Places from the Windows XP Start menu.**

   Windows opens the My Network Places window.

2. **Double-click the Network Place folder icon representing your SharePoint site.**

   Windows opens the Network Place window for your SharePoint site, showing all its folders.

3. **Double-click the folder icon representing the document library into which you want to add files.**

   Windows opens a window for your document library showing all its files and subfolders.

4. **Click the Start button on the Windows taskbar and then choose My Documents from the Start menu.**

   Windows opens the My Documents folder.

5. **From the My Documents folder, open the folder on your computer's hard drive or a network drive that contains the files you need to upload.**

   Now, you just need to select the files to upload.

6. **Select the icons of all the document files you want to upload in the active Explorer window.**

   After selecting the files, you can use either the drag-and-drop or copy-and-paste method to upload the selected files to the document library folder on your SharePoint site via the Network Place Explorer window.

7. **To use the drag-and-drop method, drag the selected document files over to your document library's Network Place Explorer window and then drop them. To use the copy-and-paste method, press Ctrl+C to copy the selected files to the Clipboard and then click your document library's Network Place Explorer window before you press Ctrl+V.**

   No matter which method you use, Windows uploads copies of the selected files to your SharePoint document library. When Windows finishes uploading the selected documents, their file icons appear in the library's Network Place window on your desktop.

If you have your document library open in a Web browser window at the time you perform this upload, don't forget to click the browser's Refresh button (F5 in the Internet Explorer) to have the newly uploaded documents displayed in the file list.

Mapping the SharePoint site as a network drive in Windows Vista

If your computer runs a version of the new-fangled Windows Vista, follow these steps to map your SharePoint site as a network drive that is then available from the Vista Computer Explorer window:

1. **Click the Start button on the Vista taskbar and then choose Computer from the Start menu.**

   Windows opens the Computer Explorer window.

2. **Click the Map Network Drive button at the top of the Computer window.**

   Windows opens the Map Network Drive dialog box, with the next available drive letter automatically assigned in the Drive drop-down list box (going from Z to A in descending order).

3. **(Optional) To select another network drive letter from among those still available on your computer, click the Drive drop-down button and choose its letter from the drop-down menu.**

4. **In the Folder text box, type the complete URL address (including the `http://` prefix) of your SharePoint site and then click Finish.**

   If you want Vista to connect to your SharePoint site and map it as a network drive each time you log on to your computer, be sure that you leave the Reconnect at Logon check box selected.

5. **If the Connect To dialog box appears, enter your username (if it's not already displayed) in the User Name text box and enter your SharePoint site password in the Password text box. If you want Windows to be able to automatically log you in each time you open the Network Place you're creating, also click the Remember My Password check box before you click OK.**

   Windows opens an Explorer window showing the contents of your SharePoint site, including folders for all the document libraries it contains.

Uploading files to a document library via a Vista network drive

After mapping your SharePoint site to a network drive on your Windows Vista computer, you can upload files to your document libraries by following these steps:

1. **Click the Start button on the Windows taskbar and then choose Computer from the Vista Start menu.**

   Windows opens an Explorer window showing all the physical and virtual drives on your computer.

2. **Double-click the Network Location folder icon representing your SharePoint site.**

   Windows displays the contents of your SharePoint site, showing all its folders, in the same Explorer window.

3. **Double-click the folder icon representing the document library into which you want to add files.**

   Windows opens a window for your document library showing all of its files and subfolders.

4. **Click the Start button on the Windows taskbar and then choose Documents from the Start menu.**

   Windows opens an Explorer window showing all your local documents.

5. **Open the folder on your computer's hard drive or on a network drive that contains the files you need to upload.**

6. **Select the icons of all the document files you want to upload in the active Explorer window.**

   Next, you'll want to use the drag-and-drop or copy-and-paste method to upload the selected files to the document library folder on your SharePoint site.

7. **To use the drag-and-drop method, drag the selected document files over to your document library's Explorer window and then drop them. To copy and paste, press Ctrl+C to copy the selected files to the Clipboard and then click your document library's Explorer window before you press Ctrl+V.**

   Windows then uploads copies of the selected files to your SharePoint document library. When Windows finishes uploading the selected document, their file icons appear in the library's Explorer window on your desktop.

If you have your document library open in a Web browser window at the time you perform this upload, don't forget to click the browser's Refresh button (F5 in the Internet Explorer) to have the newly uploaded documents displayed in the file list.

Creating a New Word Document for a Library

Not only can you copy your existing document and data files to a SharePoint library, but you can also create new Word documents for the library (assuming that Microsoft Word 2003 or higher is installed on your computer).

To create a new Word file using the site's word processing document template, follow these steps:

1. **Log on to your SharePoint site and then open the Web page containing the document library to which you want to add a new Word document.**

2. **Choose New Document from the New drop-down menu.**

   SharePoint displays an alert dialog box warning you that you're about to open a file called `template.doc` that exists on your SharePoint site.

3. **Click OK in the alert dialog box.**

   Windows then opens Word on your computer. If the Connect To dialog box appears, prompting you to enter your password, type your password and click OK to download the template from your SharePoint site and use it to open a new Word document.

4. **Create your new Word document using any and all of the program's features. Then save the new document by clicking the Save button or pressing Ctrl+S.**

   Word opens the Save As dialog box, showing the current SharePoint document library as the place where the new document file will be saved.

5. **Replace the default filename given to the file (using the document's initial text) with your own filename in the File Name text box and then click the Save button.**

   Windows saves the file in the current SharePoint library.

6. **Press Alt+F4 to exit Word and close the new document you just saved.**

   Windows returns you to the open Web browser window containing your document library.

7. **Click the Web browser's Refresh button (or press F5, if you use Internet Explorer).**

   SharePoint redraws the library's Web page, adding the new document you just created and saved in Word to its file list.

SharePoint launches Word and opens the template.doc file in this application when you select the New Document option from the New drop-down menu because Microsoft Office Word 97–2003 Document is the default template file for the Shared Documents library (as it is for any new document library you create). Keep in mind that you can select another application template file at the time you create a new document library. (See the section "Creating a new document library" later in this chapter for details.) You can also edit this template file in its native application by opening the Document Library Advanced Settings page (by clicking the Settings button in the library and then choosing Document Library Settings from the drop-down menu and Advanced Settings on the Customize page) and then clicking the Edit Template link that appears immediately beneath the Template URL text box.

Adding New Libraries and Folders to Your SharePoint Site

Typically, when you start working with a new SharePoint site, you have only the Shared Documents library to work with. You can, however, have as many additional document and new picture libraries as you need on your SharePoint site to house all the information that your teams need to successfully collaborate. You create document libraries for the text and data documents that your teams need access to and picture libraries for all the photos and graphic images they need.

You can create specific libraries for the various team subsites that you've created (as covered in Chapter 2) so that each team has easy access to the supporting documents they need in collaborating. You can also organize the documents in these libraries using folders and subfolders just as you do for the files on your local computer.

Creating a new document library

To create a new document library on your SharePoint site, follow these steps:

1. **Log on to your SharePoint site and then open the site where you want to add the new document library.**

   If you want to add the document library to the top-level site, remain on the SharePoint home page after you log on to the site.

2. **Choose Create from the Site Actions drop-down menu.**

   SharePoint opens the Create Web page.

3. **Click the Document Library link in the Libraries column.**

   SharePoint opens a New page, similar to the one shown in Figure 5-8.

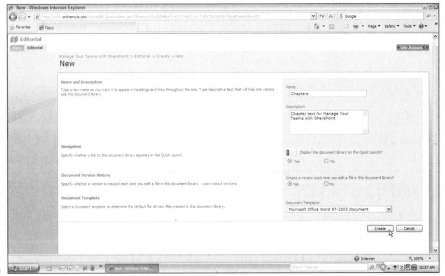

Figure 5-8: I'm creating a new Chapters SharePoint document library in the Editorial subsite.

4. **Type the name for the new document library in the Name text box and then press Tab.**

   SharePoint advances you to the Description text box.

5. **Type a description of the new document library in the Description text box.**

6. **(Optional) Make any desired changes to the Navigation, Document Version History, and Document Template settings that you want.**

By default, SharePoint displays a link to the new document library in the Documents section of the site's Quick Launch. Click the No radio button under the Display This Document Library on the Quick Launch heading if you don't want this link to appear (in which case, your teams must open the library from the All Site Content page for the site — not the most convenient way to do it).

SharePoint doesn't automatically track the version history for the document files you add to the new library (including when they were modified and by whom). To turn on versioning for the new document library, click the Yes radio button under the Create a Version Each Time You Edit a File in This Document Library heading (a step I strongly recommend if managing the versions in the library is at all important to you).

SharePoint automatically uses the Microsoft Office Word 97–2003 Document as the default template for any new documents you or your team members create in the new library. If the library is intended to primarily house files of another type (such as Excel workbooks or PowerPoint presentations), you may want to select a different document template (such as the Microsoft Office Excel Spreadsheet or Microsoft Office PowerPoint Presentation) for any new files created there. In which case, SharePoint will then launch Excel or PowerPoint and open a new file from the template in Excel or PowerPoint whenever you or another team member selects the New Document option from the library's New drop-down menu.

7. **Click the Create button.**

   SharePoint creates the new library and then opens the Web page for the new document library. You can then use its Upload options to add the text and data files you want to make available to your teams. (See "Uploading Documents to a Documents Library" earlier in this chapter for details.)

Creating a new picture library

To create a new picture library on your SharePoint site, follow these steps:

1. **Log on to your SharePoint site and then open the site where you want to add the new picture library.**

   If you want to add the picture library to the top-level site, remain on the SharePoint home page after you log on to the site.

2. **Choose Create from the Site Actions drop-down menu.**

   SharePoint opens the Create Web page.

3. **Click the Picture Library link at the bottom of the Libraries column.**

   SharePoint opens a New Web page.

4. **Type the name for the new picture library in the Name text box and then press Tab.**

   SharePoint advances you to the Description text box.

5. **Type a description of the new picture library in the Description text box.**

6. **(Optional) Make any desired changes to the Navigation and Picture Version History settings that you want.**

   By default, SharePoint displays a link to the new picture library in the Pictures section of the site's Quick Launch. Select the No radio button under the Display This Picture Library on the Quick Launch heading if you don't want this link to appear (in which case, your teams must open the library from the All Site Content page for the site).

   SharePoint doesn't automatically track the version history for the graphic files you add to the new picture library (including when they were modified and by whom). To turn on versioning for the new picture library, click the Yes radio button under the Create a Version Each Time You Edit a File in This Picture Library heading (a step I strongly recommend if managing the various versions of graphic files in this library is at all important to you).

7. **Click the Create button.**

   SharePoint creates the new picture library and then opens the Web page for the new picture library.

Adding graphics file to a new picture library

After creating a new picture library, you can use its Upload Picture and Upload Multiple Picture options on the Upload drop-down menu to add images to it. The Upload Picture option works very similarly to the Upload Document option in a document library: You browse for the image file from the Add Picture page and then, after selecting its graphics, click OK to upload it. Immediately after uploading the picture, SharePoint opens an Edit Item page where you can a title, the date the image was created, a description of the image, and keywords that you can use to filter the images in a particular view of the picture library.

If you have more than one image to upload at a time and you have the Office Picture Manager installed, use the Upload Multiple Pictures option to add the graphic files you want to make available to your teams. Here's how it's done:

1. **Choose Upload Multiple Pictures from the Upload drop-down menu.**

   SharePoint then opens the Microsoft Office Picture Manager, similar to the one shown in Figure 5-9.

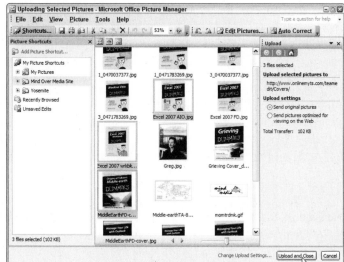

Figure 5-9: Selecting graphics files to upload to a new picture library with the Office Picture Manager.

2. **Click the Add Picture Shortcut link in the Picture Shortcuts pane on the left.**

   Windows opens the Add Picture Shortcut dialog box.

3. **Select the folder on your computer or local network that contains the graphic files you want to upload to the new picture library.**

   Windows displays thumbnails of all the graphics in the folder you've selected in the main area of the Office Picture Manager.

4. **Ctrl+click each of the pictures you want to add and then click the Upload and Close button.**

   SharePoint closes the Microsoft Office Picture Manager, uploads the selected graphics files, and returns you to an Uploading Pictures page.

5. **Click the Go Back To link followed by the name of your picture library.**

   SharePoint returns you to the picture library, where thumbnails appear for each of the images you added (in alphabetical order by filename).

Working with the images added to a picture library

When you create a new picture library, SharePoint creates three default views that you can use to display the images in the library:

- ✔ **All Pictures:** This default view shows thumbnails of each of the images with their filenames beneath the thumbnail and a check box in front of the filename that you can use to select individual pictures.

- ✔ **Explorer View:** This view shows the images added to the library in a Picture Folder Explorer window using the Filmstrip viewer, which enables you to preview larger images by selecting their thumbnails (see Figure 5-10). This view also contains a pane with Picture Tasks and File and Folder Tasks areas that enable you to perform typical file tasks, such as create a new folder or rename, copy, or delete a selected folder or even e-mail its files to another team member.

- ✔ **Selected Pictures:** This view reduces the display of the images added to the picture library down to just those thumbnails that are selected in the library at the time you choose the view.

To switch the picture library into the Explorer View or Selected Pictures view, choose the option you want from the View drop-down menu. You can also customize these views by choosing Modify This View from this drop-down menu or add to them by creating brand-new views for the picture library. To create new views, choose Create View from the same menu.

If the picture library is not in Explorer View and you need to peruse its images, choose View Slide Show from the Actions drop-down menu. SharePoint then opens an Explorer window that shows you each image in the library one at a time when you click the Play button in the image controls that appear in the upper-right corner. You can then click the Pause and Stop controls to halt the slideshow as well as the Previous and Next buttons to view the next or previous image in the library.

In addition to selecting a new view for the images in your picture library, you can also edit a library's images as follows:

- ✔ **To edit an image's metadata:** (*Metadata* is information about the graphic such as its title, creation date, verbal description, and identifying keywords.) Click to select an image's thumbnail in the picture library and then, when its image page appears, click the page's Edit Item button.

- ✔ **To edit an image:** Select the thumbnail's check box and then choose Edit from the Actions drop-down menu to open the picture in Microsoft Office Picture Manager. There, you can make such editing changes to the picture as modifying its brightness and contrast as well as cropping, rotating, flipping, resizing, and compressing the image.

✔ **To delete an image:** To remove an image from the library, select the thumbnail's check box and then choose Delete from the Actions drop-down menu. You can also remove it by clicking its thumbnail and then clicking the Delete Item button on its image page.

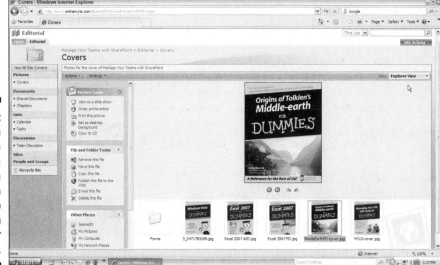

Figure 5-10:
You can view the images in a new picture library with the Filmstrip viewer in the Explorer View.

Customizing a Document Library

SharePoint makes it easy to customize any of the document libraries you add to the site. To modify a library's settings, open the library's Web page and then choose Document Library Settings from the Settings drop-down menu.

SharePoint then opens a Customize Web page for the selected document library (similar to the one shown in Figure 5-11, using the default Shared Documents library). Here, you can modify the overall library settings in one of three categories (General Settings, Permissions and Management, and Communications) as well as modify the library's columns and views.

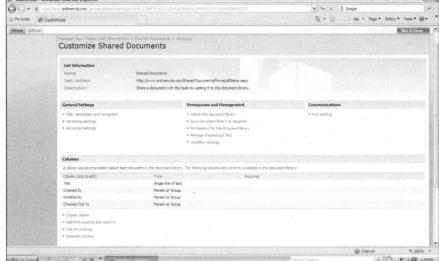

Figure 5-11:
The
Customize
Shared
Documents
Web page
showing
the various
settings you
can modify.

Modifying a library's General Settings

The General Settings options on a library's Customize Web page include

➤ **Title, Description and Navigation:** These settings enable you to rename the library, change its description, and remove the library's link from the Quick Launch area.

➤ **Versioning Settings:** These settings enable you to control whether or not content approval is in operation so that documents that other team members upload to the library remain in a draft state until you approve them. These settings also enable you to control who sees draft items waiting for approval as well as enable you to turn on and off (the default) both the Document Version History and Require Check Out settings. When you activate Document Version History, SharePoint automatically creates versions of all edits to the library documents and keeps a history of all their changes (very useful for chronicling their modifications). When you activate the Require Check Out settings, team members must individually check out the documents in a library in order to edit them (assuming they have sufficient permissions). You, as the administrator, can override a checkout and check a document back in to the library should the need arise.

✔ **Advanced Settings:** These settings govern a range of more sophisticated library functions, including

- Activating the management of content types (thus enabling you to specify how to manage diverse documents in the library that are related to the project at hand)

- Specifying a new document template that's used as the basis for all new documents you create in the library

- Specifying a custom Send To destination for copies you make of library files

- Specifying whether the New Folder option appears on the New menu and determining whether documents in the library can be displayed as part of the results from searches that you and your team members perform on the site

Modifying a library's Permissions and Management settings

The Permissions and Management settings on a library's Customize Web page include

✔ **Delete This Document Library:** This option enables you to remove the document library from the site. Note that when you delete a library, SharePoint automatically removes all of the documents you've added to it.

✔ **Save Document Library as Template:** This option enables you to save a customized document library as a template that you can then use to generate other, similar document libraries on your SharePoint site.

✔ **Permissions for this Document Library:** This option enables you to customize the permissions for just that particular document library. When you modify user access to a particular library, you break the natural parent-child inheritance of permissions — meaning that changes you make to the parent site's permissions (see Chapter 3) no longer affect this library. Note that if you use this option to edit permissions for the library and then later decide that you do want the library to once again inherit permissions from its parent site, you can do this by choosing the Inherit Permissions option from the Actions drop-down menu.

✔ **Manage Checked Out Files:** This option enables you (as an administrator) to manage files in the document library that have been checked out by various team members (assuming that you've selected the Require Check Out setting as part of the Versioning Settings for the document library). The Checked Out Files page indicates the checked in or out status of all document library files and allows you to take ownership of any file that a team member has checked out and check it back in so it's available to other team members. See Chapter 9 for details on checking files in and out of a document workspace (which works the same way as in a document library).

✔ **Workflow Settings:** This option enables you to define a new workflow or customize the workflow assigned to the contents of the document library. Workflows can automate and regulate the processing of documents, assuming that they need to follow a set procedure. (See Chapter 10 for details on creating workflows for SharePoint document libraries.)

Modifying a library's Communications settings

The Communications settings of a library's Customize Web page includes just the following two options:

✔ **Incoming E-Mail Settings:** This option, when enabled, makes it possible to designate an e-mail address on the SharePoint site that your team members can use to send files to the document library as attachments to e-mail messages. See Chapter 11 for more on using Outlook with SharePoint.

✔ **RSS Settings:** This option enables you to modify the RSS (or Really Simple Syndication, which is a special Web format used to publish regularly updated works) feed settings for the document library (referred to as a list, which it officially is). Note that, by default, SharePoint enables RSS updating for the list of documents in a new document library so that all library updates automatically appear in an RSS reader capable of subscribing to a protected SharePoint site. (See Chapter 8 for details on using Outlook 2007 and the Mozilla Firefox Web browser as your RSS reader for SharePoint components such as lists and blogs.)

Adding Columns to a Document Library

When you start using a new document library, the All Documents default view uses a list with only a few columns of information: Type, Title, Created By, Modified By, and Checked Out To (if you enable the Require Check Out setting as part of the Versioning Settings for the library). You can use the Create Column link or the Add from Existing Site Columns link on the library's Customize page to add new columns. (The procedure for adding a new column to a library is very similar to that for adding one to a list — see Chapter 4 for details on adding columns to lists.)

Here's a place where the Add from Existing Site Columns option is really, really useful. This option enables you to reuse columns defined for any other component on the SharePoint site. The Available Site Columns list box on the Add Columns from Site Columns page contains a number of file-related fields such as Author and Contributor whose columns you can readily add to a document library you're customizing.

Modifying and Adding Views to a Document Library

When you create a new document library, SharePoint creates two standard views for it:

- **All Documents:** This default library view displays the library's documents in a standard SharePoint list with four columns: Type, Name, Modified, and Modified By. You click the hyperlink attached to the document's filename in the Name column to open the document for printing or editing with its native application. To edit the document's filename or title, choose Edit Properties from the drop-down menu that appears when you position the mouse pointer over the filename in the column. This drop-down menu also contains options for customizing the file's permissions, deleting the file, sending the file to another location (or creating a document workspace for it), checking it in and out (if the Check In/Out option is enabled), and turning on modification alerts.

- **Explorer View:** This view displays the library's documents in a standard Windows Explorer window that shows icons for all its documents and folders and contains a task pane with links for performing common folder- and file-related tasks, such as renaming, moving, copying, and deleting. To open a file for editing, double-click its file icon (or right-click it and then choose Open from its shortcut menu). To delete a file or folder, click its icon and then click the Delete This Folder or Delete This File link in the pane.

If you want to customize the All Documents or Explorer View, choose Modify This View from the View drop-down menu when the library is displayed in that view. Note that customizing the All Documents view is very much like customizing a list (as described in Chapter 4) because it uses all the same types of categories: Name, Columns, Sort, Filter, and so on. When you customize the built-in Explorer View, however, you're limited to renaming the view, making it the default view, and deleting it altogether (something I really don't recommend).

In addition to customizing the built-in views, you can create new views for a document library by choosing Create View from the View drop-down menu. When you select this option, SharePoint opens a Create View page where you select a format for the new view using the same View Format options that are available when you customize list view — detailed in Chapter 4.

After you select the view format for the new list, SharePoint opens a Create View page where you name the view; select the audience (Personal View for your eyes only or Public View for everyone on the team); and then specify the columns, sort order, any filtering, grouping, totals, and so on — very much like you do when creating a list view. (For the details on creating a list view, see Chapter 4.)

Sorting and Filtering a Document Library

You can sort and filter the lists of documents you add to any of your document libraries pretty much as you sort and filter any other SharePoint list. To sort or filter the documents listed in a particular library, you need to display that library in some sort of standard column view such as the default used by the All Documents view. Then, you need to display the library list as a datasheet by choosing Edit in Datasheet from the Actions drop-down menu.

After your SharePoint library is displayed as a datasheet, you can then sort and/or filter its document list. To sort the list, click the Sort Ascending or Sort Descending option at the top of the drop-down menu for the column (or columns) by which you want the list sorted.

To filter the list on a particular entry in a column, click that entry on the column's drop-down menu. To filter the list on a range of entries in a particular column, you need to choose Custom Filter from that column's drop-down menu and then set the range of values as a condition in the Custom Filter dialog box. After filtering a library, you can restore its entire document list by then choosing Show All from the drop-down menu of the column used in filtering the library — indicated by the filter cone icon that appears next to its field name in the column heading. (See Chapter 4 for more details on the sorting and filtering of SharePoint lists.)

 In a document library with tons of files, you can help yourself quickly locate the document you need to access by filtering the library's list so that it displays only documents of that particular file's type. For example, if you need to refer to an Excel worksheet, you can filter out everything except Excel files in the list by selecting .xls or .xlsx (if you use Excel 2007 and save your workbook files in the new 2007 Excel file format) in the filter section of the Type column's drop-down menu.

Part III
Getting the Most Out of Your SharePoint Site

The 5th Wave   By Rich Tennant

"Just how accurately should my Web site reflect my place of business?"

In this part . . .

Although it's Web-based, SharePoint provides a surprisingly rich environment in which to work collaboratively. The chapters in this part look at the major ways that you can share information with your teams and work together on the projects at hand. These methods range from using meeting workspaces to manage your team meetings all the way to using task lists and workflows to assign and manage the work.

Chapter 6

Using Meeting Workspaces to Plan and Manage Team Meetings

In This Chapter

▶ Understanding how meeting workspaces can help you plan and organize team meetings

▶ Creating a meeting workspace for a team meeting from scratch

▶ Creating a meeting workspace from a calendar item in your SharePoint site

▶ Creating a meeting workspace from an Outlook 2003 or 2007 meeting request

▶ Adding a button to your meeting workspace that launches a Yugma Web conference

*Y*ou can use meeting workspaces in SharePoint 2007 to plan and manage the physical meetings and real events that take place at various times during the period of your team collaboration. Note, however, that meeting workspaces don't actually provide a place from which to launch Web conferencing applications such as Microsoft's Live Meeting, Citrix's GoToMeeting, or Yugma's Instant Web Conferencing software — the kind of applications that enable you to conduct virtual meetings over the Internet.

In this chapter, you find out what you can do with SharePoint meeting workspaces along with the various types of meeting workspaces that SharePoint supports. You also discover the different ways you can go about setting up meeting workspaces, including creating a meeting workspace from an event you place on a SharePoint calendar or from a meeting request in Outlook 2003 or 2007.

Finally, I show you how to use SharePoint's multipurpose Content Editor Web Part to add an HTML snippet to display a button on a meeting workspace page that you and your team members can then click to join a virtual meeting online using a version of the Yugma's Instant Web Conferencing program (a free Web conferencing service for meetings up to 20 attendees) directly from your SharePoint site.

Understanding How You Can Use Meeting Workspaces

Like document workspaces (discussed in Chapter 9) that are designed to facilitate the team editing of a document, meeting workspaces are special subsites designed to facilitate the planning and managing of team meetings. These meetings can be any of the various types of physical meetings and events that your teams need to participate in at different times during the period of your collaboration.

Document workspaces are often temporary and exist on the site only until the editing of the document in question is completed — at which time the updated document may be moved to a document library and the document workspace deleted. Many meeting workspaces share a similar fate, in that they need to stay up on the SharePoint site only until the scheduled meeting or event takes place. However, keep in mind that some team-sponsored events (such as special social gatherings, competitions, and even product launches) are worth memorializing on the site so that you can readily share its memories with the team. In such a case, you'd not only retain the workspace on the SharePoint site after the event takes place, but you'd also enhance it by adding photos and recaps of the event to that meeting workspace.

SharePoint 2007 supports five different types of meeting workspace, each with its own elements for planning and managing an upcoming meeting or event:

- ✔ **Basic Meeting Workspace:** Creates a meeting workspace page (see Figure 6-1) with four empty lists: Objectives (for listing your goals for the meeting), Agenda (for listing the meeting's agenda), Attendees (for listing those team members among the site's authorized users that you want to attend the meeting), and Document Library (for listing the supporting files you've uploaded for the meeting). You can then add your content to these built-in lists or customize them by modifying or adding to their Web Parts.

- ✔ **Blank Meeting Workspace:** Creates an empty meeting workspace page with three Web Part zones (Left, Center, and Right) to which you can add Web Parts for the elements you want to include in the workspace. (See Chapter 2 for details.)

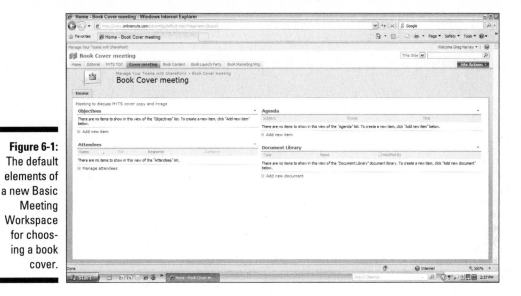

Figure 6-1:
The default elements of a new Basic Meeting Workspace for choosing a book cover.

✔ **Decision Making Meeting Workspace:** Creates a meeting workspace page with the same four lists as the basic meeting space along with a Tasks list (for listing the tasks that each team member needs to accomplish as part of the decision making) and a Decisions list (for listing all the choices that must be made as part of making the overall decision). Figure 6-2 shows what a Decision Making Meeting Workspace looks like.

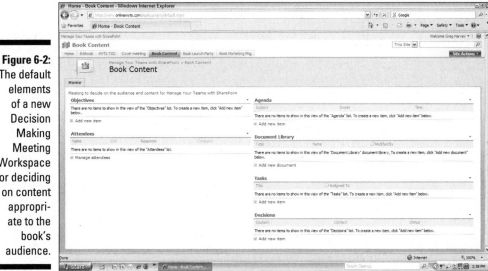

Figure 6-2:
The default elements of a new Decision Making Meeting Workspace for deciding on content appropriate to the book's audience.

✔ **Social Meeting Workspace:** Creates a meeting workspace page with three distinct pages — Home, Discussion, and Photos — as shown in Figure 6-3. The Home page of this workspace contains three empty lists: Attendees (for listing the team members invited to the event), Directions (for listing the location of the event and directions for getting there), and Things To Bring (for listing the items that each team member should bring to the event). The Discussion page contains a blank discussion board for conducting a threaded discussion on the nature of the event and/or its planning. (For more on discussion boards, see Chapter 7.) The Photos page contains a blank picture library to which you can add photos used in planning the event or taken at the event itself. This type of meeting workspace also contains a stock photo of party favors that you can, if you like, delete or replace with a photo more in keeping with the nature of your gathering.

Figure 6-3:
The default elements of a new Social Meeting Workspace for planning a book launch party.

✔ **Multipage Meeting Workspace:** Creates a meeting workspace with three pages — a Home page and two blank pages (Page 1 and Page 2). The Home page contains three of the four empty lists found in the basic meeting workspace: Objectives, Agenda, and Attendees. (See Basic Meeting Workspace at the top of this list.) Pages 1 and 2 are empty pages, each with three Web Part zones (Left, Center, and Right) to which you can add Web Parts for the elements you want to include in the workspace. (See Chapter 2 for details on how to use Web Part zones.)

Creating New Meeting Workspaces

Just as with document workspaces, SharePoint provides more than one way to add a new meeting workspace to your site. You can create a new meeting workspace from scratch by following the same procedure you use to add a new subsite (Chapter 2) or document workspace (Chapter 9). Even more to the point, you can create a new meeting workspace on the fly right at the time that you schedule the meeting or event in question on either your SharePoint calendar or your calendar in Outlook.

Creating a meeting workspace from scratch

To create a new meeting workspace from scratch, follow these steps:

1. **Log on to the SharePoint site and then open the subsite in which you want to add the new meeting workspace.**

   If you want to create the meeting workspace at the top level of your site, open the home page.

2. **Choose Create from the Site Actions drop-down menu.**

   SharePoint opens a New SharePoint Site page, similar to the one shown in Figure 6-4.

Figure 6-4:
You can create a new meeting workspace using the options on the New SharePoint Site page.

3. Enter a name for the meeting workspace in the Title text box and then press Tab.

The workspace name you enter here appears in the Quick Launch and the tab on the Top Link bar (unless you choose not to display the workspace in these areas).

When you press Tab, SharePoint advances you to the Description text box.

4. Type a description for the meeting workspace in the Description text box and then press Tab.

The description you enter here appears at the top of the workspace page when you or a team member opens it.

When you press Tab, SharePoint advances you to the URL Name text box.

5. Type a URL address for the new meeting workspace.

Follow the same conventions in naming the new workspace as you do in naming any other subsite (no spaces and no punctuation besides hyphens and underscores).

6. Click the Meetings tab in the Select a Template list box and then click the name of the type of meeting workspace you want (Basic Meeting Workspace, Blank Meeting Workspace, Decision Meeting Workspace, Social Meeting Workspace, or Multipage Meeting Workspace).

Refer to the figures and meeting workspace descriptions in the previous section, "Understanding How You Can Use Meeting Workspaces," if you need help in deciding which template to select.

7. (Optional) Make any other changes to the Permissions, Navigation, and Navigation Inheritance options you need to for the new meeting workspace.

Select the Use Unique Permissions radio button under User Permissions if you need to set workspace site use permissions for individual team members (permissions different from the ones they have as members of a user group — see Chapter 3 for details).

Select the No button under Display This Site on the Quick Launch of the Parent Site if you don't want a link to the meeting workspace to appear in the Site section of the parent site's Quick Launch.

Select the No button under the Use the Top Link Bar from the Parent Site if you don't want the new meeting workspace to have its own tab on the SharePoint site's Top Link bar.

8. Click the Create button.

SharePoint creates a new workspace using the meeting workspace template you selected and then takes you to this new workspace so that you can begin customizing its elements or adding your content to them.

Remember that you can also create a new meeting workspace from scratch by clicking the View All Site Content or Sites link in the site's Quick Launch and then clicking the Create button to open the Create page. When that page opens, click the Sites and Workspaces link in the Web Pages column of the Create list. Then on the New SharePoint Site page, after you specify the name, description, and URL of the new workspace, select the Meetings tab of the Select a Template list box and select your meeting template (Basic Meeting Workspace, Decision Making Workspace, and so on) before you specify Permission, Navigation, and Navigation Inheritance settings. Finally, click the Create button to create the subsite with the new meeting workspace.

Creating a meeting workspace from a SharePoint calendar item

If you use a Calendar page on your SharePoint site to keep track of upcoming events of interest to the team (see Chapter 1), you can create a new meeting workspace for an event at the very time you add it to the calendar.

Simply follow these steps to add the event to your SharePoint calendar and, at the same time, create a meeting workspace for it:

1. Open the Web page on your SharePoint site with the calendar to which you want to add the event that also needs a meeting workspace.

Remember that the calendar is a special type of list that enables you to add events to a facsimile of a daily, weekly, or monthly calendar.

2. Click the New button at the top of the calendar.

SharePoint opens a New Item page for the calendar, similar to the one shown in Figure 6-5. This page contains a form with various fields for adding information about the upcoming meeting or event. Note that the final option on this form is a check box that enables you to create a meeting workspace for the event you're adding.

3. Type a name for the meeting or event in the Title text box and then press the Tab key.

SharePoint advances you to the Location field.

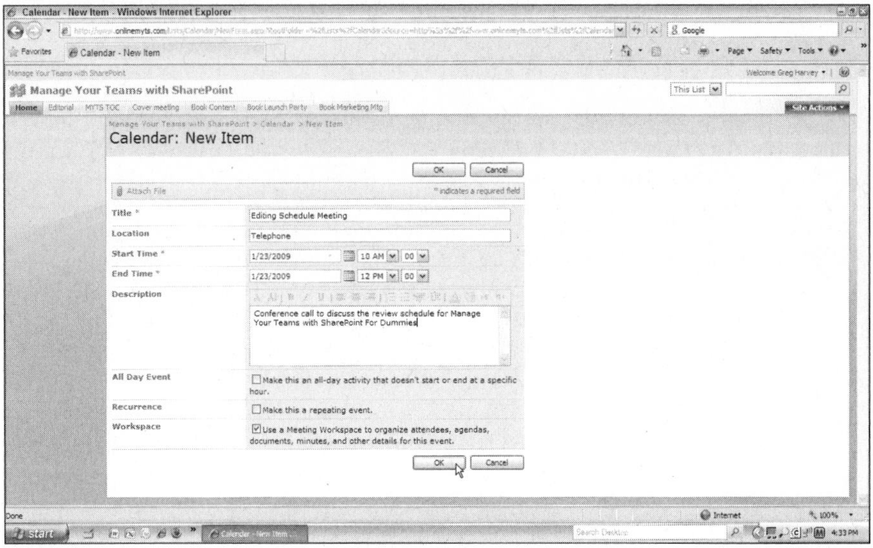

Figure 6-5:
Create a
meeting
workspace
from a
SharePoint
calendar
item on the
calendar's
New Item
page.

4. **Type the physical location of the meeting or event in the Location text box.**

   Next, you need to specify the starting and time of the meeting or event.

5. **Use the mini-calendar and time drop-down list boxes to designate the starting and ending times in both the Start Time and End Time fields.**

6. **Click the Description text box and type a description of the upcoming meeting or event.**

7. **(Optional) If the meeting or event is an affair that spans an entire day or a range of days, select the check box labeled Make This an All-Day Activity that Doesn't Start or End at a Specific Hour.**

   If you select this check box, SharePoint redraws the New Item page, removing the time drop-down list boxes from the Start Time and End Time fields.

8. **(Optional) If the meeting or event is recurring on some sort of regular basis, select the check box labeled Make This a Repeating Event. Then, after SharePoint finishes redrawing the page, specify the interval at which the event repeats using the radio button and text box options that appear beneath the check box.**

   You can choose between making a recurrence interval of Daily, Weekly, Monthly, or Yearly. The Pattern options that then appear depend upon the particular interval radio button you select.

9. **Select the check box labeled Use a Meeting Workspace to Organize Attendees, Agendas, Documents, Minutes, and Other Details for This Event. Then click OK.**

   SharePoint adds the item to the calendar (which the program does not display) and then immediately takes you to the New or Existing Meeting Workspace page, similar to the one shown in Figure 6-6.

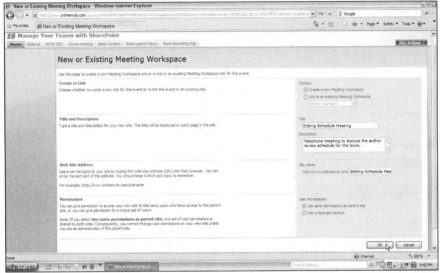

Figure 6-6: Specify the settings for the meeting workspace being created from a new SharePoint calendar item.

10. **(Optional) Edit any of the options that require modification (Choices, Title, Description, URL Name, and/or User Permissions) on the New or Existing Meeting Workspace page.**

    If you want to link the new meeting workspace to an existing workspace, select the Link to an Existing Meeting Workspace radio button and then select the name of the meeting workspace from the drop-down list immediately beneath it.

    If you want to set up individual site user permissions, select the Use Unique Permissions radio button.

11. **Click OK.**

    SharePoint displays the Template Selection page.

12. Select the name of the meeting workspace template you want to use for the new workspace in the Template list box and then click OK.

SharePoint creates the new meeting workspace using the template you selected. (Refer to "Understanding How You Can Use Meeting Workspaces," earlier in this chapter, for help with this.) The program then displays the Home page for the new meeting workspace, similar to the one shown in Figure 6-7. Note that this new workspace page not only displays the title at the top of meeting workspace, but also the meeting's date, time, and location information from the calendar item.

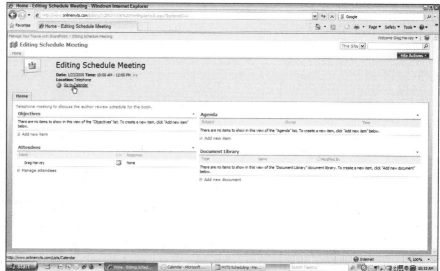

Figure 6-7:
The Home page of a new meeting workspace created from a SharePoint calendar item.

You can click the Go to Calendar link that appears immediately underneath the location information at the top of the meeting workspace page to jump immediately to the event on the calendar that generated the workspace.

Accessing a meeting workspace created from a calendar item

Keep in mind that SharePoint doesn't automatically add links to the Quick Launch for meeting workspaces that you generate from events on your calendar. To access the page for this meeting workspace, click the View All Site Content link for the site containing the workspace and then click the link attached to its name in the Sites and Workspaces section of the All Site Content page.

Alternatively, you can open the calendar containing the event used in creating the workspace, click the link attached to its calendar item, and then click the link attached to the name of the meeting workspace in the Workspace field at the bottom of the item's form page.

Adding a Quick Launch link to a meeting workspace created from a calendar item

If you want your site's Quick Launch to have a link to the meeting workspace you've created from a SharePoint calendar item, you need to manually add it. You do this by following these steps:

1. **Click the View All Site Content link above the site's Quick Launch and then click the link attached to the name of the meeting workspace in the Sites and Workspaces section.**

   SharePoint opens the page for the meeting workspace you want to add to the site's Quick Launch.

2. **Right-click the URL address in the Address bar of your Web browser and then choose Copy from the shortcut menu that appears.**

   You must supply this URL address to add the workspace to the Quick Launch, and copying it in this manner is the easiest way to ensure that you enter the correct address.

3. **Click the link to the parent site in the Content Navigation Breadcrumb that appears at the top of the page and then choose Site Settings from the Site Actions drop-down menu.**

   SharePoint opens the Site Settings page.

4. **Click the Quick Launch link in the Look and Feel column of this page.**

   SharePoint opens the Quick Launch page for the site.

5. **On the site's Quick Launch page, click the New Link button.**

   SharePoint opens the New Link page.

6. **Highlight the `http://` characters automatically entered into the Type the Web Address text box and then press Ctrl+V to replace it with the complete URL address you copied in Step 2. Then press Tab.**

   SharePoint pastes the URL address into the Type the Web Address text box and advances the insertion point to the Type the Description text box.

7. **Type a short description of the meeting workspace in the Type the Description text box.**

   The description you enter here appears as the name of the workspace link in the site's Quick Launch.

8. **Choose Sites from the Heading drop-down menu and then click OK to close the New Link page.**

   SharePoint returns you to the Quick Launch page, where your new link appears in the Sites section.

9. **Click the link to the parent site in the Content Navigation Breadcrumb at the top of the Quick Launch page.**

   A live link to your meeting workspace now appears in the site's Quick Launch on the left of the site's page.

Creating a meeting workspace from an Outlook meeting request

If you use the Calendar module in either Outlook 2003 or 2007 to schedule your meetings, you can create a meeting workspace in SharePoint for the event that you're scheduling in Outlook. To do this, follow these steps:

1. **Open the calendar in Outlook 2003 or 2007 and then right-click the date of the event and choose New Meeting Request from the shortcut menu that appears.**

   Outlook opens a new Untitled – Meeting window in the Calendar (similar to the one shown in Figure 6-8 except its window carries the name of the meeting from the Subject field).

Meeting Workspace button

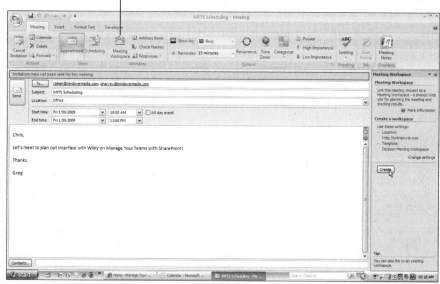

Figure 6-8:
Create
a new
meeting
workspace in
SharePoint
from a
meeting
request
in Outlook
2007.

2. **In Outlook 2007, click the Meeting Workspace button in the Attendees group on the Meeting tab of the Ribbon.**

   Outlook opens the Meeting Workspace pane on the right side of the window.

   (In Outlook 2003, press Ctrl+Shift+Q to open an Untitled – Meeting dialog box click the Meeting Workspace button to open the Meeting Workspace pane and then click its Create button.)

3. **Fill out the Outlook meeting request as you normally would, including filling in the To field with the e-mail addresses of those you intend to invite to the meeting and then adding the meeting's subject, location, and start and ending times, as well as any message to the recipients in their respective fields, and then click Create.**

   If you need help filling out the meeting request and scheduling appointments and events in Outlook, take a gander at my book *Manage Your Life with Outlook For Dummies* (from Wiley Publishing).

4. **(Optional) If the settings in the Create a Workspace area of the Meeting Workspace pane are not correct — the wrong site is indicated or the wrong template is being used — click the Change Settings link in this pane.**

   The Meeting Workspace pane refreshes to show drop-down lists for specifying a new site location, a new template language, and a new template type, as shown in Figure 6-9.

Figure 6-9: Select the SharePoint location and template to use for a new meeting workspace in the Outlook Meeting Workspace pane.

5. (Optional) Click OK in the Change Settings view of the Meeting Workspace pane to return to the Home page and then click the pane's Create button.

SharePoint creates the new meeting workspace and then Outlook adds a link to that workspace in the body of the meeting request, as shown in Figure 6-10. You can then click the Send button to send out the updated meeting request to all your recipients.

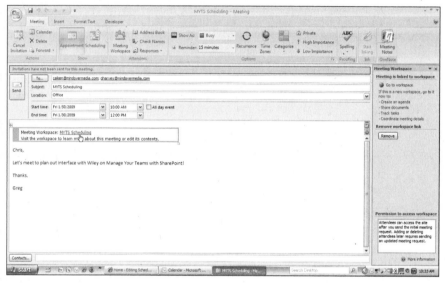

Figure 6-10: This meeting request shows the link to the new meeting workspace after creating it on the SharePoint site.

Don't forget that the team members to whom you send the meeting request with the link to the new SharePoint meeting workspace may not be able to access that workspace unless they're registered as authenticated users of that site, complete with user ID, password, and permissions to browse the site. (See Chapter 3 for details on adding authenticated SharePoint site users.)

SharePoint doesn't automatically add a link to the Quick Launch for the meeting workspace you generate from an event added to your Outlook calendar. To access the page for this meeting workspace, click the View All Site Content link for the site containing the workspace and then click the link attached to its name in the Sites and Workspaces section of the All Site Content page. Or, you can add a link to the meeting workspace in the site's Quick Launch by following the steps outlined in the section "Adding a Quick Launch link to a meeting workspace created from a calendar item," earlier in this chapter.

Linking a Calendar Event to an Existing Meeting Workspace

Instead of creating a new meeting workspace for an event that you're adding to your SharePoint or Outlook (2003 or 2007) calendar, you can create a link to an existing workspace already created on the SharePoint site. This is useful, for example, when you've set up a meeting workspace for an initial meeting that contains supporting materials that pertain not only to the initial meeting but to a subsequent meeting as well (especially if the meeting or event is a recurring one that requires only a single, supporting meeting workspace).

The process for linking a SharePoint calendar event or Outlook calendar event (if you're using Outlook 2003 or 2007) to an existing meeting workspace is almost the same as the process for creating a new meeting workspace for the event — almost, but not quite. One slight change is required, and the exact nature of that change differs depending upon which of the two calendars you're using (the SharePoint Calendar or the Outlook 2003/2007 Calendar):

- ✔ **SharePoint Calendar:** Click the Link to an Existing Meeting Workspace radio button in the Choices area at the top of the New or Existing Meeting Workspace page in SharePoint and then select the workspace you want from the drop-down list immediately beneath it.

- ✔ **Outlook 2003 or 2007 Calendar:** Click the Change Settings link in the Meeting Workspace pane of the meeting request window (opened in Outlook 2007 by clicking the Meeting Workspace button in the Attendees group of the Meeting tab on the Ribbon, whereas in Outlook 2003 you click the Meeting Workspace button in the Untitled – Meeting dialog box). Next, select the Link to an Existing Workspace radio button in the Select a Workspace area of the Meeting Workspace pane, select the name of the meeting workspace, and then click OK.

When you click OK after designating the existing workspace to link in the SharePoint New or Existing Meeting Workspace page, SharePoint takes you to the Meeting Workspace page on the site. When you click the Link button in the Meeting Workspace pane in Outlook, the program adds a link to the existing workspace in the body of the meeting request, which you can then send to all your designated recipients by clicking the Send button. You can then click the link to the existing meeting workspace that appears in the e-mail generated from the meeting request to open the home workspace page in your Web browser.

After you link a new recurring event to an existing meeting workspace, SharePoint adds a Date Selector pane on the left side of the home workspace page, and this new pane displays the dates of all the events currently connected to the workspace. You can then click the date of the particular event to display its information and calendar link on the home workspace page.

Adding a Button to Launch a Yugma Web Conference

At this point in the development of SharePoint technologies, you (unfortunately) can't actually conduct an online or Web meeting from a particular meeting workspace. The best you can do if your meeting workspace is for an upcoming online meeting is to use the workspace page(s) to provide your team members with all the information they need to prepare for the Web conference. The team member attendees will then still have to launch whatever Web conferencing software you're using — perhaps Microsoft Live Meeting, Citrix GoToMeeting, or Yugma Instant Web Conferencing — from your Web browser outside of the SharePoint site.

If, however, you use Yugma Instant Web Conferencing to conduct your online meetings, you can easily add a command button to the Home page of any SharePoint meeting workspace capable of supporting an online meeting component. You and your team members can then click this button at the appointed meeting time to launch Yugma (in its own window) and join the Web conferencing session. And even if you don't use Yugma Instant Web conferencing and don't have any interest in getting it, you may still want to follow along with the steps, as doing so provides you with a good opportunity to see how easy it is to use SharePoint's Content Editor Web Part to bring readymade HTML code into your site.

To add this Yugma Now button to a meeting workspace you've created on your SharePoint site, all you have to do is download the Yugma Widget (a tiny file containing the snippet of HTML code you need to launch the Yugma program as well as the graphic used by its command button) and then add the HTML code from this snippet to a Content Editor Web Part you've added to the meeting workspace.

You can do all this by following these simple steps:

1. **Point your browser to the Yugma home page (www.yugma.com) and then click the Support link that appears in the column on the left side of the page.**

   The Yugma Support page appears in your browser.

2. **Click the Yugma Widget link and fill in the information in the online form to customize the widget. Then click the Save This HTML Snippet link.**

   Windows opens a dialog box asking whether you want to open or save the snippet.

3. **Click the Save button and then designate a place on your computer to save the Yugma_now widget.**

   As a general principle, you should always save such files to your hard drive.

4. **Navigate to where you saved the Yugma_now widget folder; then open the folder and click the Yugma_now HTML icon inside.**

   The Yugma_now HTML page appears in your browser.

5. **Use the browser's command to open the HTML source code (View⇨Source in Internet Explorer and View⇨Page Source in Mozilla FireFox).**

   The browser displays the HTML code for the page in a separate window.

6. **Select all the HTML code for the Yugma snippet and then choose Edit⇨Copy or press Ctrl+C.**

   Windows copies the selected HTML code to the Windows Clipboard.

   Now, you're ready to add the Content Editor Web Part to the appropriate page of the meeting workspace in SharePoint.

7. **Open the page in the meeting workspace in your SharePoint site where you want the Yugma Now button to appear and then choose Edit Page from the Site Actions drop-down menu.**

   SharePoint places the workspace page in Edit mode, displaying the Web Part zones.

8. **Click the Add a Web Part button at the top of the Web Part zone where you want the Yugma Now button to appear.**

   SharePoint opens the Add Web Parts dialog box for the Web Part zone you select.

9. **Select the check box in front of the Content Editor Web Part in the Miscellaneous section of this dialog box and then click the Add button.**

   SharePoint closes the Add Web Parts dialog box and adds the Content Editor Web Part to the top of the selected zone.

10. **Choose Modify Shared Web Part from the drop-down menu attached to the Content Editor Web Part's Edit button.**

    SharePoint opens a Content Editor Web Part task pane on the right side of the workspace page.

11. Click the Source Editor command button in the task pane.

The button appears under the heading To Type HTML Source Code, Click Source Editor.

SharePoint opens a Text Entry – Webpage Dialog window.

12. Press Ctrl+V to insert the HTML code you copied earlier into the Text Entry – Webpage Dialog window, as shown in Figure 6-11, and then click the Save button.

SharePoint saves the HTML code you pasted into the dialog box and then closes the dialog box. The program then redraws the current page of the meeting workspace, displaying the graphic of the Yugma Now button in the Content Editor Web Part (see Figure 6-12).

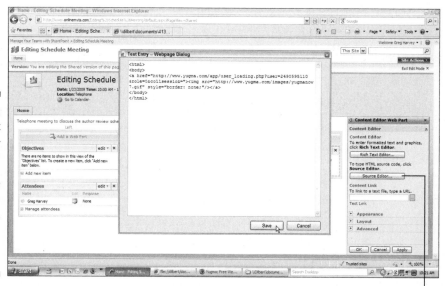

Figure 6-11:
The Text Entry – Webpage Dialog window after pasting the HTML code for the Yugma button into it.

Source Editor button

13. (Optional) Click the Expand button in front of Appearance in the Content Editor Web Part task pane and edit the name that appears in the Title text box to something a bit more descriptive than Content Editor Web Part.

Now, you're ready to close the task pane and exit Edit mode.

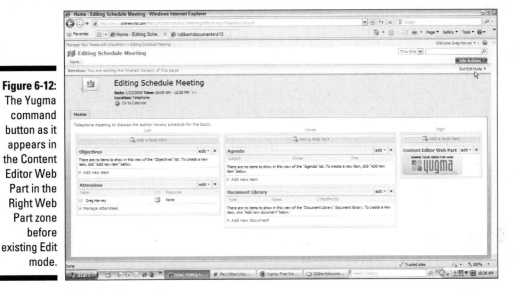

Figure 6-12:
The Yugma
command
button as it
appears in
the Content
Editor Web
Part in the
Right Web
Part zone
before
existing Edit
mode.

14. **Click the OK button in the Content Editor Web Part task pane and then click the Exit Edit Mode button in the upper-right of the meeting workspace page.**

    SharePoint redraws the meeting workspace page with a fully functional Yugma Now button that you and your team members can use to launch Yugma Web Conferencing and start a new online meeting or join one in progress.

Chapter 7

Getting Team Feedback via Surveys and Discussion Boards

In This Chapter

▶ Understanding how SharePoint surveys work and what you can do with them

▶ Creating a new survey to poll your teams and get their opinions

▶ Using threaded discussions to garner ideas and get feedback from your teams

▶ Creating new discussion boards on your SharePoint site

▶ Connecting discussion boards to Outlook

SharePoint 2007 makes it easy to get feedback from your team members during the course of the SharePoint collaboration. To this end, SharePoint supports two special types of lists:

✔ **Surveys** that team members can take to record their opinions on topics of interest to the team and/or some aspect of the collaborative project in the form of an online questionnaire

✔ **Discussion boards** where team members can share their ideas and opinions on these kinds of topics following the format of a newsgroup-style threaded discussion

In this chapter, you find out how to create and use SharePoint surveys to poll your teams and record their responses to various questions. The SharePoint surveys you put together can be straightforward questionnaires that simply record a team member's responses to a series of simple questions or they can be somewhat more complex, branching out to include different series of questions based on the particular responses given to key questions.

In this chapter, you also find out how to use SharePoint discussion boards to provide forums for your team members so that they can easily share their views and opinions on various topics. You can also use discussion boards to facilitate conversations about issues that arise in the course of the collaboration and to elicit ideas for improvements that you can incorporate in future collaborations.

Using Surveys to Poll Your Teams

When you set up a new survey in SharePoint 2007, you do so by creating a series of questions meant to elicit informative responses from the team members taking your survey. These survey questions can be one of two general types:

- ✔ **Closed:** These survey questions offer limited responses and require a definite answer such as Yes, No, or even Unsure. Closed questions are fairly easy to analyze statistically, but such questions can be a challenge to compose in such a way that they cover the full range of responses that your respondents may possibly want to give.

- ✔ **Open-ended:** These survey questions offer no specific responses and require no particular answer from the respondents. Open-ended questions tend to call for an opinion or some sort of analysis of a topic. Questions of this type are often easier to compose than closed questions, but their responses are more of a challenge to catalogue and analyze. An open-ended question often comes on the heels of a particular response to an earlier closed question. For example, if a respondent answers in the negative to a closed Yes or No question asking whether he or she felt that a particular meeting workspace on the SharePoint site contained all the materials needed to adequately prepare for a team meeting, you can then compose an open-ended, follow-up question that asks the respondent to list specific additional resources that would have helped his or her preparation.

As with the fields in SharePoint lists, the answers to particular survey questions can be any one of many different types. As you see in Table 7-1, some of these answer types are better suited to different general types of questions.

Table 7-1	The Types of Answers Supported in SharePoint Survey Questions	
Answer Type	*Question Type*	*When to Use*
Single Line of Text	Open-ended	Used for short answers of a few words or a single sentence. You can restrict the total number of characters in this single line.
Multiple Lines of Text	Open-ended	Used for longer answers of a few sentences or a short paragraph. You can specify three kinds of text for the multiple lines: Plain; Rich (enabling respondents to change the font, text color, and alignment); and Enhanced (enabling respondents to add pictures, tables, and hyperlinks).

Answer Type	Question Type	When to Use
Choice (Menu to Choose From)	Closed or open-ended	Used to restrict the answer to particular selections (such as Yes, No, Maybe) in a closed question and to allow the respondent to enter his own answer in an open-ended question. You can present the choices in a drop-down list, as radio buttons, or as check boxes (which enables the respondent to select more than one answer).
Rating Scale (a Matrix of Choices or a Likert Scale)	Closed	Used to restrict the answer to a closed question to a preference rated on a numeric scale (1 to 5 by default), where a value at one end of the scale indicates strong agreement with the question, and a value at the other end indicates strong disagreement.
Number (1, 10, 100)	Open-ended	Used to restrict the answer in an open-ended question to a value. You can specify the number of decimal places displayed in the numeric answer as well as the highest and lowest allowable value.
Currency ($, ¥, €)	Open-ended	Used to restrict the answer in an open-ended question to an amount of money. You can specify the currency format and number of decimal places displayed in the monetary answer as well as the highest and lowest allowable amounts.
Date and Time	Open-ended	Used to restrict the answer in an open-ended question to a date or a date and time.
Lookup (Information Already on This Site)	Closed	Used to restrict the answer in a closed question to a choice of entries in another list that exists on the SharePoint site.
Yes/No (Check Box)	Closed	Used to restrict the answer in a closed question to either true (Yes) or false (No).
Person or Group	Closed	Used to restrict the answer in a closed question to a particular authenticated SharePoint user or user group.

Keep in mind that you can specify whether any question in the survey is mandatory or optional (the default setting). You can also specify the most likely answer for a particular question as the default that's presented in the survey, which the respondent may then override with a different choice.

Understanding branching in surveys

The ability to have a survey *branch* depending upon a respondent's answer to a question is a very cool new feature of SharePoint Services 3.0. Branching enables you to keep the survey simple by offering your respondents mostly multiple-choice answers, while still enabling you to get more information when a respondent gives you a particular response that requires more details.

For example, a question in your survey can be a Yes/No question that asks, "Do you need more SharePoint training in order to effectively use its technology for team collaboration?" Then, if the respondent selects the No check box, the survey simply ends, but if he answers Yes, the survey then branches to another page containing a set of Rating Scale questions that query the respondent on how strongly he feels about receiving training on particular SharePoint features (subsites, lists, document libraries, and so forth). After the respondent answers that question, the survey ends or goes on to a new line of questioning.

You and your team members can always tell when a question in a survey is branched because it will always be the last question on a particular survey page. This is because SharePoint always inserts a page break after a branching-enabled question.

The only trick is that you must add the actual branching to the survey *after* you've finished creating the survey and entering all its questions. This requirement almost always means that you need to plan out the order of the questions and the logic of their branching in the survey before you actually start creating the survey and entering its questions in SharePoint. (To plan your survey, you can use paper, or you can use a program such as Excel or Word 2007, taking advantage of organization diagrams using SmartArt graphics.)

Creating a new SharePoint survey

To create a new SharePoint survey, follow these steps:

1. **Open the subsite where you want the survey to be available to the team members who are to take it.**

   If you want the survey to be available from the top-level site, open the home page.

2. **Choose Create from the Site Actions drop-down menu.**

   SharePoint opens the Create page.

3. **Click the Survey link at the bottom of the Tracking column.**

   SharePoint opens a New survey page similar to the one shown in Figure 7-1.

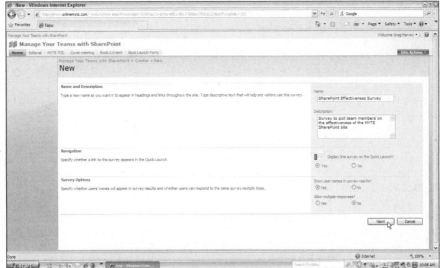

Figure 7-1:
Create a new survey for the SharePoint site.

4. **Enter a name for the new survey in the Name text box and then press Tab.**

   SharePoint advances the cursor to the Description text box.

5. **Type a description of the survey in the Description text box to let your team members know the survey's purpose and/or scope.**

6. **(Optional) Make any desired changes to the Navigation and Survey Options sections.**

   By default, a new survey appears in the Quick Launch, the results show the respondent's name, and SharePoint does not allow a respondent to take the survey more than once. If you need to change any of these default settings for your survey, you can do so at this point.

7. **Click the Next button.**

   SharePoint opens a New Question page, where you compose the survey's first question. Figure 7-2 shows the top part of this New Question page, where you type the question and then select its answer type. (See Table 7-1, earlier in this chapter, for details on the various answer types.)

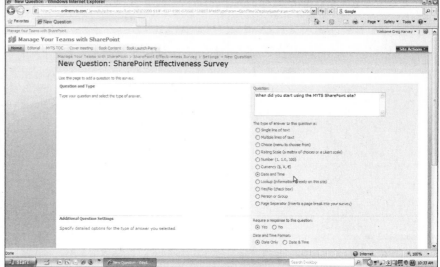

8. **Type your question in the Question text box and then select the radio button of its answer type under the heading The Type of Answer to This Question Is.**

   By default, each new question in the survey is optional, and the other question settings — the number and types of options, for example, or the default answer — depend upon the type of answer you select in this step. Figure 7-3 shows you the Additional Question Settings that appear when you select Date and Time as the answer type.

9. **(Optional) Make any necessary changes to the settings in the options that appear in the Additional Question Settings area of the page.**

   If you need to, select the Yes radio button under the Require a Response to This Question heading to make answering this question mandatory.

   You now continue to compose the survey questions in the order in which you want them to appear.

10. **Click the Next Question button at the bottom of the page and repeat the process of composing your next survey question, as outlined in Steps 8 and 9.**

    Repeat the process as many times as needed. After you've composed all the survey questions, you're ready to create the survey.

11. **When you're done composing questions, click the Finish button at the bottom of the New Question page.**

SharePoint compiles your survey questions and then, after creating the survey, displays the survey's Customize page — similar to the one shown in Figure 7-4 — where you can make last-minute changes to the survey and its questions, and add branching.

Figure 7-3: I've selected the Additional Question Settings for a question with a Date and Time answer.

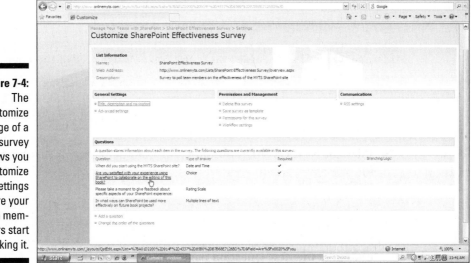

Figure 7-4: The Customize page of a new survey allows you to customize its settings before your team members start taking it.

Editing a survey

Keep in mind that, after creating a survey, you can still edit it from the survey's Customize page. To open this Customize page, click the survey's link either on the Quick Launch (assuming that the survey has such a link) or in the Surveys section of the All Site Content page and then choose Survey Settings from Settings drop-down menu.

From a survey's Customize page, you can change the survey title, its description, and whether a link to the survey appears on the Quick Launch. To access these settings, click the Title, Description, and Navigation link in the General Settings column.

You can edit individual questions (for example, changing their answer type, making them mandatory, or adding branching) by the particular question in the Question column. SharePoint then opens an Edit Question page for the selected question so that you can modify the question type and its other settings.

You can also add new questions to the survey by clicking the Add a Question link on the survey's Customize page. SharePoint opens a New Question page where you create the question. You can modify the order in which the questions appear in the survey by clicking the Change the Order of the Questions link, which opens a Change Question Order page. Here you designate the order of the questions (from top to bottom) by selecting a number that corresponds to the new question's order in the survey in the drop-down list located to the right of each question.

Adding branching to a survey

If you want to add branching to a survey so that the survey skips to a particular question when a respondent answers in a certain way, you need to add the branching logic to the question whose answer triggers the branching to the alternative question.

To do this, follow these steps:

1. **Select the survey's page by clicking the survey's link either on the Quick Launch or in the Surveys section of the All Site Content page.**

2. **Choose Survey Settings from the Settings drop-down menu.**

   SharePoint opens the Customize page for the survey.

3. **In the Question section of the survey page, click the link attached to the particular question whose answer is to trigger the branching.**

   SharePoint opens an Edit Question page for the particular question you select. The Branching Logic section is at the bottom of the page (see Figure 7-5) where you add a branch to a response or responses (in the case of Choice question) that indicates the question to which it jumps.

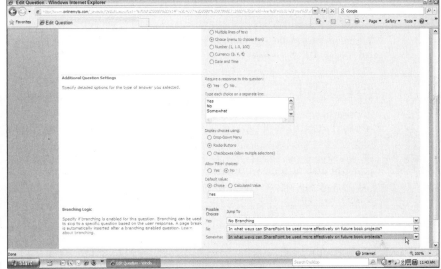

Figure 7-5:
Add branching to a question with a Choice answer type on its Edit Question page.

4. **Click the drop-down button for the answer (or answers) under the Jump To heading and then select the question to which the question branches from the drop-down menu. Then click OK.**

   SharePoint returns you to the Customize page where, in the Questions area, a new Branching Logic column has been added. In the row of the question you just edited, a check mark appears in the Branching Logic column.

Responding to the survey

After you finish composing questions and editing the branching logic for a new survey, you can alert your team members to its existence by adding an invitation to take the survey in the home page Announcements list. You can also send out an invitation e-mail message using the survey's Alert Me option on the Actions drop-down menu.

Then, team members can respond to the survey on the SharePoint site by opening its Survey page (which displays descriptive information about the survey and summarizes its results) and then clicking the Respond to This Survey button.

SharePoint opens the first page of the survey (assuming that the survey has more than a single page) where the respondent can record his answers. When the survey contains more than one page (which is always the case when a survey uses branching), he clicks a Next button when he's finished answering the questions on the current page.

When a respondent answers the final question on the survey, he can save his responses to the entire survey by clicking the Finish button at the bottom of the page, as shown in Figure 7-6. SharePoint then returns him to the main Survey page where summary information about the survey is displayed.

If a respondent doesn't complete the survey and clicks the Cancel button instead of the Finish button, an alert dialog box appears, indicating that SharePoint has saved a partial survey response that can be viewed in the All Responses survey view. To delete the partial response so that the respondent can still take the survey at a later time (assuming that the survey can be taken only once), he needs to click OK in this alert dialog box rather than Cancel.

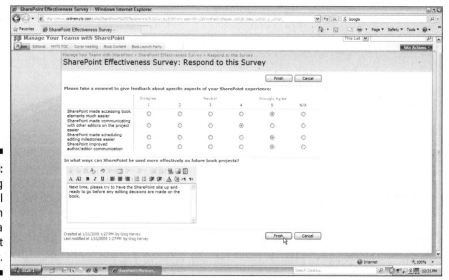

Figure 7-6:
Responding
to the final
question
in a
SharePoint
survey.

Viewing the survey results

When you create a survey in SharePoint 2007, the program automatically creates three views for the survey:

- ✔ **Overview:** This is the default view that appears on the Survey page with a list showing the survey name, description, date and time it was created, and the total number of responses to the survey.

- ✔ **All Responses:** In this view, SharePoint displays a list of responses to the survey, showing the number of responses, the team member who completed the survey (unless you elected not to show a respondent's name in the results), the date he took it, and whether the survey was completed. To view individual answers to a question, click the link to its number in the list. To switch to this view, either click the Show All Responses link when the Survey page is in Overview or select All Responses from the View drop-down list.

- ✔ **Graphical Summary:** In this view, SharePoint displays statistics about the answers to each of the survey questions in bar and column chart form, as shown in Figure 7-7. To switch to this mini-graph view, either click the Show Graphical Summary of Responses link when the Survey page is in Overview or choose Graphical Summary from the View drop-down list.

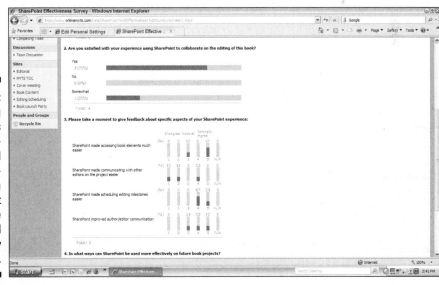

Figure 7-7: Displaying the results to the second and third questions in a SharePoint survey in the Graphical Summary view.

Unlike most of the other lists and libraries in SharePoint that enable you to customize the program's default views and create ones of your own, be aware that you can't create custom views for your surveys. The three built-in views (Overview, All Responses, and Graphical Summary) are the only ones you can use to display survey results, and these views must be used as is.

Using Web Parts to add a survey summary list to the home page

During the time that you're actively eliciting responses to a survey from your team members, you can make it easier for them to respond to the survey by adding the survey's Web Part to the home page. That way, the minute your team members log on to the SharePoint site, they'll see a summary of the survey along with a Respond to This Survey link that they can click to take the survey.

To see how this works, follow along with the steps for adding a summary list to the Left Web Part zone of my site's home page, immediately below the Announcements list:

1. **On the home page of the SharePoint site, choose Edit Page from the Site Actions drop-down menu.**

   SharePoint displays the home page in Edit mode.

2. **Click the Add a Web Part button at the top of the Left Web Part zone.**

   SharePoint opens the Add Web Parts to Left dialog box.

3. **Select the check box in front of the SharePoint Effectiveness Survey Web Part in the List and Libraries section and then click the Add button.**

   SharePoint adds the SharePoint Effectiveness Survey in Overview to the top of the Left Web Part zone of the home page.

4. **Drag the SharePoint Effectiveness Survey Web Part by its title bar and drop it between the Announcements and Calendar Web Part and then click the Exit Edit Mode button.**

   SharePoint exits Edit mode and redraws the home page with the Overview of the SharePoint Effectiveness Survey displayed between the Announcements and the Calendar lists, along with its Respond to This Survey link (see Figure 7-8).

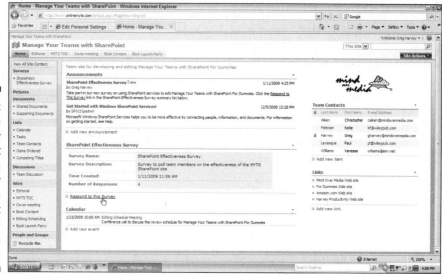

Figure 7-8:
The home
page of my
SharePoint
site showing
a summary
list of the
SharePoint
Effective-
ness
Survey.

If you want your team members to see the results of a survey you're currently conducting in graphical form, switch the Survey Web Part on the home page from the default Overview to the Graphical Summary view. While in the home page's Edit mode, click the survey's Edit button and then choose Modify Shared Web Part from the drop-down menu to display the survey's task pane on the right. When the pane is on-screen, choose Graphical Summary from the Selected View drop-down menu before you click OK.

Exporting survey results to an Excel worksheet

If you have Excel 2003 or 2007 installed on your computer, you can easily export your survey results to an Excel worksheet (as a Web query) and then use Excel's extensive analytical features to further evaluate the results.

To export the results of a survey to an Excel worksheet, follow these steps:

1. **Choose Export to Spreadsheet from the survey's Actions drop-down menu.**

   SharePoint displays a File Download dialog box.

2. **Click the Open button in the File Download dialog box.**

   Windows launches Excel (if it's not already running) and then displays an Excel Security Notice alert dialog box.

3. **Click the Enable button in the Excel Security Notice dialog box. (Supply your SharePoint User ID and password, if prompted for it.)**

   Excel then copies the survey results into a spreadsheet table as shown in Figure 7-9. In Excel 2007, you can then easily summarize the results in an Excel Pivot Table by clicking the Summarize with PivotTable button in the Tools group of the Table Tools: Design tab on the Ribbon. (See my book *Excel 2007 All-in-One Desk Reference For Dummies,* from Wiley Publishing, for loads more on analyzing summary data with Excel Pivot Tables.)

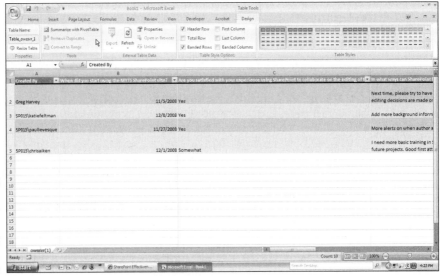

Figure 7-9: I've exported the results of the SharePoint Effectiveness Survey to Excel as a worksheet table.

Using Discussion Boards to Get Team Feedback

SharePoint 2007 supports the use of newsgroup-style discussions to enable you and your team members to easily exchange views on various topics of interest through the use of its discussion boards. Discussion boards enable you to create new discussion topics as well as to track all the postings and replies that you and your team members make as part of the online discussion.

When you open a discussion board, you see a list of all the discussion topics that you add to the board (using the Discussion option on the board's New drop-down menu). SharePoint displays this list using the Subject view.

The Subject view is the only ready-made view available for a new discussion board (although you can customize this view and create new views in addition to using the Modify This View and Create View options on the board's View drop-down menu). In this view, each discussion topic that you add to a discussion board is displayed in a simple list with four columns: Subject, Created By, Replies, and Last Updated.

Then, to view the particular postings and replies to a particular topic on the discussion board and to add to them, you click the link attached to the topic in the Subject column of the list itself. SharePoint then displays a page showing the posts and replies in what's called a Flat view, one of the two pre-defined views for a discussion that you can select from the discussion's View drop-down menu:

- ✔ **Flat:** This is the default view afforded of a particular discussion topic that displays a straight, sequential listing of all posts and replies in the order in which they were created.

- ✔ **Threaded:** This is an alternative view you can select for a particular discussion topic that groups replies to a particular post under that post in the order in which the replies were created.

Typically, when you start using a new SharePoint site, create a subsite from the Team Site template (Chapter 2), or create a workspace using the Document Workspace template (Chapter 9) or Social Meeting Workspace template (Chapter 6), the program automatically adds a discussion board to the subsite or workspace.

When working with a discussion board created from a Team Site or Document Workspace template, start the discussion by clicking the Team Discussion link in the Quick Launch. As for discussion boards created from a Social Meeting Workspace template, you access those by clicking the workspace's Discussion tab.

Adding a new topic to a site's discussion board

To start an online roundtable discussion about a particular topic using the Team Discussion board that comes with a new site, follow these steps:

1. **Open the home page and then click the Team Discussion link in the site's Quick Launch.**

   SharePoint opens a blank Team Discussion page.

2. **Choose Discussion from the New drop-down menu.**

   SharePoint opens a New Item page with a blank form for adding a new discussion topic, similar to the one shown in Figure 7-10.

3. **Type a title for the new discussion topic in the Subject text box and then press Tab.**

   SharePoint advances the cursor to the Body text box.

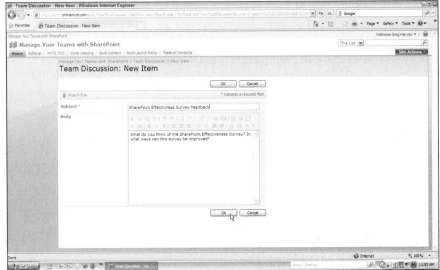

Figure 7-10:
Add a new discussion topic to the site's default Team Discussion board.

The title you've chosen appears in the Subject column on the discussion board, so make it as informative as possible.

4. **Type in a description or question that indicates the nature of the new discussion topic and the type of information you want discussed.**

   Some topics are probably better phrased as questions for the team ("What do you think of . . . ?"), but others are better phrased as polite commands eliciting their feedback ("Please give me your ideas on . . .").

5. **(Optional) To attach a supporting document file to the new discussion topic, click the Attach File link at the top and then use the Browse button to select the file in the Choose File to Upload dialog box. After selecting the file, click Open and then click OK.**

   SharePoint closes the Choose File to Upload dialog box and returns you to the original New Item form with the Subject text box and Body text box.

6. Click the OK button at the bottom of the New Item form.

SharePoint closes the New Item page and returns you to the Team Discussion page, where the new subject of the new discussion topic appears along with your name and the date and time you created it.

Posting a message to a discussion topic

After adding a discussion topic as a new item on your Team Discussion board, you can post messages to it by following these steps:

1. Open the Team Discussion page for your site by clicking the Team Discussion link on its Quick Launch.

2. Click the link attached to the discussion topic in the Subject column of the discussion list on this page.

SharePoint displays a page displaying the subject and description of your new discussion topic.

3. Click the Reply button on the far right of the title bar above the new discussion topic.

SharePoint displays a New Item page similar to the one shown in Figure 7-11, where you can respond to the message posed in the original discussion topic. The Body text box contains the original discussion subject and description beneath the area where you enter your response.

Figure 7-11:
You can respond to the original message of the discussion topic.

4. Type your thoughts and feelings about the discussion topic and then click OK.

SharePoint returns you to the discussion page that now shows your response immediately beneath the original post.

Replying to someone's post

When someone posts a response to a comment that you make about a topic on a discussion board, you can easily post a reply directed to that person's comments. All you have to do is open the topic's discussion page and then click the Reply button that appears on the far right side of the title bar of his post. (See Figure 7-12.)

SharePoint then opens a New Item page that shows the text of the person's response immediately beneath the area where you type your reply. When you click OK on this New Item page, SharePoint returns you to the discussion page containing all the posts, where your reply now appears immediately below the person's response to your original comment.

Figure 7-12: Sometimes you might need to reply directly to somebody's response to the topic being discussed on the discussion board.

Switching to a Threaded view of a discussion

By default, SharePoint displays the messages and replies posted to a particular topic on the discussion board in a Flat view, whereby each post and reply is simply listed one after the other in the order in which they were posted (as shown in Figure 7-12).

To get a better idea of the relationship between original posts and replies made specifically to them, you can switch the discussion page to the Threaded view. To do this, choose Threaded from the View drop-down menu on the discussion page that contains the threads of a particular discussion.

SharePoint then redraws the discussion page, slightly indenting replies to posts and simplifying all responses by removing the pictures assigned to the users (or the place for the person's picture even when no picture is available). Figure 7-13 gives you an idea of how the posts and replies appear in this view. Note that when you switch a discussion to the Thread view, SharePoint automatically adds a Show Quoted Messages link to each message. You can click this link to expand a particular response in the discussion so that it includes all of the previous posts and replies, thus detailing its history.

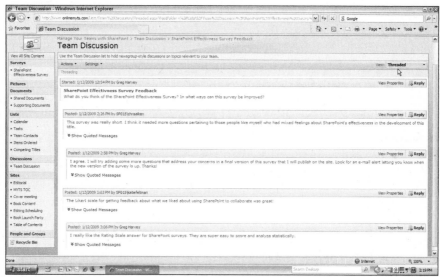

Figure 7-13: You can display the posts and replies in a particular discussion in the Threaded view.

Creating a new discussion board

You can create discussion boards for each of the subsites that you set up on your SharePoint site (see Chapter 2) that don't automatically create them (as is the case with subsites that use the Team Site template). To create a new discussion board for a SharePoint subsite that doesn't automatically have one, follow these steps:

   1. **Open the subsite for which you want to add a new discussion board and then choose Create from the Site Actions drop-down menu.**

      SharePoint opens the Create page for the subsite.

   2. **Click the Discussion Board link in the Communications column.**

      SharePoint opens a New page, where you specify the discussion board settings.

   3. **Type the name for the new discussion board in the Name text box and then press Tab.**

      SharePoint advances the cursor to the Description text box.

   4. **Type a description of the new message board in the Description text box.**

      By default, the Leave the Share List Items Across All Meetings (Series Items) option is set to No. Provided that you don't want to share the discussion topics that you add to this new discussion board with all the other discussion boards on the SharePoint site, leave the No radio button selected under Change Items Into Series Items.

   5. **Click the Create button.**

      SharePoint creates the new discussion board and then displays its page on the current subsite.

You can then start adding discussion topics to the newly created discussion board following the general steps outlined in the section "Adding a new topic to a site's discussion board," which appears earlier in this chapter.

Connecting a discussion board to Outlook 2007

If you're using Outlook 2007, you may want to connect your SharePoint discussion board to Outlook so that you can then view the posts made to particular topics within it and make replies to them from right within Outlook itself. This is a super way to stay on top of a team discussion and to make it super easy for your team members to actively participate in the discussion.

To connect a discussion board to Outlook, open the board in SharePoint and then choose the Connect to Outlook option from the Actions drop-down menu. Doing so adds a folder for the board in the SharePoint Lists section of the Mail Folders in Outlook's Navigation pane.

When you select this discussion folder in the Navigation pane, Outlook adds an Arrange By button at the top of the pane to the right. You can click the Arrange By button to modify the way the individual posts and replies for a particular conversation (topic) are displayed there.

To reply to a post displayed in this pane, right-click the post and then choose Post Reply to Folder from the shortcut menu. Outlook opens a pre-addressed e-mail window that contains the text of the post or reply below a blank line where you can type a reply. After you finish typing your reply, click the Post button at the top of this window to post your reply to the discussion topic on your SharePoint site.

Chapter 8

Stimulating Team Interaction with Blogs and Wiki Pages

In This Chapter

▶ Using blogs and Wiki page libraries to facilitate team interaction

▶ Creating and using a new SharePoint blog site

▶ Setting up the categories for your new blog and making your first post

▶ Creating and maintaining a new SharePoint Wiki page library

▶ Using RSS feeds to stay informed of additions to SharePoint blogs

SharePoint sites now support blogs and wikis, two of the latest Web-related technologies for fostering interactive communication. *Blogs* (short for Web logs) enable you to conduct an online conversation with your teams by posting comments to which your team members add their two cents. Wiki page libraries (*wikiwiki* is Hawaiian for quick) enable any of your team members to easily contribute to or modify the contents that you place there (including pictures, tables, and links to other Web sites and pages within the SharePoint site itself).

In this chapter, you find out how to set up and maintain both SharePoint blogs and Wiki page libraries to encourage members of your team to actively communicate about issues and participate in the maintenance of library pages that require this kind of very active interaction and collaboration.

Using Blogs to Elicit Your Team's Ideas

SharePoint blogs enable you to readily float new ideas with your team members, elicit their feedback, and then have them post their own spinoff thoughts. As with blogs on traditional Web sites, the team members who start and maintain the blogs post their ideas in a series of linear, chronological posts. Then the other team members who visit the blog reply to particular posts with their own comments (which, of course, other members can comment on as well, in addition to commenting on the original posts).

Keep in mind that team members who have access to your blog pages on a SharePoint site can comment freely on the original thoughts and questions you and others post there, but they can't edit or alter the content of these posts. This setup contrasts to Wiki pages on the SharePoint site (discussed at length later in the chapter), where team members with access to the pages can freely edit and amend any material you or others place there.

In SharePoint, a blog is a subsite (see Chapter 2) that uses a special Blog template found in the Collaboration group of site templates. This Blog template enables you to create and manage the posts that you and others make to the blog as well as the comments that you and your team members make to the posts and comments of others. As with other types of SharePoint subsites, you can create as many blogs as you need for the individual teams that you manage.

Setting up a SharePoint blog subsite

The procedure for setting up a SharePoint blog is very simple and straightforward. The only catch is that you're generally going to want to change at least one default Blog template setting (covered in the following steps) before you start posting to your new blog and inviting your team members to come visit and add their comments.

The default setting you routinely need to change is the Content Approval site setting that defaults to Yes and that needs to be set to No so that you don't have to stop and approve each and every comment that your team members make to your posts before they appear on the blog pages. Leaving this default setting at Yes makes sense in a blog that's open to anyone on the Web, where you really do need to screen the contents of user comments before publicly posting them. Screening contents shouldn't be a real concern with a SharePoint blog restricted to a professional team under your direct supervision. (If it is a concern, you probably need to address this issue in person with the team members, instructing them on what constitutes appropriate and inappropriate posts on the team's SharePoint site, rather than relying on the blog site's Content Approval setting.)

To create a new blog for your SharePoint site, follow these steps:

1. **Log on to the SharePoint site and open the subsite under which you want the new blog to appear.**

   If you want the blog to be available under the top-level SharePoint site, display the home page.

2. **Choose Create from the Site Actions drop-down menu.**

   SharePoint opens the Create page.

3. **Click the Sites and Workspaces link in the Web Pages column at the far right.**

   SharePoint opens the New SharePoint Site page, the top of which is shown in Figure 8-1.

Figure 8-1: I need to create a new blog subsite for my SharePoint site.

4. **Type the name of the new blog in the Title text box and then press Tab.**

   SharePoint advances the cursor to the Description text box.

5. **Type a description of the blog into the Description text box and then press Tab.**

   SharePoint advances the cursor to the URL Name text box.

6. **Type a name for the blog subsite (without spaces) into the URL Name text box.**

   The name you choose here will form the basis for the blog site's URL.

   Next, you need to select the Blog template.

7. **Click the Blog option on the Collaboration tab of the Select a Template list box.**

   As with other, more traditional subsites that you add to the SharePoint site, the program automatically assigns the same user permissions as those in effect for the blog's parent site. To assign different individual permissions, click the Use Unique Permissions radio button.

   Likewise, SharePoint displays a link for the new blog in the Sites section of the parent site's Quick Launch. The program also displays a tab for opening it on the SharePoint site's Top Link bar.

8. **(Optional) Make any necessary changes to the Permissions, Navigation, and Navigation Inheritance settings that your new blog requires.**

   If you don't want your team members to access the blog from the Quick Launch or Top Link bar or you don't want the blog site to have the same Top Link bar buttons as the parent site, you need to change these Permissions, Navigation, and/or Navigation Inheritance settings.

9. **Click the Create button.**

   SharePoint creates your new blog and then displays the home page of the new blog subsite with its Welcome information, similar to the one shown in Figure 8-2. Note that this home page contains a series of Admin Links in a column on the right side of the page along with the blog site's Quick Launch in three sections (Categories, Other Blogs, and Links) on the left side of the page.

Figure 8-2:
A new blog
subsite
looks like
this after
you first
create it.

10. Click the Manage Posts link in the Admin Links column on the right.

SharePoint opens the Posts page for the new blog that contains the single, automatic Welcome to Your Blog post.

11. Choose List Settings from the Settings drop-down menu.

SharePoint opens the Customize Posts page.

12. Click the Versioning Settings link in the General Settings column.

SharePoint opens the List Versioning Settings page, similar to the one shown in Figure 8-3.

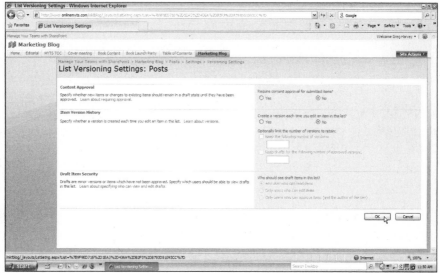

Figure 8-3:
You can modify the Content Approval settings for the new blog.

13. Select the Content Approval's No radio button under the Require Content Approval for Submitted Items heading.

You see an alert dialog box warning you that any pending and rejected items may show up in the blog posts after disabling content approval.

14. Click OK. After the alert dialog box closes and you're brought back to the List Versioning Settings page, click that page's OK button.

SharePoint returns you to the Customize Posts page.

15. Click the name of the blog's button on the Top Link bar.

SharePoint displays the home page of the new blog subsite with its Welcome to Your Blog post. Here, you can customize the blog's categories before making your first post and inviting other team members to start participating in the blog.

Setting up the categories for your blog

Categories in a blog enable you to classify and arrange the posts and comments you and your team members make by the major subject they address.

When you create a new blog in SharePoint, it automatically creates three generic categories called Category 1, Category 2, and Category 3. You can then rename these generic categories to something descriptive of the intended content and audience of the blog as well as add more categories of your own.

To customize and add to the blog's categories, follow these steps:

1. **Click the Categories link in the blog's Quick Launch.**

   SharePoint opens the Categories page for your blog site, similar to the one shown in Figure 8-4 (except that your Categories page still contains the generic categories that I've already replaced with real category names in this figure).

2. **To rename the generic categories, click each category name and then choose Edit Item from its drop-down menu or simply click its Edit button in the column on the far right.**

   SharePoint opens the Categories page for the particular item.

Figure 8-4:
You can modify and add to a new blog's categories.

Edit buttons

3. **Edit or replace the category name displayed in the Title text box and then click OK.**

4. **To add a new category for your blog posts, choose New Item from the New drop-down menu.**

   SharePoint opens a Categories: New Item page.

5. **Type the name of the new category in the blank Title text box and then click OK.**

   SharePoint returns you to the Categories page, and your new category appears at the bottom of the list.

6. **When you finish editing the three generic categories and adding any of your own, click the blog's tab on the Top Link bar.**

   SharePoint returns you to the home page of your blog, where your changes to the generic categories and any additions are displayed.

Posting to your new blog

After you've set up the categories for your new blog, you're ready to start posting items to it. To make your first post from your SharePoint blog, follow these steps:

1. **Click the Create a Post link in the Admin Links column.**

   SharePoint displays a Posts: New Item page, similar to the one shown in Figure 8-5.

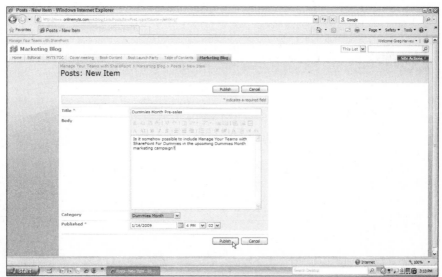

Figure 8-5: Add a new post to the blog and assign its category.

2. Type a brief title for the new post that quickly identifies its subject in the Title text box and then press Tab.

SharePoint advances the cursor to the Body text box.

3. Type the contents of the post in the Body text box.

The only thing left to do before publishing the post to the blog is to select the blog category.

4. Choose the category to which you want to associate the new post from the Category drop-down list and then click the Publish button.

SharePoint returns you to the home page of the blog, where the new post appears at the top of its list (which always shows the most recent post at the top). In addition to the title and body of the post, this list displays the date and time along with links to the author of the post as well as links for viewing only posts in the same category, for commenting on the post (called *permalink*), for sending a link to the post to a team member in an e-mail message, and for listing all the comments made to the post.

After making a new post to your blog, other team members can respond to it by posting their own comments. Here's how posting comments works:

1. Click the link attached to the title of the post or click the Permalink hyperlink that appears under its body.

SharePoint opens a new page that displays the post to be commented on at the top of the page with an area for recording comments below, similar to the page shown in Figure 8-6.

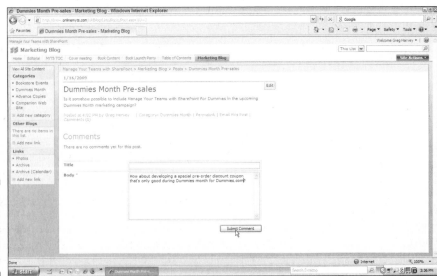

Figure 8-6:
You can add comments to a blog post.

2. **(Optional) If you want to add a title for your comments that is different from the one used to identify the post, click in the Title text box and then enter a title for your comments.**

   Note that you usually don't need to give a title to your comments unless they introduce a new subject related to the post. When your comments simply address the subject matter of the original post, a new title is not needed.

3. **Click the Body text box and then type your comments to the original post there. Then finish up by clicking the Submit Comment button.**

   SharePoint returns you to the Post page, where a Comments section with the comment you just published appears immediately beneath the original post. In addition, this page contains an Add Comment section with its own optional Title text box and Body text box where others (especially the team member who made the original post) can respond to your comments.

Posting to your SharePoint blog via an Outlook e-mail message

If you're using Outlook 2003 or 2007 and your SharePoint IT team allows your site to receive e-mail, you and your team members can e-mail posts to the blog from Outlook. Before you can do this, however, you must give the blog an e-mail address using the blog site's Incoming E-mail Settings. (See Chapter 11 for details.)

After you create an e-mail address for the blog site, you and your team members can post to the blog simply by opening a new e-mail message in Outlook and following these simple steps:

1. **Enter the blog site e-mail address in the To field.**

2. **Enter the title of the blog post in the Subject field.**

3. **Enter the body or contents of the post in the body of the new e-mail message.**

4. **Click the Send button.**

That's all there is to it. When you switch back to SharePoint and open the blog's home page or Posts page (by clicking the Manage Posts link on the home page), the new post you sent in an Outlook e-mail message will eventually appear at the top of the list. (You may have to give it some time and click the browser's refresh button — e-mail's not instantaneous after all.)

At the time you create and publish a post via e-mail, you can't assign the post to a particular blog category. You must do this from the SharePoint blog site: Open the blog and then click the link to the post to which a category needs to be assigned. Then, click the Edit button on the post page and select the desired post category on its Edit Item page from the Category drop-down menu before you click the Publish button.

Posting to your SharePoint blog via Word 2007

If your office uses Word 2007, you can create posts in a Word document and then publish them on the SharePoint blog from within the Word application. The easiest way to do this is from the SharePoint blog site, as follows:

1. **Open the home page of the blog site and then click the Launch Blog Program to Post link at the bottom of the Admin Links.**

   SharePoint launches Word 2007 and then displays a New SharePoint Blog Account dialog box that contains the Blog site's URL.

2. **Click OK in the New SharePoint Blog Account dialog box and then click Yes.**

3. **If an alert dialog box appears, warning you about sending your user-name and password to your blog service provider, click Yes. Also, if you're prompted for it in another Connect To dialog box, provide your password.**

   Word displays an alert dialog box telling you that your account registration is successful and indicating that you can change settings for this account by clicking Manage Accounts on the Blog Post tab on the Ribbon.

4. **Click OK in the Word alert dialog box indicating that you have successfully set up an account to your blog site.**

   Word selects the Blog Post tab on the Ribbon and opens a new document with a field at the top of a horizontal rule that says [Enter Post Title Here].

5. **Click the [Enter Post Title Here] field's text to select it and then replace it by typing the actual title of the new post.**

   The title you type appears in bold letters above the horizontal rule that divides the blog post's title from its body.

6. **Position the cursor at the beginning of the first blank line beneath the horizontal rule and then type the body text of the blog post.**

   Word 2007 fortunately enables you to assign a blog category to the post from within Word.

7. **Click the Insert Category button on the Blog Post tab of the Ribbon and then click Yes if an alert dialog box warning you about sending your username and password to your blog service provider appears.**

   Word adds a Category drop-down list box to the blog document, as shown in Figure 8-7.

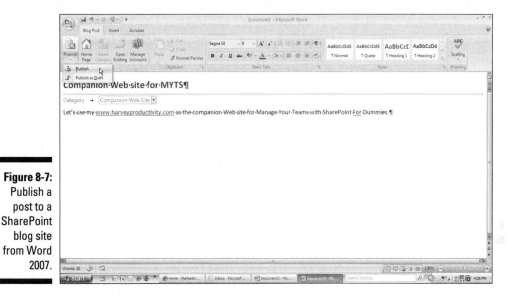

Figure 8-7:
Publish a
post to a
SharePoint
blog site
from Word
2007.

8. **Choose the category of the blog post from the Category drop-down menu.**

9. **Choose Publish from the Publish drop-down menu and then click Yes if an alert dialog box appears, warning you about sending your user-name and password to your blog service provider.**

   Note that Windows doesn't close Word after publishing the post to your SharePoint blog site. If you want, you can check that the post is pub-lished before you close Word without saving the new post as a Word document.

10. **Click the blog site's Home button on the Windows taskbar and then click the Refresh button in the Web browser.**

    The new post that you just created in Word 2007 appears at the top of the blog posts.

11. **Click the Document button on the Windows taskbar that contains the new blog post you just published.**

12. **Click the window's Close button and click No in the Word dialog box asking you to save the post as a Word document.**

    SharePoint closes Word without saving the document, returning you to the home page of the SharePoint site with your new blog post.

Involving Your Teams in the Care and Feeding of Wiki Page Libraries

Wikis in SharePoint are actually a special type of library called, appropriately enough, a Wiki page library. A Wiki page library comes equipped with controls that enable you (and the team members to whom you give access) to edit its layout and content as well as link it to other Wiki pages.

An important feature of a Wiki page is that you and your users can easily create links to other Wiki pages on the SharePoint site. And unlike links to other Web pages on the site that require you to know and enter the page's URL address, links to other Wiki pages merely require you to enter the name of the page enclosed in two pairs of square brackets. For example, to create a link from the home page to a new Wiki page that takes your team members to an existing Wiki page named How To Use This Wiki Library, you simply enter the name of the page enclosed in double square brackets as follows:

```
[[How To Use This Wiki Library]]
```

SharePoint then converts all this text into a live hyperlink that you and your wiki users can click to visit this very informative page on how to edit Wiki pages as well as how to create new Wiki pages and links to them.

Creating a new SharePoint Wiki page library

The steps for adding a new Wiki page library to your SharePoint site couldn't be simpler:

1. **Open the subsite where you want the wiki to appear.**

   If you want the wiki added to the top-level site, open the SharePoint home page.

2. **Choose Create from the Site Actions drop-down menu.**

   SharePoint opens the Create page.

3. **Click the Wiki Page Library link in the Libraries column.**

   SharePoint opens the New page, similar to the one shown in Figure 8-8. Here's where you assign a name and description, and indicate whether or not the new Wiki page library should appear on the site's Quick Launch.

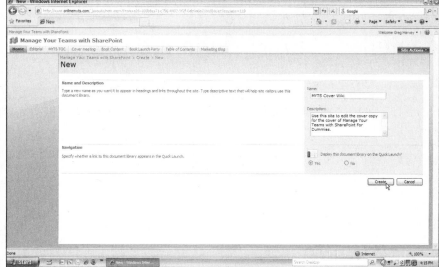

Figure 8-8:
Creating a
new Wiki
page library
for my
SharePoint
blog site
from Word
2007.

4. Type a name for the new wiki site in the Name text box and then press Tab.

SharePoint advances the cursor to the Description text box.

5. Type a description for the new wiki site that tells your team members what kind of information to expect there.

6. (Optional) Select the No radio button if you don't want a link to the new Wiki page library to appear in the Documents section of the site's Quick Launch.

If you click No, you and your team members can still access the Wiki page library by clicking the View All Site Content link on its parent site's page and then clicking the link to its name that appears in the Document Libraries section of the All Site Content page.

7. Click the Create button.

SharePoint creates the new Wiki page library and displays its home page, similar to the one shown in Figure 8-9. The home page gives your users basic information about Wiki pages and contains a How To Use This Wiki Library link that they can click to get more information about actively editing the library.

When you create a new Wiki page library, the library automatically contains two Wiki pages: Home and How To Use This Wiki Library. You can then add as many other Wiki pages to these original two as your library requires. (See the "Adding new pages to a Wiki library" section that immediately follows.)

Figure 8-9:
The home
page of my
brand-new
Wiki page
library.

Adding new pages to a Wiki library

After you've created the basic Wiki page library, it's easy to add Wiki pages to them:

1. **Click the site's View All Site Content link and then click the link to the Wiki page library in the All Site Content's page Document Libraries section.**

   SharePoint opens a Wiki library content page that contains a list showing all the Wiki pages currently added to the library.

2. **Choose New Wiki Page from the New drop-down menu.**

   SharePoint opens a page called New Wiki Page, similar to the one shown in Figure 8-10.

3. **Type a name for the new Wiki page in the Name text box and then press Tab.**

   SharePoint advances the cursor to the Wiki Content list box, where you type and format the text for the new Wiki page, as well as insert any other content such as tables, links, and graphic images.

   Note that as soon as you press the Tab key (or click the cursor in the Wiki Content list box), the various editing buttons at the top of the list box become active. You can then use these buttons to format the text you enter as well as to create tables, insert links and graphic images, and even edit the HTML source code of the page (if you're already familiar with the Hypertext Markup Language).

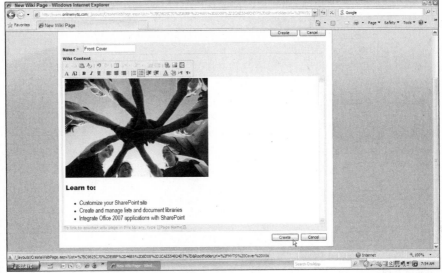

Figure 8-10:
I need to
add a new
page to my
Wiki page
library.

4. **Enter the text for the new Wiki page in the Wiki Content list box and insert and format any other elements you want to add using the command buttons at the top of the list box.**

5. **Click the Create button.**

   SharePoint creates the new Wiki page and then displays the contents of that page in your browser.

Editing Wiki pages and reviewing changes and earlier versions

After you add the pages that your new Wiki page library needs, you and any team member to whom you give library access can edit the contents of the pages at will. To edit a Wiki page, display the page in your SharePoint site and then click the Edit button that appears in the cluster of three (Edit, History, and Incoming Links) in the upper-right corner of its page.

SharePoint then opens an Edit Item page containing the page's original contents. At that point, you can change the page using the Wiki Content editing buttons to delete, replace, or add to its text and other non-textual elements.

After you finish making your editing changes, click OK to return to the updated Wiki page in your browser. Then, if you later want to review the additions and deletions made to the page, you can click its History button to view them.

When you click History, SharePoint displays the current version of the page, with all of the text deletions and insertions that have been highlighted in blue and tan, respectively, as shown in Figure 8-11 (in shades of gray). Note, however, that changes made to the page's Web Parts, images, or HTML code aren't displayed in the current version of the page.

Figure 8-11:
Reviewing
the editing
history of a
Wiki page.

To then display the way the Wiki page appeared in an earlier version, you need to click the link attached to its version number — complete with the date and time of the revision — that appears in a chronological list in the panel on the left side of the page.

To view a chronological listing of the various versions of the Wiki page together, one version above the other from the most recent version to the least recent version, click the Version History button that appears in the row of buttons at the top of the page's Page History. You can then compare differences to the page's Web Parts and graphic images that appear in each of the different versions.

Creating forward links to other Wiki pages

One of the great features of Wiki pages is how easy it is to add links to other pages in the Wiki library. All you have to do is type the name of the Wiki page enclosed in a double pair of square brackets.

For example, for my MYTS (Manage Your Teams with SharePoint) Cover Wiki, I created both Front Cover and Back Cover Wiki pages to enable the book's editorial and marketing teams to mark up and change the book's front cover image and front and back cover copy. I then created a link at the bottom of the Front Cover Wiki page — a link that, when clicked, takes you to the Back Cover Wiki page — by typing the text:

```
[[Back Cover]]
```

Then, on the Back Cover Wiki page, I created a link to the Front Cover Wiki page simply by typing the text:

```
[[Front Cover]]
```

If you make a typo when entering the name of the page to which you're meaning to link, SharePoint indicates this by displaying a series of dots underneath the text of the link in the Wiki page instead of the solid underline when you position the mouse over the text (indicating a live link).

Syndicating Blogs with RSS Feeds

RSS (Real Simple Syndication) feeds in SharePoint 2007 enable you and your team members to stay informed of when changes occur on your SharePoint site. Although RSS feeds aren't limited to SharePoint blogs, this is the one component where this particular kind of subscription makes perfect sense. By subscribing to RSS feeds for your team's blog, you can automatically stay informed of when additions actually take place.

Using RSS feeds versus SharePoint Alert Me e-mail notification

You might be wondering when to use an RSS feed to keep informed of changes to a SharePoint subsite, list, or library as opposed to using its Alert Me e-mail notification feature. The solution is simple, really: Use Alert Me e-mail notification when your team needs to know about any changes to the site's, list's, or library's contents (including deletions). Use RSS feeds when your team needs to stay informed only of additions to the site, list, or library. This is why subscribing to an RSS feed for a SharePoint blog is so right: Your teams are informed as soon as the new additions happen.

The key to using RSS feeds with the various elements of SharePoint (anything from a list or document library all the way to your favorite blog site) is to use an RSS reader that can deal with password-protected sites. Not all RSS readers are able to do this, sometimes including Microsoft's own Internet Explorer 7. Because your SharePoint site is password-protected and open only to authenticated users, you must use an RSS reader — such as Outlook 2007 or Mozilla's Firefox Web browser — that can deal with feeds to this type of restricted site.

Adding an RSS feed to a blog in Outlook 2007

If you regularly use Outlook 2007, you can use its RSS feed capabilities to make it act as your RSS reader when subscribing to a SharePoint blog. To add an RSS feed for a SharePoint blog in Outlook 2007, follow these steps:

1. **In SharePoint, open the blog to which you want to subscribe.**

   You can usually do this by clicking its button on the Top Link bar or clicking its link in the Sites section of the Quick Launch.

2. **Click the RSS Feed button below the Links section of the blog's Quick Launch.**

   SharePoint opens a Posts page containing a banner with RSS feed information, similar to the one shown in Figure 8-12.

3. **Right-click your Web browser's address bar and then choose Copy from the shortcut menu.**

   SharePoint copies the URL of the blog's RSS feed into the Windows Clipboard.

4. **Switch to Outlook 2007 or, if it's not running, launch the program. Then right-click the RSS Feeds folder in the Mail Folders section of the Outlook Navigation pane and choose Add a New RSS Feed from its pop-up menu.**

   Outlook opens the New RSS Feed dialog box.

5. **Press Ctrl+V and then click the Add button in the New RSS Feed dialog box.**

   Outlook pastes the URL of the SharePoint blog's RSS feed into the Enter the Location of the RSS Feed You Want to Add to Outlook dialog box and then displays the Add This RSS Feed to Outlook alert dialog box.

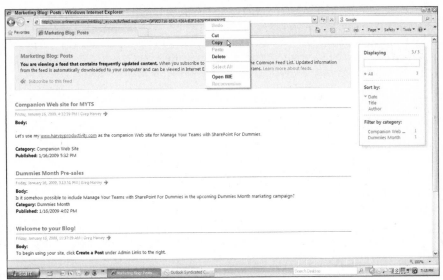

Figure 8-12:
Copy the
URL of a
blog's RSS
feed.

6. **Click the Yes button in the Add This RSS Feed to Outlook dialog box (and then enter your SharePoint password if the Connect To dialog box appears and click OK).**

   SharePoint then adds a subfolder for the particular blog to the RSS Feeds section of the Mail Folders in the Outlook Navigation pane, while at the same time displaying a list of all the posts the blog currently contains in the new folder in the center pane.

After subscribing to a SharePoint blog in Outlook, Outlook automatically adds all new posts that are made in that blog to the blog subfolder you just added to the RSS Feeds section of the Mail Folders.

Adding an RSS feed to a blog in Firefox

Firefox is a good example of a Web browser that does support RSS feeds to password-protected sites (unlike Microsoft's very own Internet Explorer). You can therefore use it to subscribe to various SharePoint lists and libraries.

The great thing about RSS feeds in Web browsers such as Firefox is that new items in the list or library show up immediately in the browser (assuming that it's open in Windows). This isn't the case with RSS feeds in Outlook 2007, where you may have to wait some time before new items appear in the appropriate mail folder.

To add an RSS feed for a SharePoint blog in the Mozilla Firefox Web browser, follow these steps:

1. **Open your SharePoint site in the Firefox browser and display the blog to which you want to subscribe in SharePoint.**

   You can normally do this by clicking the blog's button on the Top Link bar or by clicking its link in the Sites section of the Quick Launch.

2. **Click the RSS Feed button below the Links section of the blog's Quick Launch.**

   SharePoint opens a blog page with an RSS feed banner for Firefox that suggests subscribing to the feed using its Live Bookmarks.

3. **Click the Subscribe Now button in the banner on the blog page in Firefox.**

   Firefox opens an Add Live Bookmark dialog box that suggests a name and location for the new RSS feed bookmark.

4. **If you want to change the name or location of the new RSS feed bookmark, do so before you click the Add button.**

   Firefox adds an option to its Bookmarks menu with the name of the RSS feed bookmark you just assigned. When you position the mouse pointer over this option, Firefox displays a submenu with individual options for all the posts currently in the blog. You also see options to open the blog pages on your SharePoint site or to open each of the individual posts on the blog in separate Web pages with their own tabs.

After subscribing to a blog in Firefox, you can have the browser add all new posts made to the blog to the submenu attached to the blog's bookmark option. To activate this feature, right-click the blog's option on the Bookmarks menu and then choose Reload Live Bookmark from the shortcut menu that appears.

Chapter 9

Editing Collaboratively with Document Workspaces

....

....

A document workspace is a subsite of your SharePoint site that uses the special Document Workspace site template. This site template provides Web Part elements that make it easy to edit a particular document collaboratively or to work together on a project that involves a series of related documents (such as preparing an annual report or a special budget proposal).

As with other subsites that you create for your SharePoint site (see Chapter 2), when you set up a new document workspace, SharePoint imbues it with the typical Announcements, Links, and Calendar lists you'd expect as well as a Team Discussion board. In addition, the Document Workspace template also adds a distinctive Shared Documents and Tasks list.

You can then use all these standard document workspace elements to outline the document-related project to your team members, provide them with the documents they need, assign particular project tasks to them, and provide them with the deadlines and milestones they need to reach in accomplishing these tasks.

Creating a New Document Workspace

SharePoint provides three main methods for adding a new document workspace to your SharePoint site:

- ✔ **From scratch** following the same general steps you would take if you were adding a new standard subsite to SharePoint

- ✔ **From a document in a SharePoint document library** that your teams need to edit in the course of the collaborative project

- ✔ **From an Office 2003 or 2007 document** (created with an application such as Microsoft Word or Excel) that your teams need to edit in the course of the collaborative project

Creating a document workspace from scratch

To create a document workspace from scratch, follow the same basic steps you use when creating a new subsite:

1. **Open the home page of the parent site to which you want to add your document workspace.**

   If you want to add the document workspace as a subsite to the top-level site, open the home page of the entire SharePoint site.

2. **Choose Create from the Site Actions drop-down menu.**

   SharePoint opens the site's Create page.

3. **Click the Sites and Workspaces link in the Web Pages column.**

   SharePoint opens a New SharePoint Site page similar to the one shown in Figure 9-1.

4. **Type the name of the new document workspace in the Title text box and then press Tab.**

   SharePoint advances the cursor to the Description text box.

5. **Type a description of the purpose of the new document workspace in the Description text box and then press Tab.**

   SharePoint advances the cursor to the URL Name text box.

Figure 9-1:
You can
create
a new
document
workspace
from scratch
with the
Document
Work-
space site
template.

6. Type the name you want to use as the last part of the URL address of the new document workspace in the URL Name text box.

Now, you need to select the Document Workspace template for the new subsite.

7. Click the Document Workspace option on the Collaboration tab in the Select a Template list box.

8. (Optional) Make any changes necessary to the Permissions, Navigation, and Navigation Inheritance options of the new document workspace.

If you don't modify any of these default settings, your team members have the same permissions in the new document workspace as they do in its parent site, and a tab for the new document workspace appears in the Top Link bar as well as under the Sites heading in the parent site's Quick Launch.

9. Click the Create button.

SharePoint creates the new document workspace and then displays its Web page in your browser. This new document workspace page contains all the lists shown in Figure 9-2, which you can then customize (see Chapter 2). You can also add your own content to it (see Chapter 4 for details).

Figure 9-2:
Your finished new document workspace is up and running.

Creating a document workspace from a file in an existing document library

If you have a document already uploaded to an existing document library and you determine that your teams need to edit that document collaboratively, you can create the document workspace and copy the document to that workspace as part of a single procedure:

1. **Open the document library containing the document you want to copy to the new document workspace and then click the document's name and highlight the Send To option on the drop-down menu that appears.**

   SharePoint displays the Send To option's submenu, as shown in Figure 9-3.

2. **Choose Create Document Workspace from the Send To submenu.**

   SharePoint opens a Create Document Workspace page that tells you that a new document workspace is going to be created and a copy of the selected document is going to be stored there. This page also informs you that you can publish the (edited) document from the new workspace back to its original location in the document library if desired.

3. **Click the OK button on the Create Document Workspace page.**

SharePoint creates the new document workspace and displays its page, similar to the one shown in Figure 9-4. This new document workspace page carries the name of the selected document as its page name, already contains a welcome message in its Announcements list, and shows that a copy of the document has been put into its Shared Documents list.

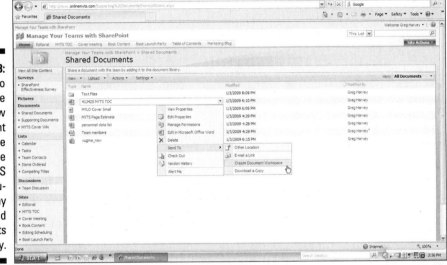

Figure 9-3:
I need to create a new document workspace with the 413425MYTS TOC document in my Shared Documents library.

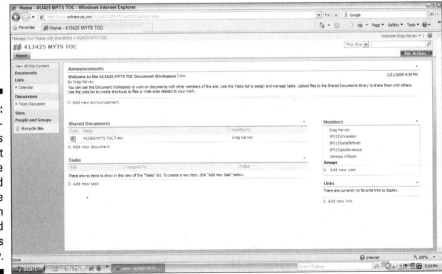

Figure 9-4:
I created this document workspace created from the document in my Shared Documents library.

The Members and Groups list that appears in a Web Part on the right side of this new document workspace may list your name as the sole member of the document workspace. When this is the case, you need to add the other team members who need access to this document workspace (or their user groups) as members, as spelled out in the next step.

4. **Click the Add a New User link under the Members and Groups list.**

   SharePoint displays the Add Users page for the document workspace.

5. **Use the Add Users, Give Permission, and Send E-Mail options on the Add Users page to add individual team members or their groups to the document workspace and then click OK.**

   Use the options on the Add Users page (see Chapter 3 for details) to add individual users or their groups to the workspace.

   After you click OK, SharePoint adds the users and groups you selected and displays the Permissions page for the document with a list showing the level of permissions you assigned.

6. **In the Content Navigation Breadcrumb at the top of the Permissions page, click the link to the document workspace (which is identical to the name of the document used to create the workspace).**

   SharePoint once again displays the document workspace page, which now displays the names of the individual team members or their groups that you just added to the site.

When you create a document workspace from a document in an existing document library, SharePoint doesn't automatically add a link to the new document workspace to the parent site's Quick Launch. This means that either you must manually add a Quick Launch link or your team members need to access the document workspace from the Sites and Workspaces section of the site's All Site Content page. See the following section for details on creating this link.

Adding a document workspace to the parent site's Quick Launch

To add a link for a document workspace to the parent site's Quick Launch when you create the workspace from an existing document, follow these steps:

1. **Click the Sites link in the parent site's Quick Launch in SharePoint.**

   SharePoint opens the All Site Content page for that site, using the Sites and Workspaces filter.

2. **Click the link to the document workspace you want to add to the Quick Launch.**

   SharePoint opens the document workspace.

3. **Right-click the document workspace's URL address in your Web browser's address bar and then choose the Copy option from the shortcut menu.**

   SharePoint copies the workspace's URL to the Windows Clipboard.

4. **Click the link to the parent site in the Content Navigation Breadcrumb at the top of the document workspace page.**

   SharePoint opens the parent site's home page.

5. **Choose Site Settings from the Site Actions drop-down menu to open the Site Settings page, and once you're there, click the Quick Launch link in the Look and Feel column.**

   SharePoint opens the Quick Launch page for the site.

6. **Click the New Link button at the top of the Quick Launch page.**

   SharePoint opens the New Link page.

7. **Select http:// in the Type the Web Address text box, press Ctrl+V, and then press Tab.**

   Windows pastes the document workspace's URL into the Type the Web Address text box and then advances the cursor to the Type the Description text box.

8. **Type a brief description of the document workspace's Quick Launch link into this text box.**

9. **Select Sites from the Heading drop-down list and then click OK.**

   SharePoint returns you to the Quick Launch page, where the link to the document workspace appears in the Sites section.

10. **Click the parent site's link in the Content Navigation Breadcrumb at the top of the Quick Launch page.**

    SharePoint displays the parent site's home page, where the new link to your document workspace appears at the bottom of the Sites section of its Quick Launch.

Creating a document workspace from an Office document

The last method for creating a document workspace on your SharePoint site is to create it *locally* (that is, on your computer rather than on the SharePoint server) using the very Office application (such as Word 2007 or Excel 2007) used to create the document you want your teams to edit collaboratively in that new workspace.

To create a document workspace from an Office document, follow these steps:

1. **Open the document you want uploaded to a new document workspace in its native Office 2007 application.**

   Note that you do *not* have to open the SharePoint site where you want to create the new document workspace at the time you take this step. You can create a new document workspace from an Office 2007 application even when you're not currently logged in to your SharePoint site.

2. **Click the Office button in the upper-left corner of the Office program and then highlight the Publish option.**

   The Office program opens a Distribute the Document to Other People submenu similar to the one shown in Figure 9-5.

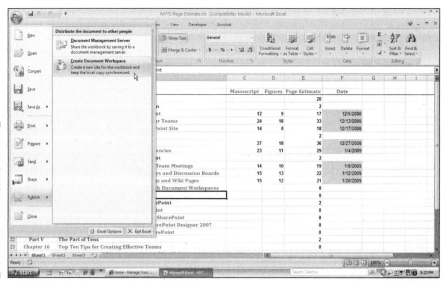

Figure 9-5: Creating a new document workspace for a worksheet open in Excel 2007.

3. **Choose Create Document Workspace from the bottom of the Distribute the Document to Other People submenu.**

   The Document Workspace pane opens in the Office application on the right side of the window. This pane displays general information about document workspaces and contains two boxes: Document Workspace Name text box (with the name of the document opened in your Office application) and a Location for New Workspace combo box.

4. **(Optional) Edit or replace the current document name automatically entered in the Document Workspace Name text box if you want the workspace to have another name.**

   Next, you need to specify the URL address of your SharePoint site.

5. **Enter the URL address of your SharePoint site in the Location for New Workspace combo box (or select this URL if you've previously connected a document to this site in this Office application) and then click the Create button.**

   Your Office application may display an alert dialog box warning you that your SharePoint site is not among its trusted sites, if it's not already listed as one. If you receive this alert, click OK and then open your Web browser and use its Internet Options to add your SharePoint site to its trusted sites list. (In some corporate environments, you will choose your local intranet instead.) If you're using Internet Explorer 7 or 8, you do this by pressing the Alt key to display the pull-down menus. Then, choose Tools➪Internet Options. In the Internet Options dialog box that appears, click the Security tab and then click the Trusted Sites button. Next, click the Sites button, type the URL of your SharePoint site into the Add This Website to the Zone, and click Add — if your site is not secure and therefore doesn't use the `https://` prefix, be sure to deselect the check box labeled Require Server Verification (`https:`) for All Sites in This Zone.

   If your SharePoint site is hosted by a third-party vendor, you'll probably receive a Connect To dialog box asking for your user ID and password. Provide this information and then click OK.

   After you get through all this necessary but unpleasant security stuff, Office then goes ahead and creates the document workspace on your SharePoint site, while at the same time saving the current Office document to it.

When you create a document workspace from a document open in an Office application, SharePoint does *not* automatically add a link to the new document workspace to the parent site's Quick Launch. This means that either you must manually add a Quick Launch link or your team members need to access the document workspace from the Sites and Workspaces section of the site's All Site Content page. See the section "Adding a document workspace to the parent site's Quick Launch," earlier in this chapter, for details on adding this link.

Using the command buttons in the Document Management pane

After your Office application finishes creating the new document workspace on your SharePoint site, the Document Workspace pane in its program window is replaced by a Document Management pane, similar to the one shown in Figure 9-6.

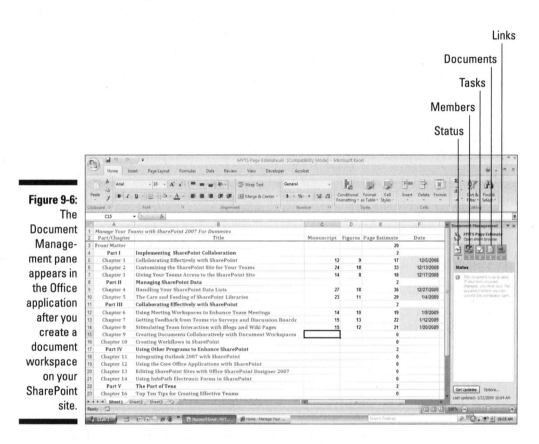

Figure 9-6: The Document Management pane appears in the Office application after you create a document workspace on your SharePoint site.

As you see in this figure, the Document Management pane indicates the current status of the document on the workspace (which is up-to-date when you first create the workspace). This pane also contains a series of very useful buttons for managing your new workspace from the document in your Office application:

✔ **Status:** This button is selected by default and shows you whether or not the document saved on the SharePoint site is currently up-to-date (which it is when you first create the document workspace).

✔ **Members:** Click this button to display the names of the members who currently have access to the document workspace. When you first create a document workspace, you are the only member. You can, however, use the Add New Members link and the Send E-mail to All Members link that appear when the Members button is selected to add members and then invite them to visit the workspace, respectively.

✔ **Tasks:** Click this button to display all the tasks assigned to team members and to use its Add New Task, Alert Me About Tasks, and View Workflow Tasks links to assign new tasks, send out alerts, and display any workflow settings you've set up for the document (see Chapter 10 for details), respectively.

✔ **Documents:** Click this button to display all the documents added to your new workspace. (Only the document currently open in the Office application is listed in the pane when you first create the workspace.) You can use the Add New Document, Add New Folder, and Alert Me About Documents links that appear when the Documents button is selected to add other documents to the workspace, create new sub-folders, and send out alerts about changes to the documents in the workspace, respectively.

✔ **Links:** Click this button to display the links that are added to the work-space. You can use the Add New Link and Alert Me About Links hyper-links that appear when the Links button is selected to add new links and send out alerts about changes to the links list in the workspace, respectively.

Synchronizing changes saved locally with the workspace copy of a document

When you or other team members save editing changes locally to a copy of the workspace document on your computer, you still have to synchronize those changes with the copy of the document saved on the SharePoint work-space. The Document Management pane in the your Office program tells you when the copies need to be synchronized by displaying an alert in the Status area telling you that your local changes have *not* been updated in the copy of the document stored on your SharePoint document workspace.

To synchronize your changes by updating this copy on the SharePoint site, you need to click the Update Workspace Copy link that appears beneath this message in the Manage Document pane. Office then updates the copy on your SharePoint site, and the status of the document reported in the Document Management pane becomes up-to-date once again.

Getting updates on the current status of the document workspace

To check for and get updates on the latest changes made to the Members, Tasks, Documents, and Links lists on the workspace, click the Get Updates button that appears at the bottom of the Document Management pane.

You can use the Options link to the immediate right of the Get Updates button to open the Service Options dialog box (shown in Figure 9-7), where you modify the settings that control when the Document Management pane appears in the document saved on the workspace and how and when workspace updates are made.

Figure 9-7: You can modify the update settings for the document used to create a document workspace in the Service Options dialog box.

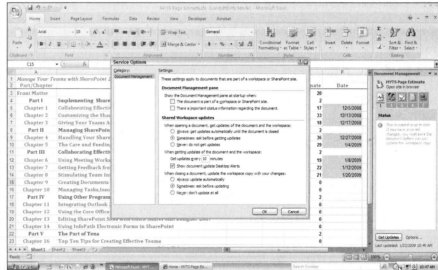

For the Document Management Pane settings, it's generally a good idea to select the There Is Important Status Information Regarding the Document check box under the Show the Document Management Pane at Startup heading so that your Office application automatically opens this pane whenever the program detects new updates to the workspace's Members, Tasks, Documents, or Links lists.

Setting Versioning Settings for the Document Workspace

Before you and your team begin collaboratively editing a document that you've placed in the default Shared Documents library on a new document workspace, you may want to modify its versioning settings. Versioning is an umbrella term that covers three distinct areas of document security: Document Version History, Content Approval, and Require Check Out.

When you activate the Document Version History settings, SharePoint creates a version of the document each time it is edited by someone on the team. To turn on these settings, you choose between having SharePoint save major and minor versions of the document. When you select major versions, SharePoint creates a version only when you or a team member saves and closes the document. When you select minor versions, SharePoint creates a minor version each time you or a team member saves editing changes (without closing the document).

Keep in mind when selecting minor versions of the document that this results in many more versions of the document. This can be a great thing when you have lots of team members editing collaboratively and want to track document changes closely. However, it also can result in lots of copies of the same document to keep track of — copies which, when added together, can start to take up quite a bit of valuable storage space on the server.

At the time you activate the Document Version History settings for a workspace, you may also activate Content Approval. When you do this, you as the administrator of the document workspace must approve each version of the document. Until you make this approval, the edited document resides in a special draft items section of the workspace that only the team members designated by the Draft Item Security settings can access.

The final version setting is the Require Check Out setting. You activate this setting to prevent multiple team members from being able to edit the same document saved in the workspace at the same time, thus preventing your team members from making conflicting edits to the document.

When Require Check Out is turned on, a document in the workspace is automatically checked out to you when you create a new document in that workspace or save a new document to that workspace. Any team member to whom the document is checked out must check it back in before the other members of your team can see the document when they access the workspace.

When you or a team member opens a document that's saved in the work-space for editing, SharePoint automatically checks the document out to you or to that team member. While the file is checked out, no one else on the team can open it for editing. (SharePoint indicates that the file is checked out with a special icon in the library list; it also indicates the person to whom the document is checked out when you position the mouse pointer over the document name.)

When the person to whom the document is checked out checks it back in, he's prompted to record comments indicating the types of editing changes he may have made. If the Document Version History settings are also acti-vated, his comments are saved as part of the version history. Should a team member ever forget to check a document back into a workspace, you as the workspace administrator can check the document back in and make it avail-able to others on the document workspace.

Keep in mind that you activate these same versioning settings for regular document libraries and not just for the libraries you add to your document workspaces.

To modify the versioning settings for the document(s) you upload to the Shared Documents library in a new document workspace, follow these steps:

1. **Open the document workspace in SharePoint and then click the Shared Documents link for the default document library containing the document(s) whose version settings you want to modify.**

   SharePoint opens the Shared Documents page for that library.

2. **Choose Document Library Settings from the Settings drop-down menu.**

   SharePoint opens the Customized Shared Documents page.

3. **Click the Versioning Settings link in the General Settings column.**

   SharePoint opens the Document Library Versioning Settings page for the Shared Documents library, similar to the one shown in Figure 9-8.

4. **(Optional) If you want to approve a team member's changes before the modified document is available in the document library, select the Yes radio button in the Content Approval section of the page.**

   When you select this option, edited versions of the document remain in the Draft Items area until you approve them.

   Once this Yes radio button is selected, the radio button options in the Draft Items Security section of the Document Library Versioning Settings page become active. You can use these options to determine who gets to see the documents placed in the Draft Items area: Any User Who Can Read Items, Only Users Who Can Edit Items, or Only Users Who Can Approve Items (and the Author of the Item), which is the default Draft Items Security setting.

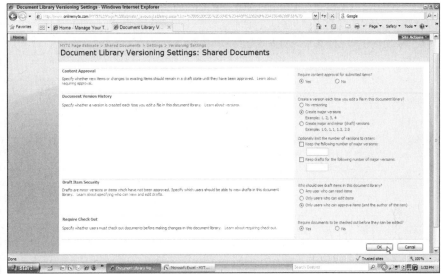

Figure 9-8:
You can
modify the
versioning
settings
for the
documents
added to
the Shared
Documents
library of a
document
workspace.

5. **(Optional) If you want SharePoint to create numbered versions each time the document is edited, select the Create Major Versions or the Create Major and Minor Versions radio button in the Document Version History section of the page.**

   When you select either of these radio buttons, the Optionally Limit the Number of Versions to Retain check box and text box settings in the Document Version History section of the Document Library Versioning Settings page become active. You can then use these options to limit the total number of major versions SharePoint should keep as well as the total number of drafts of the major versions to store.

6. **(Optional) If you want to require your team members to check out the document before they can edit it, select the Yes radio button in the Required Check Out section.**

   When you select the Yes radio button, each team member must formally check the document out before making any edits to it.

7. **After making all the changes you want to the versioning settings, click OK.**

   SharePoint makes the changes to the Shared Documents library versioning settings and then returns you to the Customize Shared Documents page. You can then return to the document workspace page by clicking its link in the Content Navigation Breadcrumb at the top of this page.

Chapter 10

Managing Tasks, Issues, and Workflows in SharePoint

In This Chapter

▶ Understanding Tasks, Project Tasks, and Issue Tracking lists

▶ Using the Tasks list that comes with SharePoint and switching its views

▶ Adding the Gantt view to the default Tasks list

▶ Creating and maintaining an Issue Tracking list

▶ Automating the business process in an Issue Tracking list

*D*ividing your collaborative projects into discrete tasks and then assigning them to teams or particular team members and tracking their progress are frequently important functions of a SharePoint site. To that end, SharePoint supports three types of task-oriented lists:

✔ **Tasks:** Provides a simple Tasks list with Title, Assigned To, Status, Priority, Due Date, and % Complete fields as its columns. Typically, when you start a new SharePoint site, the site contains a Tasks list (simply called Tasks) that you can start using to assign tasks to your team members and keep track of their progress.

✔ **Project Tasks:** Tracks the exact same information as a Tasks list except that a Project Tasks list comes with a special, graphical Gantt chart display (simply called Project Tasks) as its default view. The Gantt chart uses bar graphs to give you a visual sense of where project tasks overlap in time and when their due dates are coming up. Note that you can create a custom view for the default that gives you this Gantt chart display of the tasks you track in a regular Tasks list. (See "Creating a custom Gantt view for your site's Tasks list," later in this chapter, for details on how to create this Gantt chart custom view for your site's default Tasks list.)

✔ **Issue Tracking:** Designed to enable you to track particular issues that your teams need to deal with and resolve, either in the course of their SharePoint collaboration or in the course of their regular job duties. The fields tracked by an Issue Tracking list include Title, Assigned To, Issue Status, Priority, Description, Category (which you must customize), Related Issues, Comments, and Due Date.

In this chapter, you find out about how to use the Tasks and Project Tasks lists to track the tasks that you and your team members need to collaborate on and get done. You also find out how to use Issue Tracking lists to track the issues that you need to deal with and bring to some sort of resolution.

As part of learning the ins and outs of using these very useful Tasks and Project Tasks SharePoint lists, you also find out how to integrate them with the task-tracking capabilities of Outlook 2007 so that the tasks assigned specifically to you automatically show up in your Outlook 2007 To-Do Bar!

Finally, you get an introduction to SharePoint workflows. Workflows simplify common business processes by automatically taking certain steps at particular junctions in the process when you and your team members complete certain tasks. In this chapter, you find out how to use the default three-state workflow that comes with SharePoint Services 3.0 to create a workflow that automates the process for resolving issues pertaining to a particular SharePoint Issue Tracking list.

Using the Default Tasks List

When you start a new SharePoint site created with a Team Site (as so many are), you already have a Tasks list (named, appropriately enough, Tasks). This default list has its own Tasks link in the Lists section of the Quick Launch on the SharePoint site's home page. When you click this link, SharePoint opens the empty Tasks list shown in Figure 10-1, where you can start adding the tasks that you and your fellow team members need to begin working on.

The default Tasks list contains a simple list with columns that identify the following information for each of its tasks:

✔ **Title:** This field gives you the name of the task.

✔ **Assigned To:** This field shows you the name of the team member to whom the task is assigned.

✔ **Status:** This field shows you the current condition of the task. The choices include Not Started, In Progress, Completed, Deferred, and Waiting on Someone Else.

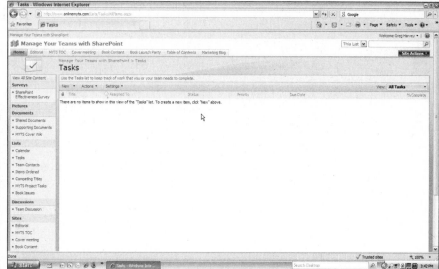

✔ **Priority:** This field shows you the relative importance of the task. The choices for this field include (1) High, (2) Normal, and (3) Low.

✔ **Due Date:** This field shows you the date by which the task needs to be completed.

✔ **% Complete:** This fields shows you the relative percentage of the task that's been completed.

When you add a new task to the Tasks list, the form you fill out contains two extra fields that don't automatically appear in the default All Tasks view: Description (for entering a brief description of the task) and Start Date (for entering the date that you intend work to begin on the task — by default, the current date). You can customize the All Tasks view to include one or both of these fields, or you can simply add them to a new list view that you create. Also note that you can attach files to a task when you add the task to the list. When you do so, a tiny paperclip icon is added to the very first Attach File field, indicating that a file has been attached to the task.

Getting SharePoint to send e-mail when tasks are assigned

Before you start adding tasks for yourself and your fellow team members, you're first going to want to change one of the default list settings for the Tasks list. By default, the E-Mail Notification setting is set to No — you need to change that to Yes. That way, SharePoint automatically sends an e-mail to individual members or to members of a group. (You can assign tasks to entire SharePoint groups as well individual users.)

To make this change for the Tasks list in your SharePoint site, follow these steps:

1. **Log on to your SharePoint site and then click the Tasks link in the Lists section of the Quick Launch on the site's home page.**

   SharePoint opens the Tasks page.

2. **Choose List Settings from the Settings drop-down menu.**

   SharePoint opens the Customize Tasks page.

3. **Click the Advanced Settings link at the bottom of the General Settings column.**

   SharePoint opens the List Advanced Settings page for the Tasks list, similar to the one shown in Figure 10-2.

4. **Click the E-Mail Notification option's Yes radio button under the heading Send E-Mail When Ownership Is Assigned and then click the OK button at the bottom of the page.**

   SharePoint saves the change to the E-Mail Notification option and returns you to the Customize Tasks page.

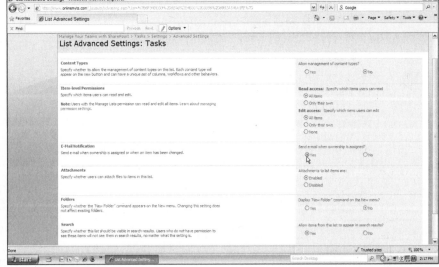

Figure 10-2:
Change the
Send E-mail
Notification
setting for
the Tasks
list from No
to Yes.

5. **Click the Tasks link in the Content Navigation Breadcrumb at the top of the Customize Tasks page.**

   SharePoint displays the Tasks page, where you can start adding your tasks.

You can tell that the E-Mail Notification has been turned on for a SharePoint Tasks list because the program displays an alert at the top of the data form indicating that the content of the task item you just created will be sent to the person or group assigned the task (see Figure 10-3).

Adding new items to the Tasks list

As with the other more generic types of lists you create in SharePoint (see Chapter 4), you can add new items to your Tasks list by one of two methods:

✔ **Data form (opened by choosing New Item from the New drop-down menu):** The data form contains all of the fields used in the All Task view of the list: Attach File, Title, Priority, Status, % Complete, Assigned To, Description, Start Date, Due Date, and Attachments. (See Figure 10-3.)

✔ **Datasheet format (opened by choosing Edit in Datasheet from the Actions drop-down menu):** The datasheet format enables you to enter the information for the Title, Assigned To, Status, Priority, Due Date, and % Complete fields using a spreadsheet-like table right on the Tasks page. (See Figure 10-4.)

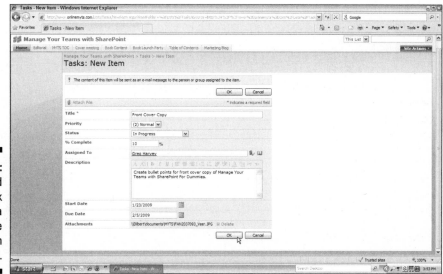

Figure 10-3: You can add a new task in the data form on the New Item page.

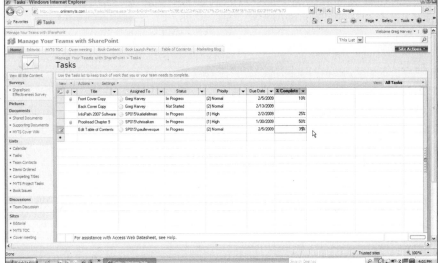

Figure 10-4:
You can add a new task in the datasheet format directly on the Tasks page.

If you enter a new task in the datasheet format, remember that you can still attach files to the task and add a description and modify or remove the start date for it (which is automatically the date you created the task). All you have to do is switch back to the Standard view by choosing Standard View from the Actions drop-down menu and then click the link to the task in the Title column. When the Task page for the item appears, click the Edit Item button. SharePoint opens the data form for the task, where you can attach a file, add a description, change the date in the Start Date field, and modify any other field in the form.

Sorting and filtering the Tasks list in the All Tasks view

After you've added all the tasks to your SharePoint Tasks list, you can use the columns of the list to sort and filter the tasks. By default, SharePoint displays the Tasks list using its All Tasks view.

In All Tasks view, the tasks you add to the list are sorted by the ID field. Unfortunately, the ID field doesn't have a column included in the New Item data form — or in the All Tasks view, for that matter. This leaves the Tasks list unsorted, in essence, so that each task you add to the list automatically appears in the bottom row.

To sort the tasks in the list, position the mouse over the name of the field by which you want to sort the list. Then, when a drop-down button appears to the right of the field's name, click the button and then select one of the two sorting options at the top of the drop-down menu:

✔ **Ascending:** Sorts the tasks in the list in A to Z, smallest to largest, or least recent to most recent order, depending upon whether the field type is text, numeric, or a date, respectively.

✔ **Descending:** Sorts the tasks in the list in Z to A, largest to smallest, or most recent to least recent order, depending upon whether the field type is text, numeric, or a date, respectively.

In addition to rearranging the order of the tasks in this list, you can also filter the list so that only tasks of a particular type appear. For example, you might want to filter the Tasks list so that you see only tasks that aren't yet started or only tasks that have been assigned High priority.

To filter the Tasks list on a particular entry in a field, click that particular entry on the field's drop-down menu. For example, to filter the list so that only tasks that haven't yet been started are displayed, click the Not Started entry on the Status field's drop-down menu. To once again display all the entries in the Tasks list, choose Clear Filter from Status from the Filter field's drop-down menu.

Switching the Tasks list to a new view

Although the All Tasks view is the default view for the SharePoint Tasks list, it is by no means the only view available. SharePoint Tasks lists (and Project Tasks lists, for that matter) come with several very handy built-in list views that you can switch to by choosing their names from the View button's drop-down menu:

✔ **Active Tasks:** SharePoint filters the Tasks list so it displays all tasks except for those whose Status field entries are Completed. Tasks with all other Status field entries (Not Started, In Progress, Deferred, and Waiting on Someone Else) remain displayed.

✔ **By Assigned To:** SharePoint sorts the Tasks list so its tasks are arranged in ascending order by the team members to whom the tasks are assigned.

✔ **By My Groups:** SharePoint sorts the Tasks list so its tasks are arranged in ascending order by the user group member to whom the tasks are assigned.

  ✔ **Due Today:** SharePoint filters the Tasks list so it displays only the tasks with a due date that is the same as the current date.

  ✔ **My Tasks:** SharePoint filters the Tasks list so its displays only the tasks that are assigned to you.

Remember that you can customize any of these built-in list views. Simply switch the Tasks list to that list view and then choose Modify This View from the View drop-down menu. (See Chapter 4 for more on customizing list views.)

Creating a custom Gantt Chart view for your site's Tasks list

One built-in view missing from the Tasks list is the Gantt Chart view. (*Note:* It *is* available in the Project Tasks list.) In a Gantt Chart view, SharePoint displays the tasks using mini bar charts (and some symbols) against a calendar background to graphically depict how the tasks extend in time and overlap one another. Viewing the tasks in this graphically enhanced view often makes it easier to spot potential bottlenecks and problem areas.

To create a custom Gantt Chart view for your SharePoint site's Tasks list, follow these steps:

1. **Open the Tasks list in your SharePoint site and then choose Create View from the View drop-down menu.**

   SharePoint opens the Create View page for the Tasks list where you choose a view format.

2. **Click the Gantt View link in the Choose a View Format section of the page.**

   SharePoint opens another view of the Create View page for the Tasks list, this time where you select the particular options for the Gantt View format you selected.

3. **Type a name in the View Name text box.**

   You can name this view **Gantt Chart** if you'd like. Also, if you want to make this new Gantt Chart view the new default view for your SharePoint Tasks list, be sure to select the Make This the Default View check box.

4. **Scroll down to the Gantt Columns section of the Create View page and then choose Title from the Title drop-down menu, choose Start Date from the Start Date drop-down menu, choose Due Date from the Due Date drop-down menu, and choose % Complete from the Percent Complete drop-down menu.**

5. **Choose ID from the First Sort By the Column drop-down menu in the Sort section and then click the OK button.**

   SharePoint creates the Gantt Chart view and then returns you to the Tasks list, whose tasks are now displayed using the custom Gantt Chart view. (See Figure 10-5 to get an idea of how this view graphically depicts typical tasks.)

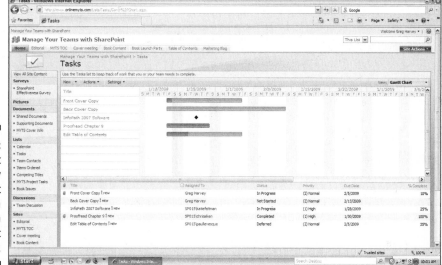

Figure 10-5:
Check out the My Tasks list displayed in the custom Gantt Chart view.

Note that in the Gantt Chart view, the Gantt Chart itself appears in a separate pane above the regular Tasks list display. In the Gantt chart in the upper pane, SharePoint depicts each task to which you assign a start date and due date as a bar on the calendar. Any task that has no due date shows a black diamond symbol. Typically, the uncompleted part of the task appears in light blue in its bar, and the completed part of the task appears in dark blue. (A task whose status is Completed is entirely dark blue.)

Editing items in the Tasks list

You need to know to how to edit the items you place in your SharePoint Tasks list because this is the way that you change and update the status of the tasks you track there.

To edit an item in the Tasks list, click the link attached to its name in the initial Title column in the list. SharePoint duly displays a page with the data form for that task. To then change the entries made in one or more of the fields in this task's data form, you need to click the Edit Item button at the top of the form. Doing this causes SharePoint to display an editable version of the data form where you make your changes before clicking OK.

Don't forget about using the Alert Me feature to help you oversee and manage the tasks added to your Tasks list. You can use this handy feature to have SharePoint send you e-mail updates whenever your team members (specifically those to whom the task is assigned) edit particular tasks. These e-mail alerts can come when any team member changes an item or just when they update the item's status to Completed. To set up e-mail alerts for a particular task, click the Alert Me button that appears at the top of the editable version of its data form. If you want SharePoint to alert you whenever any task in the list changes, choose the Alert Me option from the Actions drop-down menu attached to this button at the top of the list and select the appropriate options on its New Alert page.

Connecting the Tasks list to Outlook 2007

As with other more conventional types of SharePoint lists, you can connect your Tasks list to Outlook 2007. When you do this, SharePoint creates an Outlook folder for the Tasks list that displays all of the tasks. And as an extra special benefit, those tasks in the SharePoint Tasks list that are assigned to you are then automatically added to your Outlook To-Do bar. (Note that some hosted SharePoint service providers don't support this automatic updating in Outlook 2007.)

To connect your Tasks list to Outlook 2007, follow these steps:

1. **Open the Tasks list in your SharePoint site and then choose Connect to Outlook from the Actions drop-down menu.**

   Internet Explorer opens an alert dialog box asking you to confirm that you want to allow SharePoint to open the Outlook program on your computer.

2. **Click the Allow button in the Internet Explorer alert dialog box.**

   SharePoint launches Outlook 2007 (if it's not already open on your computer) and Outlook displays an alert dialog box asking you to confirm your intention to connect the SharePoint Tasks list to Outlook.

3. Click the Yes button in the Outlook alert dialog box.

If your SharePoint site is on a hosted SharePoint server, a Connect To dialog box asking for your username and password may appear. Enter any missing information and click OK.

Outlook then displays the Tasks module, where a new folder bearing the name of your SharePoint site appears in the Other Tasks section of its Navigation pane and those tasks currently in the Tasks list appear in the center pane. (See Figure 10-6.)

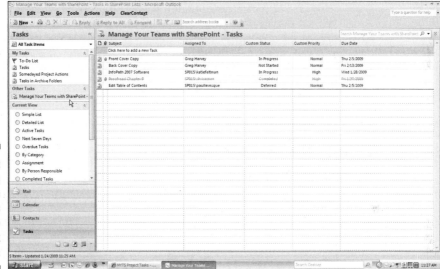

Figure 10-6:
Connecting my Share Point Tasks list to Outlook 2007.

Adding a Project Tasks List

As I mention earlier in this chapter, a Project Tasks list is nothing more than a Tasks list whose default view is a Gantt Chart view (simply called the Project Tasks view). Otherwise, the Project Tasks list is almost identical to a Tasks list, containing all the same fields in its data form and offering most of the other built-in list views. This is the reason that many SharePoint 2007 users simply add the Gantt Chart as a custom view to the default Tasks list (as outlined in the section "Creating a custom Gantt Chart view for your site's Tasks list," earlier in this chapter) and forget all about the Project Tasks list.

However, if you don't want to go through the rigmarole of creating a custom Gantt Chart view for your Tasks list, you can easily get all the benefits of a Gantt Chart view simply by adding a Project Tasks list to your SharePoint site:

1. **Open the subsite where you want the new Project Tasks list added.**

   To add the list to the top level of the SharePoint site, open its home page.

2. **Click the Lists link in the site's Quick Launch.**

   SharePoint opens the All Site Content page, filtering out everything but the lists on the site.

3. **Click the Create button at the top of the All Site Content page.**

   SharePoint opens the site's Create page.

4. **Click the Project Tasks link in the Tracking column.**

   SharePoint opens a New page.

5. **Type a name for the new Project Tasks list in the Name text box and then press Tab.**

   SharePoint advances the cursor to the Description text box.

6. **Type a description of the new Project Tasks list in the Description text box.**

7. **(Optional) Select the No Navigation radio button to prevent SharePoint from adding the new Project Tasks list to the site's Quick Launch and/or select the Yes E-Mail Notification radio button to have SharePoint send e-mail alerts to a team member whenever a task is assigned to him.**

   Be sure to select the Yes radio button for E-Mail Notification if you want SharePoint to let your team members know when you've assigned them a task to complete.

8. **Click the Create button.**

   SharePoint creates the new Project Tasks list and then displays its empty list page (in the default Project Tasks list view with its Gantt chart), which is similar to the one shown in Figure 10-7.

You can then use the New button at the top of the Project Tasks list page to add tasks to the new list or you can switch the list to Datasheet view (by choosing Edit in Datasheet from the Actions drop-down menu) and then add them in the spreadsheet-like table.

Keep in mind that the moment you switch a Project Tasks list into Datasheet view, the Gantt chart in the top pane disappears from the page, and only the datasheet table is displayed there. However, as soon as you switch the Project Tasks list back into Standard view (by choosing Show in the Standard View from the Actions drop-down menu), the Gantt Chart pane immediately reappears, updated with whatever tasks you added to the datasheet.

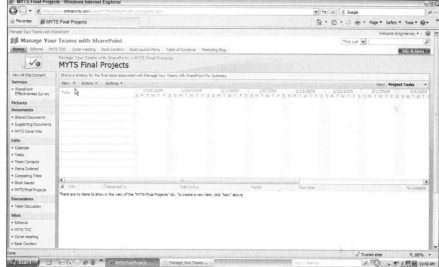

Figure 10-7:
I've added a
new Project
Tasks
list to my
SharePoint
site.

Working with Issue Tracking Lists

Issue Tracking lists are just like Tasks lists except that, in addition to helping you track the priority and status of a particular issue that you and your teams must resolve, they enable you to categorize the issues you're dealing with and record detailed comments about the steps you took at each stage in its resolution.

Moreover, Issue Tracking lists have a special Related Issues field that enables you to link issues that are related to each other. This field is helpful when you're dealing with a larger issue that can't be resolved until smaller, related issues are fixed. For example, if you're tracking an order fulfillment problem for a customer, you may have to resolve a related issue with a discrepancy between the customer's billing and shipping addresses before it can be cleared up.

Adding an Issue Tracking list

To add an Issue Tracking list to your SharePoint site, follow these steps:

1. **Open the subsite where you want the new Issue Tracking list added.**

   To add the list to the top level of the SharePoint site, open its home page.

2. **Click the Lists link in the site's Quick Launch.**

   SharePoint opens the All Site Content page, filtering out everything but the lists on the site.

3. **Click the Create button at the top of the All Site Content page.**

   SharePoint opens the site's Create page.

4. **Click the Issue Tracking link in the Tracking column.**

   SharePoint opens a New page.

5. **Type a name for the new Issue Tracking list in the Name text box and then press Tab.**

   SharePoint advances the cursor to the Description text box.

6. **Type a description of the new Issue Tracking list into the Description text box.**

7. **(Optional) Select the No Navigation radio button to prevent SharePoint from adding the new Issue Tracking list to the site's Quick Launch and/or select the Yes E-Mail Notification radio button to have SharePoint send e-mail alerts to a team member whenever an issue is assigned to him.**

   Be sure to click the Yes radio button for E-Mail Notification if you want SharePoint to let your team members know when you've assigned them an issue to resolve.

8. **Click the Create button.**

   SharePoint creates the new Issue Tracking list and then displays an empty list page in its default All Issues list view.

In the All Issues list view, an Issue Tracking list contains columns for displaying the entries in the Issue ID, Title, Assigned To, Issue Status, Priority, and Due Date fields. In addition to the default All Issues view, a new Issue Tracking list contains an Active Issues list view that filters out all issues that are resolved or closed and a My Issues list view that filters out all issues that are not assigned to you.

Keep in mind that an Issue Tracking list is the one kind of SharePoint list that you can't connect directly to Outlook 2007. If this kind of connectivity is really important to you — perhaps because you're on Outlook all day long and it serves as your early warning system for all things project related — you can get around this limitation by creating a new Tasks list (that you can connect to Outlook) to which you add the following custom fields: Issue Status, Category, Related Issues, and Comments using the Add Columns from Site Columns link. (See Chapter 4 for details on adding custom fields to SharePoint lists.)

Adding issues to the list and tracking their resolution

You can add items to your new Issue Tracking list just as you would add items to a SharePoint Tasks or Project Tasks list: by using the data form (opened by choosing New Item from the New drop-down menu) or the datasheet format (opened by choosing Edit in Datasheet from the Actions drop-down menu).

When you add a new issue to the list using the data form, you have an opportunity to fill in many of the same fields as you do in a SharePoint Tasks or Project Tasks list, including Title, Description, Assigned To, Priority, and Due Date.

In addition, the New Item page that comes with a new issue data form contains the following additional fields unique to the Issue Tracking list:

✔ **Issue Status:** This field enables you to select one of three different statuses for the issue: Active, Resolved (meaning that the issue is no longer active and has been successfully dealt with), and Closed (meaning that the issue is no longer active and may or may not have been successfully dealt with).

✔ **Category:** This field enables you to select one of three generic categories: Category1, Category2, or Category3. You can (and need to) customize the names of these generic categories so that they reflect the types of issues that you and your teams are actually dealing with. (See the section "Customizing the generic issue categories" that immediately follows for more on customizations.) Note that, as part of customizing the generic issue categories, you can also create as many additional custom categories as needed.

✔ **Related Issues:** This field enables you to connect issues in the list that are related to one another. This creates a link between the issues that you can use to track their progress and ensure that all the interrelated issues are being taken care of.

✔ **Comments:** This field enables you and your fellow team members to record a history of the steps you've taken to resolve the issue. To that end, SharePoint clears out the Comments field each time you edit the issue. This enables you to use this field to record your latest efforts to successfully resolve the issue. Your series of comments (which appear in chronological order immediately beneath the Comments list box in the issue's Edit Item page) provide you with the history of how the issue was handled each step of the way.

Customizing the generic issue categories

When you first create a new Issue Tracking list, SharePoint creates three generic categories (Category1, Category2, and Category3) for classifying the issues that you add to the list. One of the first things you'll want to do upon creating a new Issue Tracking list is to rename these generic categories and, perhaps, create additional categories for the types of issues that your list is bound to deal with.

For example, if your Issue Tracking list follows team-related issues, you might want to rename the generic categories to something like Technical, Communication, and Training and then add a couple of your own such as Leadership and Support.

To rename the generic categories in a new Issue Tracking list and add some of your own, follow these steps:

1. **Open the Issue Tracking list in SharePoint and then choose List Settings from the Settings drop-down list.**

   SharePoint opens the Customize page for the Issues Tracking list.

2. **Click the Category link in the Columns section of the Customize page.**

   SharePoint opens the Change Column page for the Category field, similar to the one shown in Figure 10-8.

3. **Select the Category1 text in the choices list box in the Additional Column Settings section and then replace its text with the name of the issue category you want in your list. Repeat this action for Category2 and Category3.**

4. **(Optional) To add more categories, type the name of the category.**

   Note that you can have less than three issue categories: To delete a generic category, however, you need to remove all of its text on its line in the list box.

5. **(Optional) Make any necessary changes to the other column settings that determine how the category choices appear, whether to allow fill-in, and what default choice to use.**

   SharePoint automatically displays the default category choice listed in the Default Value text box in a drop-down list button, and your category choices appear on a drop-down menu. If you want your category choices displayed with radio buttons instead, select the Radio Buttons option under the Display Choices Using heading. If you want your category choices displayed with check boxes, select the Checkboxes (Allow Multiple Selections) option.

   Note that by selecting the Checkboxes option, you automatically enable your users to choose more than one category for the issue. (When you select the Drop-Down Menu or Radio Buttons option, users can select only one category.)

   Also, regardless of how you display the category choices, SharePoint doesn't allow your users to choose any category other than the ones you designate when you replace the generic Category1, Category2, and Category3 categories. If you want your users to be able to enter other categories that they enter, you must click the Yes button under the Allow 'Fill-In' Choices heading.

   SharePoint also enables you to designate one of your category choices as the default value that's automatically selected when you or your team members add a new issue to the Issue Tracking list. Enter the name of the category that you think is the most likely category choice in the Default Value text box.

6. **Click the OK button.**

   SharePoint saves your changes and returns you to the Customize page.

7. **Click the Issue Tracking list's breadcrumb in the Content Navigation Breadcrumb at the top of the Customize page.**

   SharePoint returns you to your Issue Tracking list. When you next add a new issue there, you will see the custom categories that you just created for the list.

Editing items in the Issue Tracking list and following them to resolution

As you and your team members continue to work on particular issues that you've added to the Issue Tracking list, you'll need to edit them to record the steps that you've taken. To edit an issue in the list, click the link that's attached to it in the Title column and then click the Edit Item button in the page that appears, displaying the data form with the current field entries.

By clicking the Edit Item button, you tell SharePoint to open a page containing an editable version of the data form, where you can update any of its fields (similar to the one shown in Figure 10-9). When this page opens, you will notice, however, that the Comments list box is now empty (and the comments you previously made in this list box are now displayed beneath it).

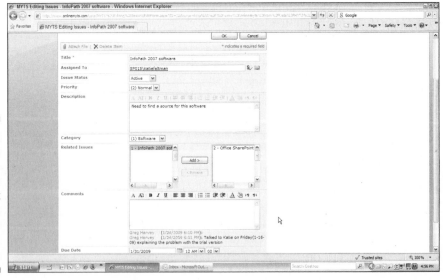

Figure 10-9:
Updating an issue in the Issue Tracking list by editing the fields in its data form.

You can then record the latest steps you've taken to resolve the issue in this empty Comments list box. When you or your team finally resolves the issue, you then open the issue's data form for editing one last time, where you change the Issue Status field entry from Active to Resolved and record your final comments in the Comments list box.

To review all the comments that you and your team members made in the course of resolving an issue, open the Issue Tracking list and then choose Version History from the issue's drop-down menu (opened by positioning the mouse pointer over the name of the issue in the Title column and then clicking the drop-down button that appears). SharePoint then opens a list showing all the versions of the issue, similar to the one shown in Figure 10-10.

This list shows the version number, the date the issue was modified, and the name of the team member who modified it. The list also shows the comments that you and your team have made in the issue's Comments fields, thus giving you a nice little history of the issue from its inception to its final resolution.

Figure 10-10:
You can review the version history of an issue in the Issue Tracking list.

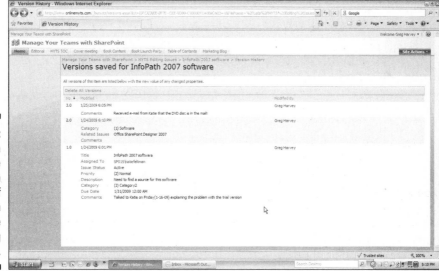

ng a SharePoint Workflow

Workflows in SharePoint enable you to use data stored on your SharePoint site to automate business processes that you and your teams routinely follow. The workflow feature represents an area in SharePoint that varies depending on whether you're using SharePoint Services 3.0 alone or with Office 2007 SharePoint Server.

If you're using SharePoint Services alone, you're probably going to be restricted to using just the three-state workflow template that comes with it to create workflows for your Issue Tracking lists. If, however, you're using Office 2007 SharePoint Server, you have access to additional built-in workflow templates for document management and document workflows that you can use in your SharePoint Tasks lists in addition to the three-state workflow template.

The good news is that if you also have access to Office SharePoint Designer 2007, you can use its Workflow Wizard to create custom workflow templates tailored to the content of your SharePoint site without having to write a single line of code. (See Chapter 13 for general information on using Office SharePoint Designer 2007 and specific information on using the Workflow Wizard to create custom workflow templates.)

Understanding the three-state workflow

True to its name, the three-state workflow tracks a typical business process through three distinct phases:

- ✔ **Active (Initial):** Before you start this initial phase, you create the list that tracks the tasks associated with the workflow (usually, an Issue Tracking list) and then assign a three-state workflow template to be used on the list. You then add the specific tasks (or issues) that your team needs to deal with and assign these tasks to your team members. Depending upon how the workflow is set up, SharePoint either automatically starts the workflow as soon as you assign new tasks to the list, or you can manually start the workflow.

- ✔ **Ready for Review (Middle):** In this second (middle) phase, team members mark their tasks as complete, and SharePoint then automatically updates the status of the workflow from Active to Ready for Review and alerts you to the fact that the tasks are now complete and ready for you to review.

- ✔ **Complete (Final):** In this third (final) phase, you review and approve the tasks in the tasks list and update them as complete. SharePoint then changes the status of the workflow from Ready for Review to Complete.

The beauty of this workflow is that SharePoint automates the transitions from the Initial/Active state to the Middle/Ready for Review state and from the Ready for Review state to the Final/Complete state. All you have to do is set up a Tasks list, assign a workflow to it, and assign the tasks to your team members as you normally would.

Using the three-state workflow to automate issue resolution in an Issue Tracking list

Although you can use the three-state workflow with custom Tasks lists that you create (provided that the list contains some sort of status field with three choices), this template is particularly well suited for the Issue Tracking list. (See the section "Working with Issue Tracking Lists," earlier in this chapter, for details.)

This is because the three-state workflow template is perfectly designed to work with the choices offered by the Issue Tracking list's Issue Status field (Active, Resolved, and Closed). These three Issue Status field choices correspond to the workflow's three states (Initial, Middle, and Final).

To assign a three-state workflow for an Issue Tracking list that you've created, follow these steps:

1. **Open the Issue Tracking list in SharePoint and then choose List Settings from the Settings drop-down menu.**

   SharePoint opens the Customize page for your Issue Tracking list.

2. **Click the Workflow Settings link in the Permissions and Management column.**

   SharePoint opens the Add a Workflow page, similar to the one shown in Figure 10-11. By default, SharePoint selects the Three-state template option in the Workflow list box. (This may be the only template available if you're using SharePoint Services 3.0 and haven't created any custom workflow templates.)

3. **Click the Name text box and then type a unique name for the new workflow.**

   By default, SharePoint adds the new workflow to the Tasks list you have open and sets it up so that you must start the workflow manually. If you want SharePoint to create a new list for the workflow, choose New Task List from the Task List drop-down menu. If you want SharePoint to initiate the workflow whenever a new item is created in your Tasks list, click the Start This Workflow When a New Item Is Created check box.

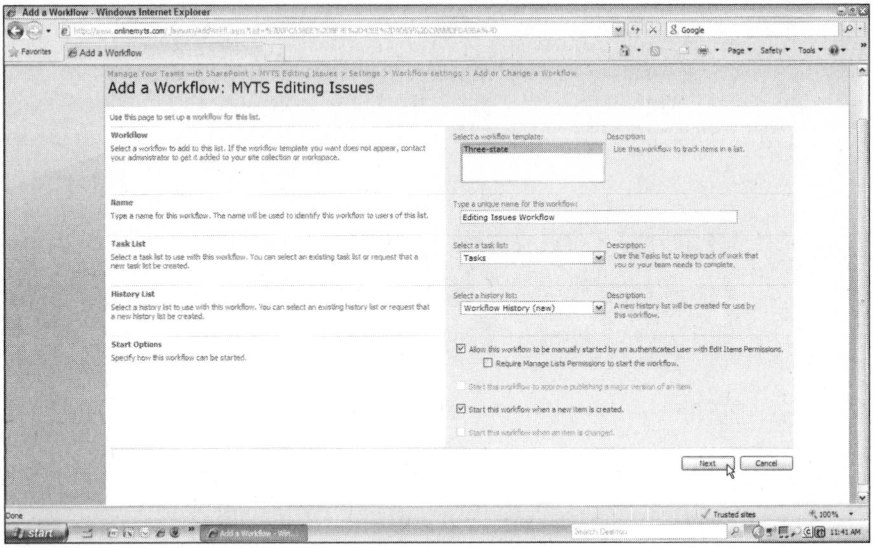

Figure 10-11:
Adding a three-state workflow for an Issue Tracking list on my SharePoint site.

4. **(Optional) Make any desired changes to the Task List and Start Options.**

5. **Click the Next button.**

   SharePoint opens the Customize the Three-State Workflow page, the top part of which is shown in Figure 10-12. This part contains the options for synchronizing the three Workflow States (Initial, Middle, and Final) with the three options in a choice field (specifically, the Active, Resolved, and Complete choices in the Issue Tracking field). This part also contains options for detailing what actions SharePoint is to take when the workflow is started.

6. **(Optional) Customize any of the messages (and fields referred to in those messages) using the options found in the Task Details section for sending out word that the workflow has been initiated.**

   Note that you can accept the default messages and Issue Tracking field lists offered by SharePoint.

7. **In the Initiated State section, specify the team members to whom messages regarding the changes in the workflow tasks are to be sent by using the Task Details message and field options. Also, under E-Mail Message Details, fill in the To and Subject text boxes as well as the Body text box.**

   When you scroll up the Customize the Three-State Workflow page to display the bottom part, you see the options for specifying what you want to happen when the workflow changes to its middle state (see Figure 10-13).

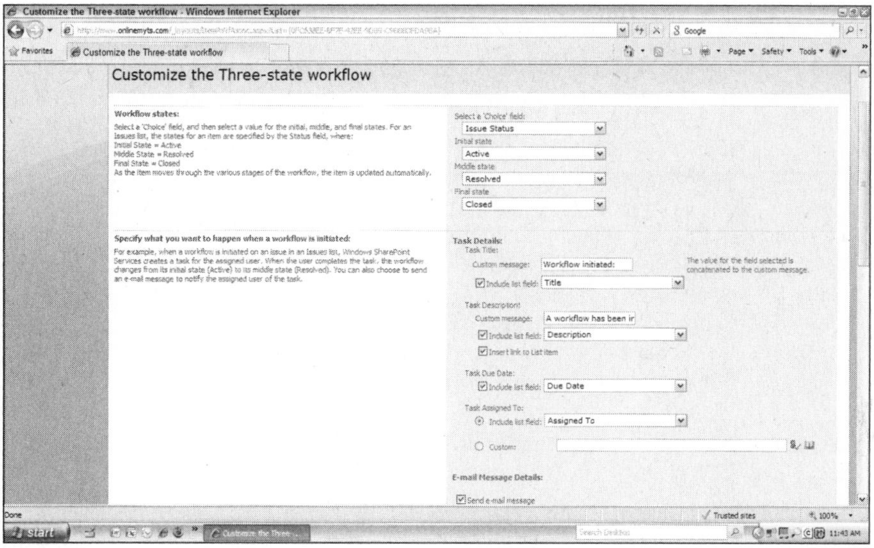

Figure 10-12:
Specifying the actions the new workflow takes when the workflow is initiated.

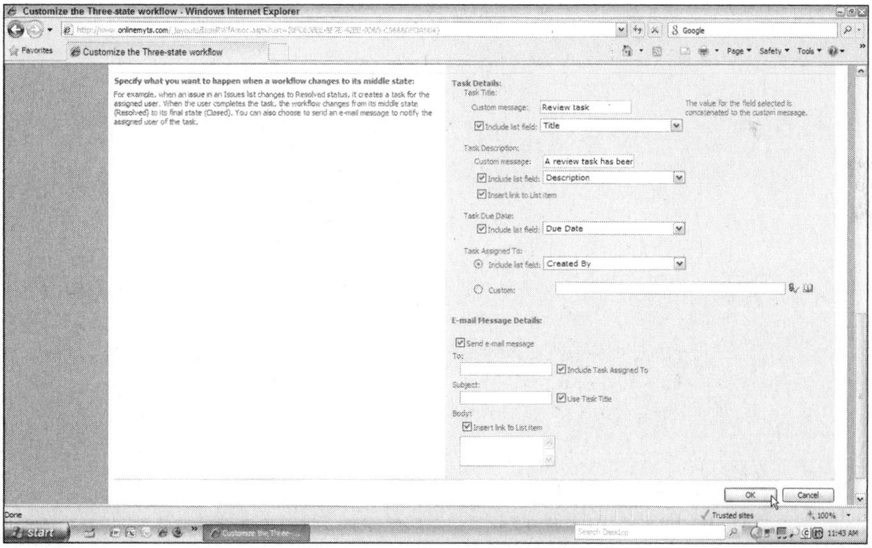

Figure 10-13:
Specifying the actions the new workflow takes when the workflow reaches its middle state.

8. **In the Middle State section, specify yourself or some other team member to receive notification that initial tasks are done and are ready for review by using the Task Details message and field options. Also, under E-Mail Message Details, fill in the To and Subject text boxes and the Body text box.**

Now you're ready to create the workflow.

9. **Click the OK button.**

SharePoint creates the workflow for the current Issue Tracking list and returns to this list.

After creating a workflow for an Issue Tracking list, you can start the new workflow for any issues that you add to the list. All you have to do is click the drop-down button that appears when you position the mouse pointer over the list item and then click the Workflow option that now appears on this drop-down menu.

SharePoint then opens a Workflows page for the particular issue item, similar to the one shown in Figure 10-14. Click the link that appears under the name of the Workflow you just created for the Issue Tracking list at the top of the Workflows page and SharePoint starts the workflow, automatically sending out e-mail messages to specified team members to inform them of the tasks that they are to perform during the Initial workflow phase.

Figure 10-14:
Starting a workflow for a particular item added to my Issue Tracking list.

Part IV
Using Office Programs with SharePoint

The 5th Wave   By Rich Tennant

"Our automated response policy to a large company-wide data crash is to notify management, back up existing data and sell 90% of my shares in the company."

In this part . . .

One of the things that makes SharePoint 2007 so impressive is its tight integration with the programs in Microsoft's Office suite, especially those in the latest version, Office 2007. This part of the book shows you how to use the core Office applications of Outlook, Word, and Excel with SharePoint. It also gives you some specific information about how you can use Office SharePoint Designer 2007 to create custom workflows for your SharePoint lists and InfoPath 2007 to create form templates and form libraries for your site.

Chapter 11

Integrating SharePoint and Outlook 2007

*O*ne of the great things about SharePoint 2007 is how tightly integrated it is with the applications in Microsoft Office 2007, especially Outlook. This chapter looks at some of the more important ways that you and your team members can access and update SharePoint site information right from the comfort of Outlook folders.

If you're like many knowledge workers, Outlook is the one program you always have open on your computer and the one in which you often spend a good part of your workday. For you, being able to access and work with information from different parts of the SharePoint site from within Outlook can't help but enhance your ability to communicate and collaborate with other members of the team.

Connecting Your SharePoint Calendar to Outlook

Outlook's Calendar module provides a convenient graphical view of your upcoming appointments, usually on a daily, weekly, or monthly basis. If you're part of a SharePoint team, you can keep track of team-related events and deadlines by connecting the team's SharePoint calendar to your Outlook Calendar module so that they stay synchronized.

To connect the SharePoint calendar to Outlook, follow these steps:

1. **Open the team's calendar page in SharePoint.**

   If your SharePoint site uses only the one default calendar, you can do this step by clicking the Calendar link in the Lists area of the home page's Quick Launch.

2. **Choose Connect to Outlook from the Actions drop-down menu.**

   SharePoint displays an Internet Explorer alert dialog box asking you to allow the browser to open Outlook on your computer.

3. **Click the Allow button.**

   Outlook displays a Connect alert dialog box asking you to confirm the connection to its Calendar.

4. **Click the Yes button in the alert dialog box.**

   Outlook downloads the SharePoint calendar, which it displays alongside the Outlook calendar that's currently open in the program (see Figure 11-1). In addition, Outlook adds your SharePoint calendar to the list of calendars displayed in the Other Calendars section of the Navigation pane.

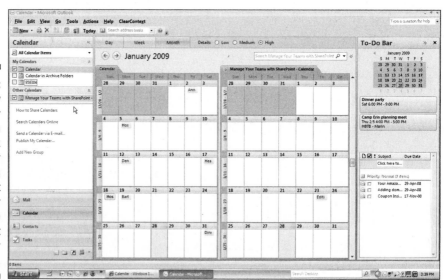

Figure 11-1: My Calendar module in Outlook 2007 after connecting the default Calendar on the SharePoint calendar to it.

Modifying the display of the SharePoint calendar in Outlook

After you connect your SharePoint calendar to your copy of Outlook and it's displayed in the Calendar module along with the Outlook calendars you have open, you can display it alone in the Calendar module: Simply deselect the check box or boxes for the calendar or calendars that are currently selected in the My Calendars section of the Navigation pane.

When your SharePoint calendar is the only one displayed in Outlook, you can then switch the view from the default monthly calendar view to the more in-depth weekly or daily view by clicking the Week button or Day button, respectively, at the top of the calendar. After clicking the Week button, you can switch between displaying the full calendar week (Sunday through Saturday) and displaying the normal workweek (Monday through Friday) by selecting the Show Work Week radio button that then appears to the immediate right of the Month button.

When you want to once again view your Outlook calendar, select its check box in the My Calendars section of the Outlook Navigation pane and then select the check box in front of your SharePoint calendar in the Other Calendars section to deselect it. Remember that there must always be at least one calendar displayed in the Outlook Calendar module, so you must always display your Outlook calendar with the SharePoint calendar before you can hide the SharePoint calendar (and vice versa).

Adding events to your SharePoint calendar in Outlook

After you've connected your SharePoint calendar to Outlook, you can then add events to the SharePoint calendar in Outlook without having to log on to the SharePoint site in your Web browser. All you have to do is follow these easy steps in Outlook:

1. **Display the SharePoint calendar in the Outlook Calendar module, as spelled out in the previous sections.**

2. **Right-click the date on the calendar where you want to add the event and then choose New Appointment from the shortcut menu that appears.**

    Outlook opens a new, Untitled – Appointment dialog box similar to the one shown in Figure 11-2. Here, you specify the subject, the location, and the event's starting time and ending time, along with a description of the event.

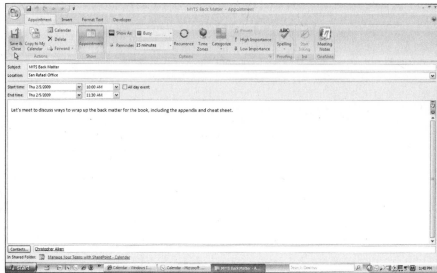

Figure 11-2:
Adding an appointment to my SharePoint calendar in Outlook 2007.

Note: If the event is something along the lines of a seminar or conference that takes all day or spans more than one day, choose New All Day Event from the shortcut menu to call up an Untitled – Event dialog box.

3. **Enter the subject of the meeting in the Subject line of the Untitled – Appointment dialog box and then press Tab.**

   Outlook advances the cursor to the Location line of the Appointment or Event dialog box.

4. **Enter the location of the meeting (Conference Room, online, telephone, and so forth).**

   Next, you need to specify the starting and ending times of the event. In the Appointment dialog box, the All Day Event check box is not selected as it is in the Event dialog box.

5. **If necessary, modify the starting and ending times of the event using the Start Time and End Time date and/or time drop-down buttons. If the event is an all-day or many-day affair, be sure the All Day Event check box is selected.**

6. **Click the text area immediately below the Start Time and End Time options and type a detailed description of the appointment or event.**

   The Appointment or Event dialog box also contains a Contacts field at the bottom, where you can add links to the contact information for particular team members who are involved in some way with the upcoming event on the SharePoint calendar.

7. **(Optional) To add a link to a contact in your Outlook Contact folder, click the Contacts button and then select the person or people in the Select Contacts dialog box before you click OK.**

   Now you're ready to save the appointment or event on your SharePoint calendar.

8. **Click the Save and Close button at the beginning of the Appointment or Event tab on the Ribbon.**

   Outlook closes the Appointment or Event dialog box and returns you to its display of your SharePoint calendar. The appointment or event you just created appears on the appropriate day (or days) on the calendar.

After adding items to your SharePoint calendar in Outlook 2007, their events automatically appear on the copy of the calendar in SharePoint the next time you open the calendar's page.

Viewing and modifying calendar events in SharePoint

To view the details of the appointment in the SharePoint site, simply click the item on the calendar in SharePoint (just as you would a calendar item in Outlook). The program then opens a page for the calendar item, similar to the one shown in Figure 11-3.

This page contains the standard appointment fields as well as a Workspace field that shows the location of any meeting workspace you may decide to set up for the event. (See Chapter 6 for more on meeting workspaces.)

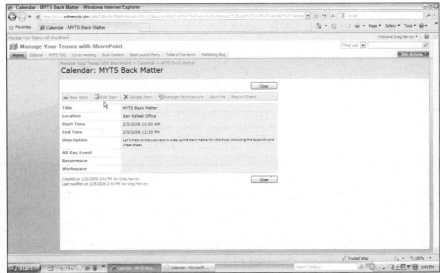

Figure 11-3: You can view the details of a calendar item added in Outlook on the SharePoint site.

If you need to edit the calendar item, you then click the Edit Item button at the top of the form on this page and make whatever changes are needed or desired in the appropriate fields. When you finish editing the event, simply click the OK button to close the page and return to the calendar.

Copying items from your local calendar to your SharePoint calendar

After you've connected your SharePoint calendar to Outlook, you can easily copy items from the local calendar or even an Internet calendar (such as a Google Calendar) to your SharePoint calendar. All you have to do is follow these few general steps:

1. **Open both the local Outlook calendar or Internet calendar that contains the items you want to copy and the SharePoint calendar to which you want to copy them.**

   Remember that you display multiple calendars in the Outlook Calendar module by selecting their check boxes in the appropriate sections (My Calendars and Other Calendars) of the Navigation pane.

2. **Drag the calendar items you want to copy from the Outlook or Internet calendar and drop them on the appropriate day in the SharePoint calendar.**

   Outlook displays an alert dialog box telling you that any incompatible content in the items you're copying will be removed when the items are synchronized. (This applies only if your Outlook calendar contains special fields that aren't supported by the SharePoint calendar feature.)

3. **Click the Yes button in the Outlook alert dialog box.**

   Outlook completes the copies, and the calendar items you dragged to the SharePoint calendar in Outlook now appear on the appropriate date on the calendar.

Keep in mind that you may have to refresh the calendar page displayed in your SharePoint site before the items that you've copied in Outlook appear in the online copy as well. If you're using Internet Explorer, you can do this by clicking the Refresh button, pressing F5, or pressing Alt and then selecting View⇨Refresh from the browser's pull-down menu.

Adding SharePoint calendar items to your Outlook To-Do Bar

If you're the type of Outlook user who mostly works in the Mail module and doesn't visit the Calendar very often, you can help remind yourself of upcoming team-related events that have been placed on your SharePoint calendar by adding them to the Outlook 2007 To-Do Bar. That way, the calendar event appears on-screen in Outlook no matter which module you have open.

To copy an event from your SharePoint calendar in Outlook 2007 to the Task List section of the Outlook To-Do Bar, do the following:

1. **In Outlook, click the text in the Task List area of the To-Do Bar that says "Click here to add a new task."**

   Outlook removes the "Click here to add a new task" text from the text box and replaces it with the cursor.

2. **Display the portion of the SharePoint calendar that contains the item or items you want to add to the Outlook To-Do Bar and then drag the item from the calendar and drop it into the empty text box in the To-Do Bar that used to contain the "Click here to add a new task" text.**

   Outlook copies the title of the event into the empty text box.

3. **Press the Enter key.**

   SharePoint adds the event as a task to the Tasks List section at the bottom of Outlook's To-Do Bar.

Because calendar events usually have start and stop times associated with them but don't have any due date, they are, at best, an imperfect fit in the Task List section of the To-Do Bar. Because they're bona fide appointments, they really should be added to the Appointments section of the To-Do Bar that appears immediately above the Task List section.

Unfortunately, Outlook 2007 only displays appointments placed on your local Outlook calendar in the To-Do Bar, so you have to add your SharePoint calendar items to its Tasks List.

 If you do add SharePoint calendar items to the Tasks List part of your Outlook To-Do Bar, you might want to edit these calendar items (by double-clicking them in the To-Do Bar) and add a Reminder to their task items. That way, Outlook will remind you before the date and time of the event like it does with appointments, and you don't have to keep the SharePoint calendar open either in Outlook or in your Web browser in order to remember to attend an important team meeting or event.

Sharing your SharePoint calendar with other team members

Outlook 2007 also makes it easy to share your SharePoint calendars with other team members. In Outlook, you can either e-mail the calendar (or a part of it) to other team members or send them an e-mail that invites them to visit the copy of the calendar on the SharePoint site.

To e-mail a copy of the calendar, right-click the SharePoint calendar's listing in the Other Calendars section of the Navigation pane and then choose Send via E-Mail from the shortcut menu that appears.

Outlook then displays a Send a Calendar via E-Mail dialog box, where you use both the Data Range drop-down list to select which part of the calendar to send and the Detail drop-down list to select the number of details to include. (In the Detail drop-down list, choose Full Details to include availability status plus all the information on each item, choose Availability Only to include availability status only, or choose Limited Details to include availability status plus the subjects of your calendar items.) If you want to include any files that are attached to particular calendar items, you need to click the Show button to the immediate right of the Advanced heading and then select the Include Attachments within Calendar Items check box.

When you click the OK button, Outlook inserts the entire calendar (or just the part you selected) into the body of a new e-mail message, as shown in Figure 11-4. You can then personalize the body of the message introducing the SharePoint calendar information and select the message's recipients by inserting their e-mail addresses from your Contacts address book into the To, Cc, and Bcc fields, as appropriate. When you're ready, click the Send button to send the e-mail with your SharePoint calendar info.

Figure 11-4:
You can send the entire SharePoint calendar in an e-mail to other team members.

To invite other team members to view a SharePoint calendar on the SharePoint site — provided they are authenticated users of the SharePoint site — right-click the SharePoint calendar's listing in the Other Calendars section of the Navigation pane and then choose the Share option followed by the name of the SharePoint calendar that appears on the calendar's shortcut menu.

Outlook then opens a Share window similar to the one shown in Figure 11-5. This window contains a new e-mail message with a link to the SharePoint site's calendar page. The team members who are the recipients of this e-mail can then follow this link to review the calendar online (assuming, of course, that they're authenticated users of the SharePoint site and are equipped with user IDs and passwords, for gaining access to the site, and permissions, for reviewing the calendar information).

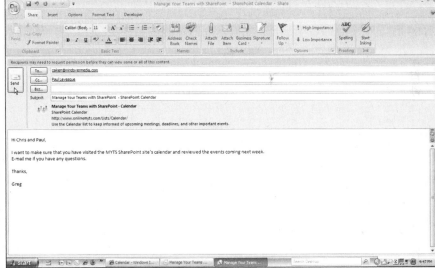

Figure 11-5:
You can share the SharePoint calendar by sending an e-mail with a link to it to other team members.

Managing SharePoint Contacts in Outlook 2007

In Chapter 4, I show you how to create a Team Contacts list for keeping track of your team's essential contact information as part of my discussion on maintaining SharePoint lists. If you use Outlook 2007, you can maintain this list right from within Outlook. All you have to do is connect the Team Contacts list in SharePoint to Outlook (by choosing Connect to Outlook from the list's Actions drop-down menu).

After you establish this connection, Outlook adds a Contacts list associated with your SharePoint site under the Other Contacts heading in the Outlook 2007 Contacts module. Selecting the list displays the contact information you've entered for your team members using the Contacts module's default Business Card view, as shown in Figure 11-6.

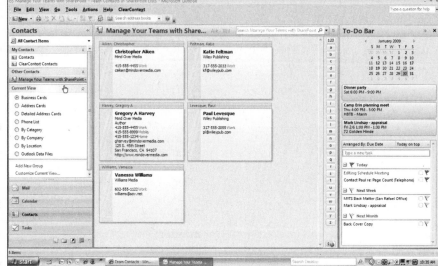

Figure 11-6:
Maintaining
a Share
Point Teams
Contacts list
in Outlook's
Contacts
module.

Remember that you can change the way that Outlook displays the records in your SharePoint contacts list by choosing View⇨Current View in Outlook and then choosing the view option you want to use (Address Cards, Detailed Address Cards, or Phone List) from the submenu. If you want the contacts to be grouped by a particular field in a phone list type of display, choose the By Category, By Company, or By Location option from this menu instead.

When you have the SharePoint contacts in Outlook, any updates you make to the information in their contact records in Outlook are automatically reflected in their records in the copy of the contacts list that resides on your SharePoint site.

To add a new record for a team member, click the New button when the SharePoint contacts list is open in Outlook or press Ctrl+N. Then fill in the contact information you have for that team member in the appropriate fields in the Untitled Contact window and click the Save & Close button.

If you have a record for a team member in your regular Outlook Contacts folder that you need to add to Outlook's copy of your SharePoint contacts list, you can add it by opening the Outlook Contacts folder and then simply dragging the contact icon and dropping it onto the SharePoint Contacts folder that appears in the Other Contacts area of Outlook's Navigation pane.

Categorizing, flagging, and communicating with your SharePoint contacts

In addition to being able to update your SharePoint contact records and add to them in Outlook, you can do any of the following things with them:

- ✔ **Assign the contact to a color category:** Outlook 2007 enables you to assign any of its items to particular color-coded categories. To assign the contact for a SharePoint team member to one of these categories, right-click the contact and then choose Categorize from the shortcut menu that appears, followed by the name and color of the category on the shortcut's continuation menu.

- ✔ **Flag the contact with a reminder:** To flag a SharePoint team member with a reminder that you should contact him in a particular manner at a particular date and time, right-click his contact record and then choose Follow Up from the shortcut menu that appears, followed by Add Reminder from the submenu. Outlook then opens a Custom dialog box where you specify what type of contact to make in the Flag To combo box (Follow Up, Call, Arrange Meeting, Send E-Mail, or Send Letter) as well as the date and time when Outlook is to display a reminder to you to initiate this contact.

- ✔ **Create a message, meeting request, or task for the contact:** To send an e-mail to a SharePoint team member, request his presence at an upcoming team meeting, or assign him a task to complete, right-click his record and then choose Create from the shortcut menu that appears, followed by New Message to Contact, New Meeting Request to Contact, or New Task for Contact from the submenu.

Reviewing the e-mail activities that involve a SharePoint contact

Outlook 2007 has the ability to search for and display all the e-mail activities involving a particular SharePoint team member in your contacts list (including sent and received messages that refer to him). Before you can review the e-mail activities of particular members in the SharePoint contacts list, though, you first need to define Outlook folders that will be searched and designate a folder in which to store the list of items. To do this, follow these steps:

1. **Open the contacts list associated with your SharePoint site in Outlook and then right-click its folder in the Navigation pane and choose Properties from the shortcut menu that appears.**

   The contacts list for your site should be located under the Other Contacts heading in the Navigation pane.

   Outlook opens a dialog box for the SharePoint list's Outlook folder.

2. **Click the Activities tab in the Outlook folder dialog box and then click the New button.**

   Outlook opens the View Title and Folders dialog box where you designate the name of the new folder to contain the list of e-mail activities as well as designate the Outlook folders that are to be included in the search.

3. **(Optional) In the Name text box, replace the generic New Folder Group name suggested by Outlook with a more descriptive name such as SharePoint Contact Activities.**

   Next, you need to designate the Outlook folders to be included in the activities search.

4. **Select the check box in front of Personal Folders in the View Title and Folders list box and then click OK.**

   Outlook returns you to the SharePoint Contacts List dialog box where the names and groups of folders you specified appear in the Folder Groups list box.

5. **Click the OK button.**

   Outlook closes the SharePoint list's dialog box and returns you to that list in Outlook.

After defining the Outlook folder to record the items and the Outlook mail folders to search, you can view all the e-mail activities involving a particular SharePoint team member by following these steps:

1. **Double-click the team member's contact record in Outlook.**

   Outlook opens the member's record in its own window, similar to the one shown in Figure 11-7.

2. **Click the Activities button in the Show area of the Contact tab on the Ribbon.**

   Outlook then displays a list of all the e-mail activities (including sent and received messages that refer in some way to the team member) in the Contact window.

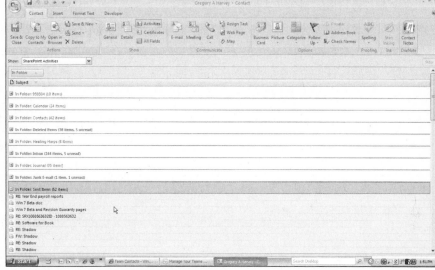

Figure 11-7:
You can
display all
the Outlook
items
(grouped
by folder)
that involve
a particular
SharePoint
contact.

You can make this list of Outlook items much more manageable by grouping them by their Outlook folders (as I've done in Figure 11-7). To do this, right-click the top row of the list with the column headings and then choose Group By Box from the shortcut menu that appears. Outlook then displays the message "Drag a Column Header Here to Group by That Column" in the Group By box that now appears at the top of the list. You then drag the In Folder column header and drop it somewhere in the area of this box. Outlook then groups the items by Outlook folder, and each folder has its own set of Expand buttons when its section of the list is collapsed; when its section is expanded, the folder has Collapse buttons.

Don't forget that you can redisplay the normal fields in the Contact window by clicking the General button in the Show area of the Contact tab on the Ribbon after you finish reviewing the contact's list of e-mail activities.

Outlook and SharePoint Document Libraries

If you and your team members use Outlook 2007 for sending and receiving e-mail and keeping track of your schedule, you can easily access the files that you've uploaded to a SharePoint document library by connecting the SharePoint site (and consequently the selected document library) to your

Outlook program. Then, all you have to do to work with the files is to open them in their client applications directly from the document library's Outlook folder on your computer. (That's assuming that the necessary client applications are installed on your computer.)

Connecting a SharePoint document library to Outlook gives you the added benefit of being able to work with the files in that library even when you can't be connected to the Internet and need to work offline. This is especially useful when you're accessing the SharePoint site on the go on a laptop computer and encounter times when you don't have Internet access but still need to access and work with site information stored in one of its document libraries.

To see how you can put this feature to work on your SharePoint site, follow along with the steps for connecting the default Shared Documents library to Outlook 2007 on my laptop computer and then using the Outlook folder that points to the SharePoint library to open one of the library's files saved in Microsoft Word:

1. **Open the Shared Documents library in the SharePoint site and then choose Connect to Outlook from the Actions drop-down menu.**

   Internet Explorer displays an alert dialog box asking you to allow the SharePoint Web site to open a program on your computer. Note that the Connect to Outlook option won't appear on the Actions menu if you don't have Outlook 2003 (or later) installed on the computer you're using to access the SharePoint site.

2. **Click the Allow button in the Internet Explorer alert dialog box.**

   Windows launches Outlook, if it's not already running on your computer, and Outlook displays an alert dialog box asking you to confirm the connection of your SharePoint document library to Outlook.

3. **Click the Yes button in the Outlook alert dialog box.**

   If you connect to SharePoint Services on an external server hosted by a third party, a Connect dialog box may appear prompting you for your username and password. After supplying your password in this dialog box, click OK.

   Outlook creates a folder for the newly connected document library with the name of your SharePoint site. This Outlook folder appears in the SharePoint Lists section of the Mail Folders area in the Outlook Navigation pane. Immediately beneath this library Outlook folder, the program creates a subfolder for any subfolders in the connected SharePoint document library. Beneath these subfolders, you find two Outlook Search folders: Offline Documents and SharePoint Drafts.

When you select a file in the Messages pane (to the immediate right of the Navigation pane), Outlook attempts to display a preview of the selected document in its Reading pane (to the immediate right of the Messages pane). If no preview is available for the file you select, Outlook informs you of this situation in the Reading pane.

4. To open the document file you've selected in the Messages pane, double-click it or right-click it and then choose Open from its shortcut menu (as shown in Figure 11-8).

Windows displays an Opening File dialog box that reminds you that you should only open files that come from a reliable source.

5. Click the Open button in the Opening File dialog box.

Windows launches the program that created the document file (assuming that this application is installed on your computer), while at the same time opening the selected document.

When you open files in standard Office applications such as Word and Excel, a message bar similar to the one shown in Figure 11-9 appears at the top of the document. If you want to edit the document (as opposed to simply printing it), you need to click the Edit Offline button in this message pane. The program then displays an Edit Offline dialog box (sometimes preceded by an alert dialog box and a Connect To dialog box) that tells you that the changes you make to the document will be saved to a copy stored in the SharePoint Drafts folder in the My Documents folder on your computer's hard drive.

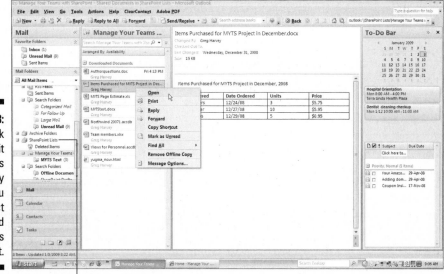

Figure 11-8:
Outlook 2007 as it appears immediately after you connect the Shared Documents library to it.

SharePoint Lists folder

After you click OK in the Edit Offline dialog box, you can make all your editing changes. After you save your changes and close the document, another Edit Offline dialog box appears, reminding you that you're currently offline and asking whether you want to update the document library on the SharePoint server with a copy of your revised document. Click the Update button in this dialog box to have the updated document saved in your SharePoint document library.

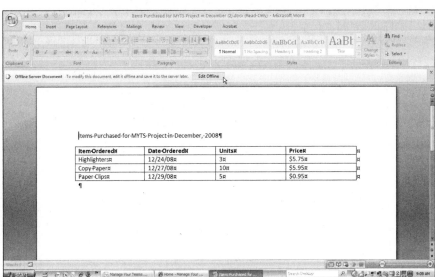

Figure 11-9:
The SharePoint library document as it appears when opened in Word 2007 via the SharePoint folder in Outlook 2007.

Chapter 12

Using Office Applications with SharePoint

In This Chapter

▶ Editing an Office document saved in a SharePoint document workspace

▶ Saving Word documents directly to your SharePoint document libraries

▶ Exporting Excel worksheet data into custom SharePoint lists

▶ Importing Excel worksheet data into custom SharePoint lists

*F*rom the perspective of the typical SharePoint user, one of the most satisfying things about using SharePoint 2007 is how well integrated it is with the later versions of Office applications (2003 and later), especially the core programs such as Microsoft Word, Excel, and PowerPoint.

A big part of this integration is provided by the Document Management pane (called Shared Workspace in Office 2003) in these core Office programs. You can use these panes to create and maintain SharePoint document workspaces (see Chapter 9) as well as to collaboratively edit their documents. Using the controls provided by the Document Management (Shared Workspace) panes, your team members can make their edits on the document saved in the workspace on the SharePoint site, and you, as the team leader, can determine which edits to save in case of conflicting changes.

When it comes to using Word 2007 with your SharePoint site, you can not only save and upload your documents to your SharePoint document libraries (see Chapter 5 for details on creating SharePoint document libraries) but also create and post your SharePoint blog entries (see Chapter 8 for details).

When it comes to Excel and your SharePoint site, you can import Excel worksheets to create new custom lists (see Chapter 4) as well as publish Excel worksheet tables directly to a new custom SharePoint list. This makes it extremely easy to share the latest worksheet data with the members of your team who rely on the data in order to make intelligent and timely decisions.

If your SharePoint site happens to use MOSS 2007 technologies, you may be able to make use of its Excel Services, which greatly enhance SharePoint integration with Microsoft Excel. This is because Excel Services enable SharePoint to maintain dynamic connections between the data in Excel worksheets and the SharePoint lists that use these data. Excel Services also includes a special Excel Web Access Web Part that enables you to display parts of Excel worksheets in various Web Part zones on your SharePoint site's Web Part pages.

Editing Document Workspace Files with Their Native Office Applications

Many of today's knowledge workers are very comfortable using the core Office programs Word, Excel, and PowerPoint to communicate their ideas and share vital information. If you had the opportunity to peruse Chapter 9, you know that SharePoint enables collaborative editing of the document files created with these applications in a special location referred to as a *document workspace.*

The great thing about SharePoint document workspaces is that not only do they enable you (as an administrator) to set up and maintain the document workspace from within the Office document (see Chapter 9 for details), but they also enable you and your team members to access these shared documents saved on the SharePoint server right within the comfort of the Office applications on their local computers.

Moreover, when the documents you place in these document workspaces are edited at the same time by different team members (all of whom must have at least Contribute-level site permissions — see Chapter 3) and this simultaneous editing results in conflicting changes, you, as team leader, can easily resolve these conflicts on the SharePoint site right within the native Office applications used to create the documents.

Figure 12-1 shows an Excel 2007 Employee Data List worksheet containing a table of personnel information. I created a SharePoint document workspace from this Excel workbook file by clicking the Office button and choosing Publish➪Create Document Workspace from the menu that appeared. When you select this command, Excel opens the Document Management pane, where you specify the name of the new document workspace and the URL address of the SharePoint site.

Links

Documents

Tasks

Members

Status

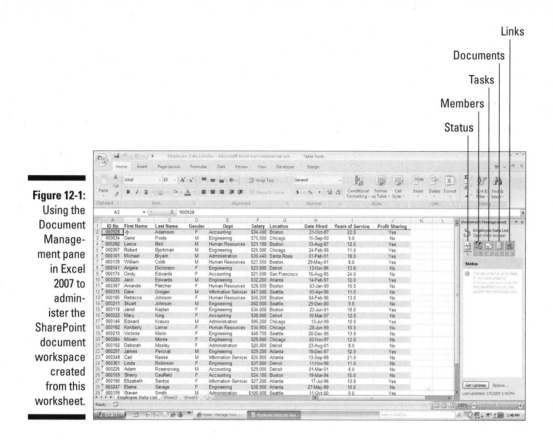

Figure 12-1:
Using the
Document
Manage-
ment pane
in Excel
2007 to
admin-
ister the
SharePoint
document
workspace
created
from this
worksheet.

If you're using Excel 2003, this pane is referred to as Shared Workspace. You open the Shared Workspace pane in an Office 2003 program by choosing View⇨Task Pane from the application's pull-down menu (or pressing Ctrl+F1) and then clicking Shared Workspace on the pane's drop-down menu. You can then create the document workspace by giving the workspace a name and specifying the SharePoint site's URL address before clicking the Create button (just as you do in Office 2007 programs).

Don't forget that document workspaces that you create from within Office applications such as Excel do not automatically show up on the SharePoint site's Quick Launch. If you don't manually add their links to the Quick Launch (see Chapter 9 for details on this procedure), you must open the workspace from the Sites section of the SharePoint site's All Site Content page.

Granting team members access to the document workspace

After creating the document workspace, you can use buttons and links that appear in the Document Management (or Shared Workspace) pane to administer the workspace. The first thing you probably want to do with a new document workspace is to give the other team members who will be reviewing and potentially editing the document access to it.

To add team members to a document workspace in Excel 2007, for example, follow these steps:

1. **Click the Members button at the top of the Document Management pane.**

   Excel displays your name as the sole member of the document workspace in the Document Management pane.

2. **Click the Add New Members link near the bottom of the Document Management pane.**

   Excel displays an Add New Members dialog box similar to the one shown in Figure 12-2. Here, you specify the e-mail addresses of the team members you want to add as members (all of whom must already be authenticated users of the SharePoint site — see Chapter 3) and select their permission level.

3. **Type the e-mail addresses or usernames of all the team members who need access to this document workspace. Separate each e-mail address or username entry with a semicolon (;).**

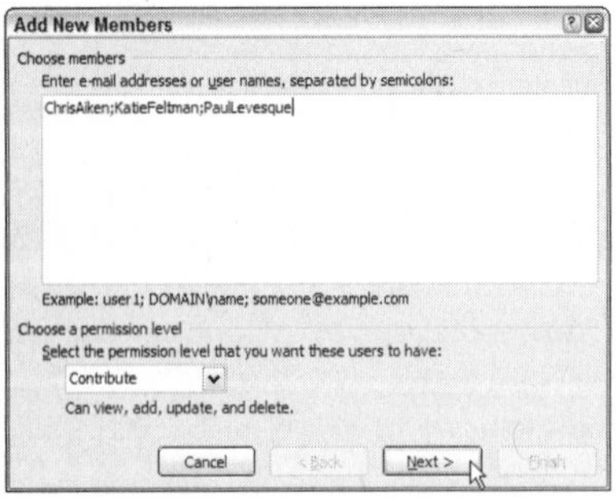

Figure 12-2:
Adding authenticated users to the document workspace in the Add New Members dialog box.

If any of your team members have more than one e-mail address, be sure to enter the e-mail address that is associated with their username on the SharePoint site in this list box.

4. **(Optional) Select a permission level (other than Design) for the team members you're adding to the document workspace by clicking Full Control, Contribute, or Read on the Choose a Permission Level drop-down menu.**

The default Design permission lets team members approve and customize the document workspace as well as view, add, and update the contents of its document(s). Select Contribute only if you want them to be able to view and edit their document(s) in the workspace or Read if you want to restrict them to reviewing. Only select Full Control when you're granting access to other site administrators to whom you want to give the ability to delete, customize, or edit the workspace and its documents.

5. **Click the Next button.**

Excel displays a second Add New Members dialog box similar to the one shown in Figure 12-3. This dialog box displays the username, e-mail address, and display name for each of the team members you just added.

6. **Verify that the list of team members displayed in the second Add New Members dialog box is complete and then click the Finish button.**

Excel displays an Add New Members alert dialog box that indicates that all your team members were successfully added to the document workspace and asks you to confirm by sending an e-mail invitation to each of them.

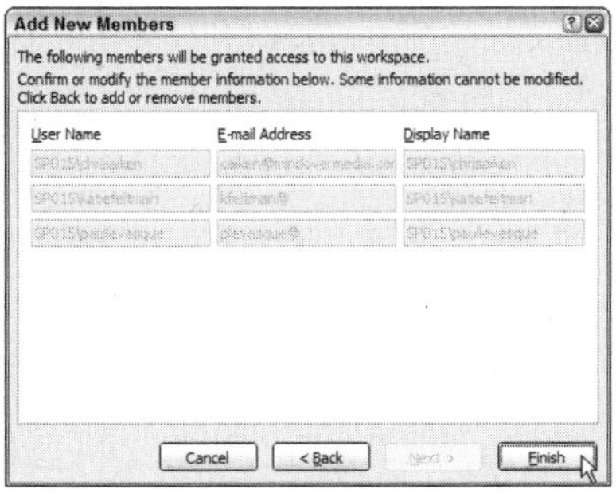

Figure 12-3:
Verifying the team members you're adding to the document workspace in the second Add New Members dialog box.

7. Click the OK button in the Add New Members alert dialog box.

Excel opens a new e-mail message in Outlook 2007 similar to the one shown in Figure 12-4. This message lets each team member know that he's been granted access to your document workspace. It also gives each member a live link to the document workspace and lets him know the permission level he has. You can then customize this e-mail message with your own comments and directives, if you wish, before you send it.

8. (Optional) Customize the message with any of your own comments or instructions that you want your team members to have as part of the initial message inviting them to visit the document workspace.

9. Click the Send button.

Outlook sends the e-mail message to each team member. Windows then closes Outlook and returns to Excel, where the Document Management pane now displays the names of all the team members you just added.

The Document Management pane divides the team members added to the document workspace into two camps: Online and Not Online. Further, should any of the currently not-online team members suddenly go online with Windows Instant Messenger or Office Communicator, this change in status is indicated in the list of display names in the Document Management pane: A color is added to the otherwise transparent ball (called the Presence icon) that appears in front of the person's name. You can chat with that team member directly by using Instant Messenger.

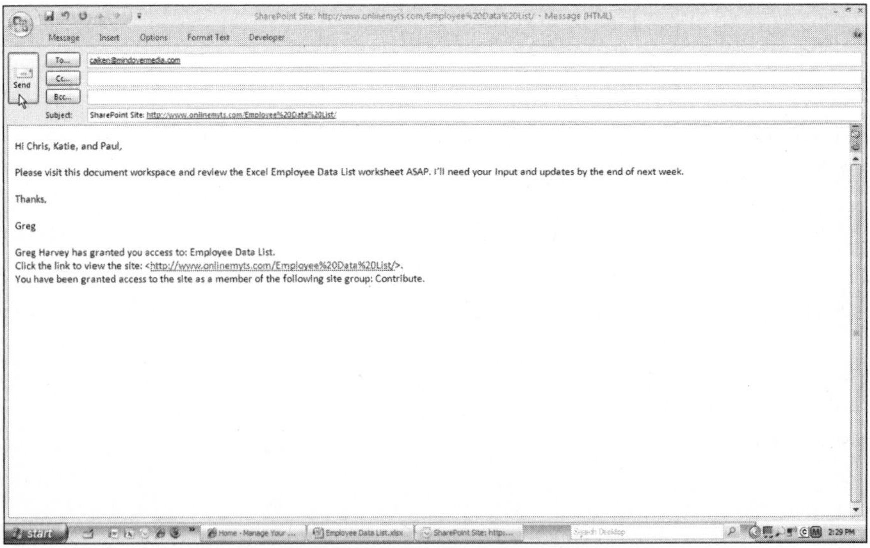

Figure 12-4:
Reviewing and editing the e-mail message before sending it to all new members of the document workspace.

Assigning editing tasks to members of the document workspace

Many times, after adding your team members to a new document workspace, you want to assign them specific tasks with appropriate milestones and deadlines. You can do this in the Office application that you use to create a new document workspace and to edit the documents you place there. Simply follow these steps:

1. **Open the document in its native Office application and then click the Tasks button in the Document Management pane.**

   To ensure that the Document Management pane automatically opens each time you open a document in its native Office program, click the Options link in the pane. Next select the check box called The Document Is Part of a Workspace or SharePoint Site that appears at the top of the Service Options dialog box under the Show the Document Management Pane at Startup When heading. Click OK.

   When you click the Tasks button in the Document Management pane, the Office program displays all the tasks currently assigned. This pane also contains links to add a new task, set up e-mail alerts, and review work-flow tasks (see Chapter 10) associated with the document workspace.

2. **Click the Add New Task link in the Document Management pane.**

   The Office program opens the Task dialog box similar to the one shown in Figure 12-5. Here, you specify a title for the task, its status, its priority, the team member to whom the task is to be assigned, a description, and a due date.

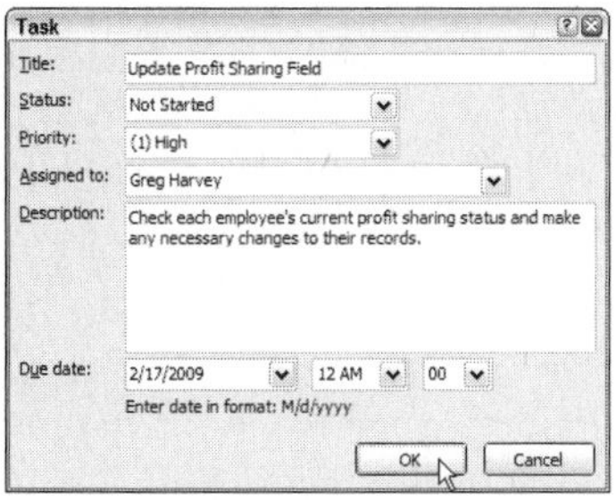

Figure 12-5:
Specifying
a new
document
workspace
task for
a team
member to
complete.

3. **In the Task dialog box, enter a title for the task, select the team member to whom the task is assigned, enter a description of the task, and select its due date and time in the appropriate fields.**

   By default, the status of a new task is Not Started and its priority is Normal. You can modify either or both of these settings if the task is already underway and needs a higher priority level.

4. **(Optional) To elevate the status or priority of a new task, select the appropriate option in the Status or Priority drop-down list box.**

5. **Click the OK button.**

   The Office 2007 application program adds the new task to its Document Management pane. To send out an alert to yourself as well as to the person to whom you've assigned the task, click the Alert Me About Tasks link in the Document Management pane and then select the appropriate settings in the New Alert page that appears on the SharePoint site before you click OK.

Resolving editing conflicts and deciding which changes to save

The beauty of using a SharePoint document workspace to edit an Office document is that different team members can all be working on local copies of the document saved to the hard disks on their own computers at the same time. However, if a team member attempts to save his changes to the workspace copy and these changes conflict with changes that some other team member has made to that copy, he then needs to resolve the conflicts by deciding which version of the document to save on the document workspace.

Note that when a team member opens the Office document from the SharePoint document workspace and then saves the document locally on the hard disk of his computer, the Office application displays an alert dialog box asking him if he wants to be able to update the workspace copy of the document with the changes he makes on his local copy.

After the team member clicks the Yes button in this alert dialog box, if there are conflicts between the version of the document on his computer and the copy on the document workspace, the Status in the Document Management pane contains a message telling him that his changes conflict with those made to the workspace copy. When the user clicks the Document Updates link that appears beneath this message in the Document Management pane, the Office application opens a Document Updates pane to its immediate right (see Figure 12-6).

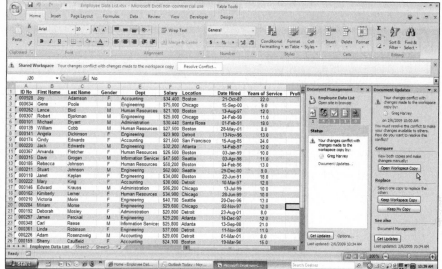

Figure 12-6:
Resolving
editing
conflicts
using the
options
in the
Document
Updates
pane.

The team member can then click the Open Workspace Copy button in the Document Updates pane to open the copy of the document in the workspace on the SharePoint site so that he can directly compare the edits made in this version on the server to those that he's made to the document on his local computer.

When he has determined which copy of the document needs to be saved (both on the workspace and on his computer), he clicks either the Keep Workspace Copy button to abandon his changes in favor of those on the workspace, or the Keep My Copy button to overwrite the server copy with his local changes. The Office application then displays an alert dialog box that reiterates which copy of the document is going to replace the other. He must click the Yes button to have the changes saved and the server and local copies synchronized.

After the Office application saves the selected version and synchronizes the server and local copies, the Document Updates pane contains only a View Previous Copy button that you can click to open the earlier version that didn't get synchronized. In addition, the Status information displayed in the application's Document Management pane now indicates that the document is up-to-date.

Saving Documents Directly on the SharePoint Site

If you're anything like me, you do almost all your writing and a good deal of the composing of your lists in Microsoft Word documents. If your office uses Word 2007, you'll find it a snap to publish these Word documents to your SharePoint site (without having to do anything with your Web browser).

To save a copy of the document you're editing in Word 2007 directly on the SharePoint site, simply use the program's Save As command (click the Office button and then select the Save As option or press F12). Word then opens the Save As dialog box, where you replace the suggested filename in its File Name text box with the URL address of your SharePoint site before you click the Save button.

Word then connects to your SharePoint site (on some systems, after prompting you for your User Name and Password if the site is hosted) and displays its Site Content page showing all its document libraries, sites, and workspaces in the Save As dialog box (as shown in Figure 12-7). You then select the SharePoint document library, site, or workspace in which to save the Word document by double-clicking its icon, or by clicking the item and then clicking the Open button. When you click the Save button after selecting the document library, site, or workspace, Word saves a copy of the document directly on the SharePoint server.

Figure 12-7:
Saving
a Word
document
directly
on the
SharePoint
site using
the Save As
command.

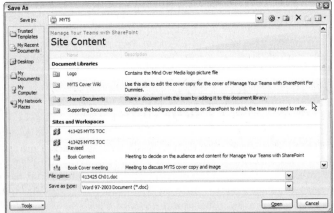

Remember that you can use this very same Save As method in other Office applications such as Excel and PowerPoint to save their native documents directly to your SharePoint site.

Excel 2007 and SharePoint Integration

Just as Word gives you mastery over the written word, Excel gives you mastery over all kinds of numerical data (especially financial and statistical data). For this reason, many SharePoint users need to be able to supply their sites with data entered into particular Excel spreadsheets (technically known as *worksheets*).

Excel 2007 provides two methods for bringing its spreadsheet data to your SharePoint site:

- ✔ **Export** the data from an Excel worksheet by creating a new custom SharePoint list.
- ✔ **Import** the data from an Excel worksheet into a new custom list that you create in SharePoint.

 Keep in mind that importing and exporting Excel worksheet data to a SharePoint site list does not create any kind of dynamic link between the original worksheet and the new list. These kinds of imports and exports are much more like making a static copy of the data. Therefore, when you update the data in the worksheet, you must remember to also manually update the custom list by repeating the import or export. Also, remember that you must manually add links to the custom lists created from exporting or importing Excel worksheet data to the SharePoint site's Quick Launch.

Exporting Excel 2007 worksheet data to a SharePoint list

To export a table of worksheet data into a SharePoint list, follow these steps:

1. **Open the worksheet in Excel 2007 and then select the first cell in the table of worksheet data that you want to export (this should be the cell that contains the first column heading).**

   Next, you need to convert the cell range containing the data (including the row of column headings at the top) into a bona fide worksheet table.

2. **Click the Format as Table button in the Styles group of the Home tab on the Ribbon.**

   Excel selects all the cells that it thinks constitutes the worksheet table, while at the same time displaying the Format As Table dialog box that shows the range's address in its text box.

3. **If necessary, adjust the cell selection to include all the cells you want to export by clicking and dragging through them in the worksheet itself, and then click OK.**

   Excel applies one of its table style formats to the cell selection. Drop-down buttons appear on the right side of the cells in the top row with the table's column headings.

4. **Click the Export button in the External Table Data group and then click the Export Table to SharePoint List option on its drop-down menu.**

   The Export Table to SharePoint List – Step 1 of 2 dialog box (similar to the one shown in Figure 12-8) appears.

5. **Enter the URL address of your SharePoint site in the Address text box and then press Tab twice.**

   The first time you press Tab, Excel advances the cursor to the Create a Read-Only Connection to the New SharePoint List check box. The second time you press Tab, Excel advances the cursor to the Name text box.

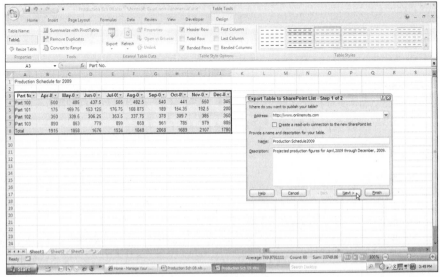

Figure 12-8:
Exporting
a work-
sheet table
to a new
SharePoint
list.

6. **Type a name for the new SharePoint list in the Name text box and then press Tab.**

   Excel advances the cursor to the Description text box.

7. **Type a description of the new list and then click the Next button.**

   Excel displays the Export Table to SharePoint List – Step 2 of 2 dialog box (similar to the one shown in Figure 12-9), displaying the data type (Text, Number, and so on) that new SharePoint list will have for each column in the table of worksheet data.

8. **Check that the data types are correct for each column of the worksheet table and then click Finish.**

   Note that if a column doesn't have the correct data type associated with it, you need to click the Cancel button in the dialog box and then apply a Number or text format to the range of cells in that column of the table that tells Excel what type of data it contains. Select the range again, click the Export button, and click the Export Table to SharePoint List option. Then repeat the steps from Step 5 on.

   After you click Finish, Excel displays a Windows SharePoint Services alert dialog box that indicates that the table was successfully exported and that it contains a direct link to the new list on the SharePoint site.

9. **Click the link to the new SharePoint list to visit the site and review it, or click the OK button to complete the export.**

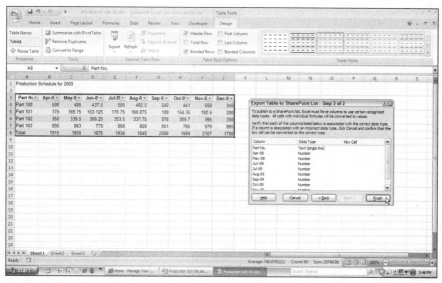

Figure 12-9:
Verifying the data type of each column in the new SharePoint list before exporting the data.

If you click the link to the list, the page with the custom list appears in the Datasheet view (see Figure 12-10). If you click the OK button, Excel closes the dialog box and you can then later open the new list by selecting its link in the List section of the SharePoint site's All Site Content page.

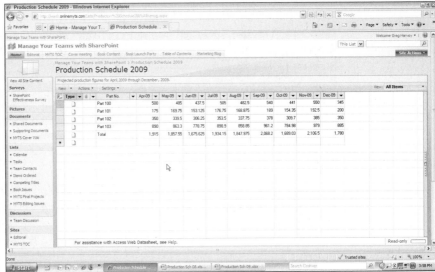

Figure 12-10: Displaying the new SharePoint custom list created from the exported table of Excel worksheet data.

Importing Excel worksheet data into a SharePoint list

The other method for getting Excel worksheet data into a new custom list is by importing the cell range or table into SharePoint. To do this, follow these steps:

1. **Open the subsite in SharePoint where you want to add the new list and then click the View All Site Content link in its Quick Launch.**

   SharePoint opens the All Site Content page.

2. **Click the Create button at the top of the All Site Content page.**

   SharePoint opens the Create page.

3. **Click the Import Spreadsheet link at the bottom of the Custom Lists column.**

SharePoint opens a New page containing a Name and Description and an Import from Spreadsheet section.

4. **Type a name for the new list in the Name text box and then press Tab.**

   SharePoint moves the cursor to the Description text box.

5. **Type a description for the new list and then press Tab.**

   SharePoint moves the cursor to the File Location text box.

6. **Click the Browse button, select the Excel workbook file that contains the data you want to import in the Choose File to Upload dialog box, and then click the Open button.**

   SharePoint closes the Choose File to Upload dialog box and inserts the path to the Excel workbook file into the File Location text box.

7. **Click the Import button.**

   SharePoint opens the workbook file in Excel 2007, displaying the data in its first worksheet along with the Import to Windows SharePoint Services List dialog box (see Figure 12-11). This dialog box contains two drop-down list boxes: Range Type (where you choose between the default Table Range option and the Range of Cells and Named Range options) and Select Range (where you actually indicate the cells whose data are to be imported).

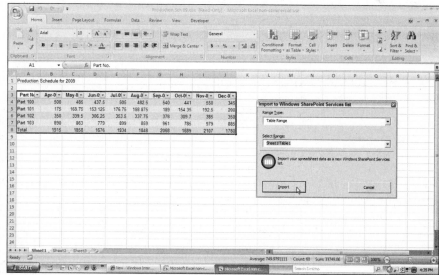

Figure 12-11:
Selecting the range of Excel worksheet data to import into the new SharePoint custom list.

8. **Select the appropriate option: Range of Cells (if the range hasn't been formatted as a worksheet table) or Named Range (if you've given the range a formal name in Excel).**

9. **If you selected Table Range or Named Range as the table type, select the name of the table or range using the drop-down button attached to the Select Range drop-down list box. If the range type is Range of Cells, click the Select Range drop-down list box and then drag through the cells in the worksheet to have the range address appear in this box.**

   As soon as you select the range of the worksheet data to import, the Import button becomes active and available.

10. **Click the Import button.**

    SharePoint creates a new custom list and then imports this data into a new list (similar to the one shown in Figure 12-12). Note that data in this list appears in the Standard view (as opposed to the Datasheet view used when you export worksheet data to a SharePoint list as shown earlier in Figure 12-10).

Figure 12-12:
A new SharePoint custom list created from the imported Excel worksheet data.

Chapter 13

Customizing Your SharePoint Site with Office SharePoint Designer 2007

● ●

In This Chapter

▶ Becoming familiar with the Office SharePoint Designer 2007 interface and environment

▶ Opening your SharePoint site in SharePoint Designer

▶ Creating a custom SharePoint workflow with Workflow Designer

● ●

*O*ffice SharePoint Designer 2007, the subject of this chapter, is a stand-alone Web designing program that Microsoft developed specifically for working with SharePoint sites. As you're very much aware if you've had the opportunity to peruse the other earlier chapters of this book, SharePoint Designer is not necessary for performing routine SharePoint customization and maintenance. In fact, the vast majority of SharePoint knowledge workers get along perfectly fine without the program when it comes to tailoring their SharePoint sites for the particular needs of the teams they supervise and collaborate with.

Nevertheless, Office SharePoint Designer 2007 does have its uses, even for the nonprogrammer with no intention of ever trying his hand at XML-driven Web solutions. SharePoint Designer's most notable use (and the real reason for including this chapter) is its very powerful Workflow Designer. This wizard enables even the most code-phobic people to develop custom workflows for a SharePoint site to supplement the default three-state workflow template, which is the only one available to you if you're using Windows SharePoint Services without MOSS 2007. (See Chapter 10 for details about the three-state workflow template.)

As you find out in this chapter, the Workflow Designer in Office SharePoint Designer takes you through each of the steps necessary to define a workflow for a particular list or library on your SharePoint site.

Getting Familiar with the Office SharePoint Designer 2007 Interface

Figure 13-1 shows you the basic Office SharePoint Designer 2007 program window as it appears when you first launch the application for customizing your SharePoint site on your local computer.

Folder List

Common Toolbar   Web Page/Site Tab   Toolbox

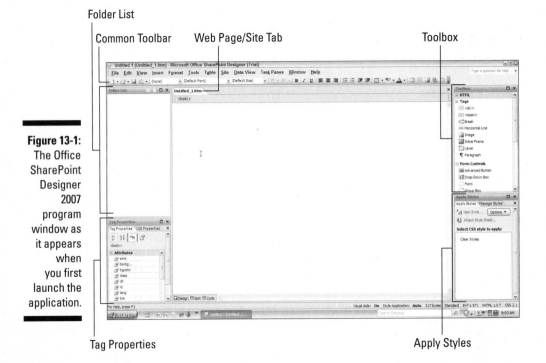

Figure 13-1: The Office SharePoint Designer 2007 program window as it appears when you first launch the application.

Tag Properties   Apply Styles

Microsoft considers Microsoft Office SharePoint Designer 2007 to be an integral part of its Office 2007 suite of programs, even though it's not automatically included in the various versions of the Microsoft Office suite (along with Word, Excel, Outlook, and the rest). For this reason, you find the menu option for starting this application on the same All Programs➪Microsoft Office submenu that contains Microsoft Word, Microsoft Excel, and so forth.

As shown in Figure 13-1, besides its pull-down menus and single Common toolbar at the top, for the most part, the SharePoint Designer window consists of different types of panes. The Folder List pane that you use to navigate the folders containing the various parts of your SharePoint site is on the upper-left side. Below it is the Tag Properties pane, which is used to display the properties of the Web page that appears in the pane in the center when a particular SharePoint page is selected.

On the right side of the central pane with its tab, you find the Toolbox pane, which enables you to select various HTML tags and forms controls when customizing a Web page. Beneath that pane, you find the Apply Styles pane, which enables you to format the various elements that appear on the Web page you're customizing using CSS (Cascading Style Sheets) styles.

Viewing Your SharePoint Site's Structure in SharePoint Designer

To be able to customize elements of your SharePoint site using SharePoint Designer 2007, you first need to open the site in the program. To do this, select Open Site from the Open drop-down list on the Common toolbar or choose File➪Open Site.

SharePoint Designer then displays an Open Site dialog box similar to the one shown in Figure 13-2. Type the URL address of your SharePoint site in the Site Name text box and then click the Open button.

Figure 13-2:
Opening your SharePoint site in SharePoint Designer.

After you're prompted to provide your username and password (if you're not already logged on to your site and it's hosted by a third-party service provider), SharePoint Designer connects to your SharePoint site. The Folder

List pane on the left displays all the subfolders currently in the site, and the central pane contains a Web Site tab that contains a table showing details of this folder structure (see Figure 13-3).

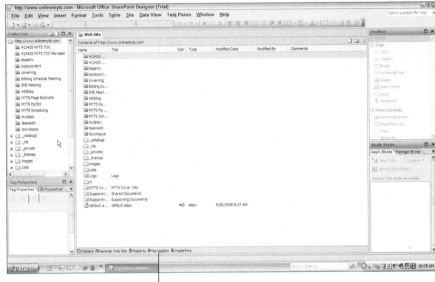

Navigation button

Figure 13-3: My SharePoint site after opening it in SharePoint Designer.

You can then switch the view of the site on the Web Site tab from its default Folders view to Navigation view (as shown in Figure 13-4) by clicking the Navigation button that appears in the row at the bottom below the Web Site tab.

The Navigation view shows the organizational structure of your SharePoint site in a diagram form that graphically depicts the connection between its various elements. In this view, you can see the relationship of all subsites, lists, libraries, and other SharePoint components to each other and all the components that are directly beneath them. This graphic view can help you visualize the hierarchy that exists between the various folders and pages and how they must be navigated on the actual SharePoint site.

When viewing your SharePoint site in Navigation view, you can narrow the hierarchical diagram displayed in the Web Site tab by right-clicking a SharePoint icon and then clicking the View Subtree Only option on the shortcut menu that appears. SharePoint Designer then temporarily removes all icons except for those that are below the one you right-clicked. To re-expand the Navigation view to once again include all the site components, you just have to click the View All button that appears as a broken arrow pointing up and to the right immediately above the Sites icon.

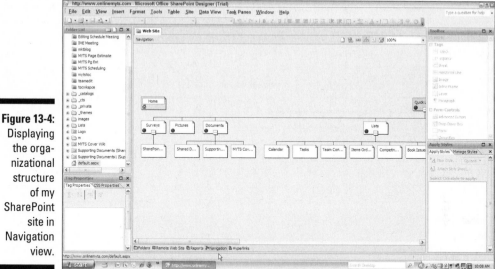

Figure 13-4:
Displaying
the orga-
nizational
structure
of my
SharePoint
site in
Navigation
view.

Creating a Custom Workflow with the Workflow Designer

One of the niftiest features of Office SharePoint Designer 2007 is its Workflow Designer. This wizard enables you to create your own custom workflows for particular Tasks and Issue Tracking lists on your SharePoint site in addition to those workflows based on the default three-state workflow provided by SharePoint Services 3.0 (see Chapter 10) and the document-processing related workflow templates offered by MOSS 2007.

To create a custom workflow in SharePoint Designer, open the SharePoint site and follow these steps:

1. **Choose File⇨New⇨Workflow.**

   SharePoint Designer opens the Workflow Designer – Workflow 1 dialog box called Define Your New Workflow, similar to the one shown in Figure 13-5. Here, you specify a name for the new workflow, associate the workflow with a particular SharePoint list, and specify whether the workflow is to begin manually or automatically.

2. **Type a name for the new custom workflow in the Give a Name to This Workflow text box and then press Tab.**

   SharePoint Designer selects the drop-down list called What SharePoint List Should This Workflow Be Attached To.

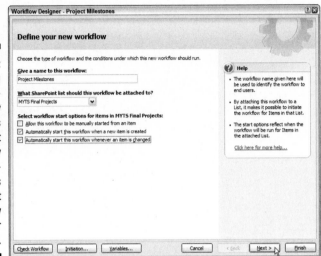

Figure 13-5:
Specifying
the work-
flow
name, its
SharePoint
list, and how
the work-
flow starts
in the first
Workflow
Designer
dialog box.

3. **Select the Tasks or Issue Tracking list with which the new workflow is to be associated on its drop-down list.**

   By default, SharePoint Designer selects the Allow This Workflow to Be Manually Started from an Item check box as its sole method for starting the new workflow. If you want SharePoint to automatically start the workflow when a new item in the associated list is created, you need to select the Automatically Start This Workflow When a New Item Is Created check box. If you want SharePoint to automatically start the workflow when a new item in the associated list is modified, you need to select the Automatically Start This Workflow Whenever an Item Is Changed check box.

4. **(Optional) To automate the starting of the workflow, click the appropriate Automatically Start check box (or boxes).**

5. **Click the Next button at the bottom of the Define Your New Workflow dialog box.**

   SharePoint Designer opens the Step 1 dialog box (similar to the one shown in Figure 13-6). Here, you specify the conditions and the subsequent actions that ensue when the first condition is met.

   For this sample workflow, I want to set up a condition whereby the workflow automatically sends out warning e-mail messages to team members whose tasks are in progress and are less than 50 percent complete. In order to set up the condition, I compare the current entries in the list's Tasks Status field and in the % Complete field. And if the status is not Completed and the % Complete is less than 50, the condition is met and workflow initiates the action that I associate with it.

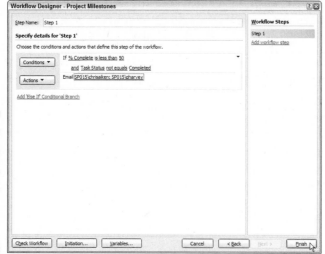

Figure 13-6:
The condi-
tions and
actions for
the new
workflow in
the Step 1
dialog box.

6. **Click the Conditions drop-down button and then click Compare Field option at the top of the drop-down menu.**

   SharePoint Designer inserts the generic condition If *field* equals *value* into the area to the immediate right of the Conditions button.

7. **Click the *field* link and then click the % Complete option in the drop-down list.**

   The condition now reads, If % Complete equals *value*.

8. **Click the *equals* link and then click Is Less Than on the drop-down menu.**

   The condition now reads, If % Complete is less than *value*.

9. **Click the *value* link and then type 50 in the text box that appears and press Enter.**

   The condition now reads, If % Complete is less than 50.

10. **Click the Conditions drop-down button and then click Compare Field option at the top of the drop-down menu.**

    SharePoint Designer inserts a second line for the condition that reads, And *field* equals *value*.

11. **Replace *field* with Task Status, *equals* with not equals, and *value* with Completed in the second line of the condition.**

    The second line of the condition now reads, And Task Status not equals Completed.

12. **Click the Actions drop-down button and then click the Send an E-Mail option at the top of its drop-down menu.**

    SharePoint Designer inserts the E-Mail *this message* action to the immediate right of the Actions button.

13. **Click the link attached to *this message* in the Actions line.**

    SharePoint Designer opens the Define E-Mail Message dialog box. Here, you specify the recipients of the message, its subject, and the actual message you want to send.

14. **Specify the recipients (these can be individual team members or user groups), the subject of the e-mail, and the body of the message in the appropriate text boxes and list box and then click OK.**

    Note that you can use the Add Lookup Body button to insert actual values from particular fields in the SharePoint list (usually those that trigger the sending of the e-mail message) into the body of the message. SharePoint then substitutes the actual value in the list for the field that appears in the body of the e-mail message.

    After you click OK, SharePoint Designer closes the Define E-Mail Message dialog box and returns you to the Step 1 dialog box. Here, you can review your condition and actions and also add another Else IF branch to it that specifies what actions the workflow is to take when the initial condition is not met.

15. **After you finish adding all the conditions and related actions for the new workflow, click the Check Workflow button to verify that workflow is complete before you click the Finish button.**

    SharePoint Designer saves the workflow and closes the Step 1 dialog box of the Workflow Designer. If you're finished using Office SharePoint Designer 2007, you can close the program and return to the list to which the custom workflow is associated on your SharePoint site.

If you specify that a custom workflow created with Office SharePoint Designer 2007 is to be started manually, you need to remember to open the associated list on the SharePoint site, click Workflow on the drop-down menu attached to one of the items in the list, and then click the link to the workflow's name in the Start a New Workflow section at the top of the Workflows page.

Chapter 14

Using InfoPath 2007 with SharePoint

. . . .

In This Chapter

▶ Using InfoPath 2007 to create standard forms for your SharePoint site

▶ Customizing InfoPath forms and publishing them to a SharePoint form library

▶ Creating a form library on your SharePoint site

▶ Creating content types for your forms

▶ Adding content types to your SharePoint form libraries

. . . .

*I*n this chapter, you find out how to use Microsoft Office InfoPath 2007 — the electronic forms application in the Microsoft Office suite of programs — to customize the forms that your teams need to have available to them on your SharePoint site. You also find out how to then publish these forms to special form libraries on the site. Here, your team members can fill out these forms, and you can easily review and collect them.

You also find out how to use SharePoint's content types to create form templates for all the standard forms that are used in all the subsites all over the entire SharePoint site. By creating a special content type for these standard forms, you make it easy to attach the forms to any form library you set up anywhere on the SharePoint site.

Using InfoPath 2007 with SharePoint

InfoPath provides a great tool for people who depend upon electronic forms for gathering and compiling all the types of information vital to their work. (There's even a free trial version that you can download from the Microsoft Office Online Web site.) InfoPath makes it a snap to customize standard electronic forms you need, such as expense reports, meeting agendas, and the like. You can customize your forms so that they contain just the fields you need and use the same layout and format as the paper forms upon which they're based.

If you're a SharePoint team leader who needs to populate your SharePoint site with standardized electronic forms that your team members can use, you'll find using InfoPath particularly beneficial. This is because you can use InfoPath not only to customize the forms you need but also to publish them directly to a new form library on your SharePoint site.

Customizing form templates in InfoPath 2007

When you first launch InfoPath 2007, the Getting Started dialog box shown in Figure 14-1 appears. You can then customize one of its sample forms, design a form template from scratch, or open a form that you've been working on for further editing.

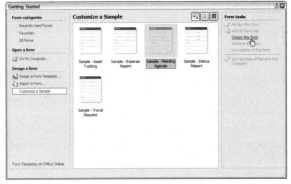

Figure 14-1:
Select a
form tem-
plate to
customize in
the Getting
Started
dialog box.

Microsoft considers Microsoft Office InfoPath 2007 to be a part of its Office 2007 suite of programs (even though it's not actually bundled as part of any of the versions of the Office 2007 suite). For this reason, you find the Microsoft Office InfoPath 2007 menu option for starting this application program on the same All Programs➪Microsoft Office submenu that contains Microsoft Word, Microsoft Excel, and so forth.

To customize one of the InfoPath sample form templates, click its icon in the Customize a Sample area and then click the Design This Form link that appears in the pane on the right side of the Getting Started dialog box. InfoPath then opens a copy of the form template in its program window (see Figure 14-2), and you can use its many features to customize its look, layout, and contents as necessary.

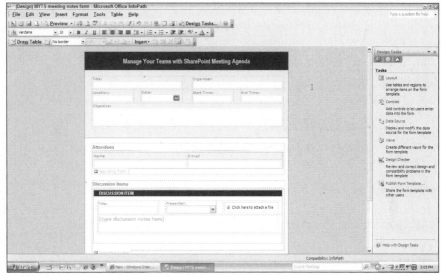

Figure 14-2:
I decided to
customize
the Meeting
Agenda
form tem-
plate for
use on my
SharePoint
site.

Publishing a customized InfoPath form to a SharePoint form library

After you save your changes to a customized InfoPath form template, you're
ready to publish the template to your SharePoint site. As part of this procedure, you can actually create a new form library on the site. All you have to
do is follow these steps:

1. **Choose File⇨Publish from the InfoPath main menu.**

   InfoPath opens the first dialog box of its Publishing Wizard, as shown
   in Figure 14-3. Here you indicate where you want to publish the customized form template. By default, InfoPath publishes the template to a
   SharePoint server.

2. **With the default To a SharePoint Server with or without InfoPath
   Forms Services radio button selected in the first Publishing Wizard
   dialog box, click the Next button.**

   InfoPath opens the second dialog box of the Publishing Wizard (shown
   in Figure 14-4), where you designate the URL address of the SharePoint
   site to which the customized form is being published.

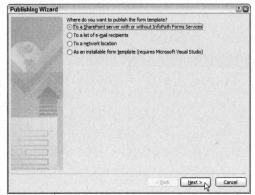

Figure 14-3:
Publish a
customized
form to your
SharePoint
site.

Figure 14-4:
Indicate the
URL address
of the
SharePoint
site to
which the
customized
form
template
is to be
published.

3. **Type the URL address of your SharePoint site in the Location text box in the second Publishing Wizard dialog box and then click Next.**

   InfoPath logs you into your SharePoint site (after prompting you for your username and password on a hosted site) and displays the third dialog box of its Publishing Wizard (shown in Figure 14-5). Here, you decide between creating a new document library (the default choice) on your SharePoint site and creating a new content type for the form on your SharePoint site. (See "Creating a content type for a form in InfoPath 2007," later in this chapter, for details on your choices here.)

Figure 14-5:
Indicate that
the form is
to be pub-
lished to a
SharePoint
document
library.

4. **With the Document Library radio button selected in the third Publishing Wizard dialog box, click Next.**

   InfoPath connects you to your SharePoint site and displays a list of all the document libraries currently on your SharePoint site in the fourth dialog box of the Publishing Wizard (shown in Figure 14-6). By default, InfoPath selects the Create a New Document Library radio button to create a new document library for the customized form.

   Note that if you had already saved the form template in the SharePoint form library and you had made some changes to it in InfoPath and then wanted to save this updated template that form library, you'd select the Update This Form Template in an Existing Document Library radio button and then click the name of the library in the Document Library to Update list box before you click Next.

Figure 14-6:
Indicate
that a new
document
library is
to be
created
for the
customized
InfoPath
form
template.

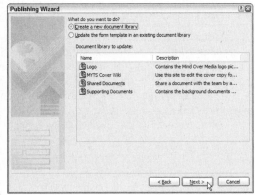

5. **With the Create a New Document Library radio button selected in the fourth Publishing Wizard dialog box, click the Next button.**

   InfoPath opens the fifth dialog box of the Publishing Wizard (shown in Figure 14-7), where you give the new document library a name and description.

Figure 14-7: Give the new document library a name and description.

6. **Type a name for the new document library in the Name text box. Press Tab and type a short description of the new library in the Description text box of the Publishing Wizard. Then click Next.**

   InfoPath opens the sixth dialog box of the Publishing Wizard (shown in Figure 14-8) which displays all the columns from the customized form template that will appear in the list displayed in the new SharePoint document library. You can modify these default list columns by adding to them, removing some of them, and/or renaming them.

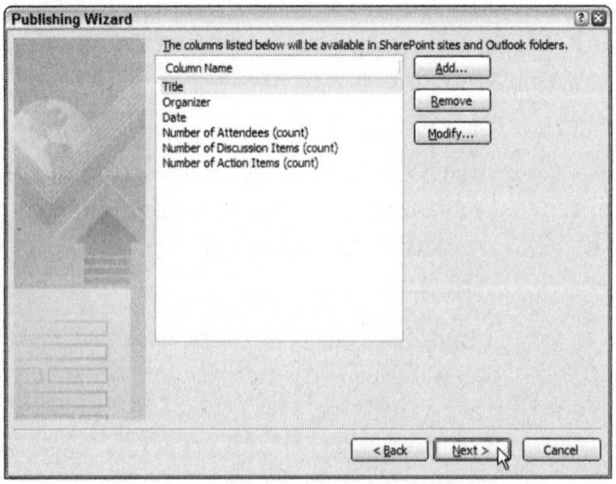

Figure 14-8: Select the columns to be displayed in the list that will appear in the new form library.

7. **After making any desired modifications to the columns that appear in the new document library in the sixth dialog box of the Publishing Wizard, click the Next button.**

   InfoPath displays the seventh dialog box of the Publishing Wizard (similar to the one shown in Figure 14-9). Here, you verify the location of your SharePoint site and its server type as well as the name of the new document library that will be created for your customized InfoPath form template.

Figure 14-9:
Verify the SharePoint site and document library information before publishing the InfoPath form template to it.

8. **After you verify the SharePoint site and document library information displayed in the seventh dialog box of the Publishing Wizard, click the Publish button.**

   InfoPath publishes the form template to the new document library that SharePoint creates for it, and the program displays the final Publishing Wizard dialog box (shown in Figure 14-10). This dialog box indicates that your form template was successfully published. It also gives you an opportunity to e-mail the customized form to your team members and open its new document library on the SharePoint site before you close the InfoPath Publishing Wizard.

9. **(Optional) Select the Send the Form to E-Mail Recipients check box if you want to e-mail the form to your fellow team members, and/or select the Open This Document Library check box to open the new form library on your SharePoint site.**

   If you select the Send the Form to E-Mail Recipients check box, InfoPath opens a new e-mail message with the customized form in the body of the message. You can then select your team members as recipients in the To:, Cc: and Bcc: fields, fill in the Subject line field, and send the form in the message by clicking the Send button.

Figure 14-10:
Indicate
whether or
not to e-mail
the custom-
ized form to
your team
members
and open
the new
document
library
on the
SharePoint
site.

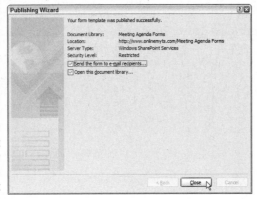

If you select the Open This Document Library check box, InfoPath opens the new document library — now a form library, for all intents and purposes — in your SharePoint site. This library contains an empty list that you can then add to. You'll also notice that SharePoint has automatically added a link to the new form library in the Documents section of the site's Quick Launch.

10. Click the Close button.

After you publish an InfoPath form to your new form library, you and your fellow team members can fill out forms by choosing New Document from the library's New drop-down menu. SharePoint then opens a fill-in version of the customized form in InfoPath. After you finish filling in the fields of this form, click the Submit button on the InfoPath Standard toolbar and then save the form; its field entries appear in the appropriate columns of the form library.

Figure 14-11 shows you my SharePoint form library after adding a couple of electronic forms using its template. Note that I open each blank form in SharePoint by selecting the Form option on the library's New drop-down menu. Doing this automatically launches InfoPath and opens the blank form in it where I fill in its fields. After submitting and saving the forms in InfoPath, they are then automatically added to the list in my form library when I return to SharePoint.

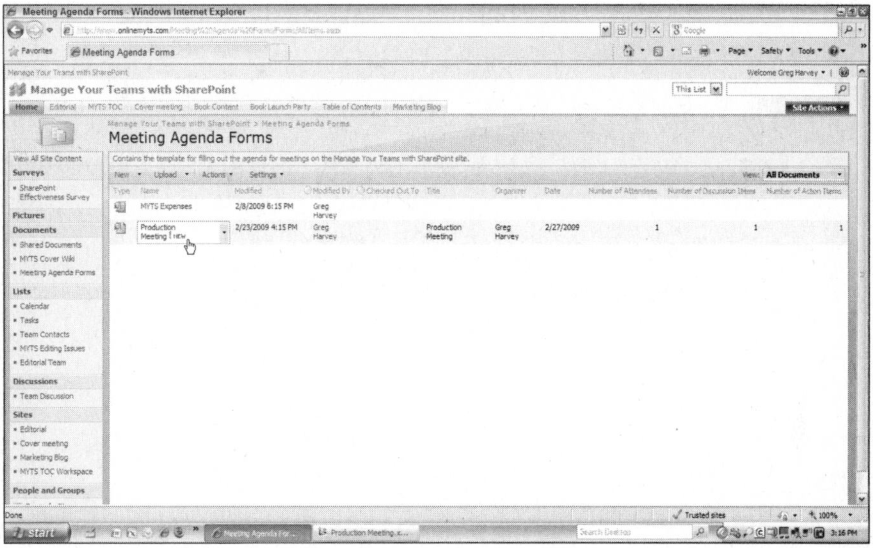

Figure 14-11:
Here's
my new
SharePoint
form library
after I
added a
couple of
forms I
filled out
in InfoPath
that were
then added
to its list.

Using Content Types in SharePoint Form Libraries

Content types in SharePoint 2007 are collections of customized settings that can then be used to add new items to any list or document library throughout the entire SharePoint site. They're particularly useful because once you've defined a new content type and associated it with a particular SharePoint subsite, list, or document library, you and your team members can use it to create new items simply by choosing its option from the site's, list's, or document library's New drop-down menu.

Creating a content type for a form in InfoPath 2007

InfoPath 2007 makes it a snap to create a new content type for a particular form template. All you do is customize the form template in InfoPath and then publish it as you would a regular form template, using the Publishing Wizard as outlined in the section "Publishing customized InfoPath forms to a new SharePoint form library" earlier in this chapter. The only difference lies in how you deal with the third screen of the Publishing Wizard (refer to Figure 14-5). Instead of accepting the default of creating a new document library on your SharePoint site, you want to choose the Content Type option:

1. **Select the Site Content Type (Advanced) radio button in the third dialog box of the InfoPath Publishing Wizard and then click Next.**

   InfoPath displays a fourth dialog box of the Publishing Wizard (shown in Figure 14-12), which lets you choose between creating a new content type and updating an existing one.

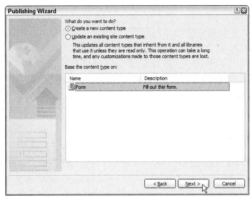

Figure 14-12: Indicate whether to create a new content type or update an existing one.

2. **With the default Create a New Content Type radio button selected in the fourth dialog box of the Publishing Wizard, click Next.**

   SharePoint displays a fifth dialog of the Publishing Wizard (shown in Figure 14-13) where you name the content type and give it a description.

3. **Type a name for the content type in the Name text box and then type a description of the function of the content type in the Description list box and click Next.**

   InfoPath displays a sixth dialog box of the Publishing Wizard (shown in Figure 14-14), where you specify the SharePoint location and filename for the new content type template you're creating.

4. **Click the Browse button, select the SharePoint document library where the template file is to be saved in the Site Content list box (see Figure 14-15), and then type the new filename in the File Name text box. Click Save.**

   InfoPath displays the dialog box of the Publishing Wizard (shown in Figure 14-16) where you add the fields you want in the new form content type template.

Figure 14-13:
Give the new content type a name and description.

Figure 14-14:
Specify the filename and location for the new content type template.

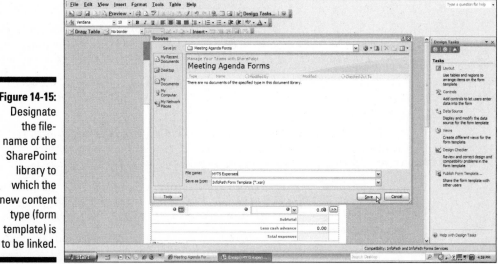

Figure 14-15:
Designate the file-name of the SharePoint library to which the new content type (form template) is to be linked.

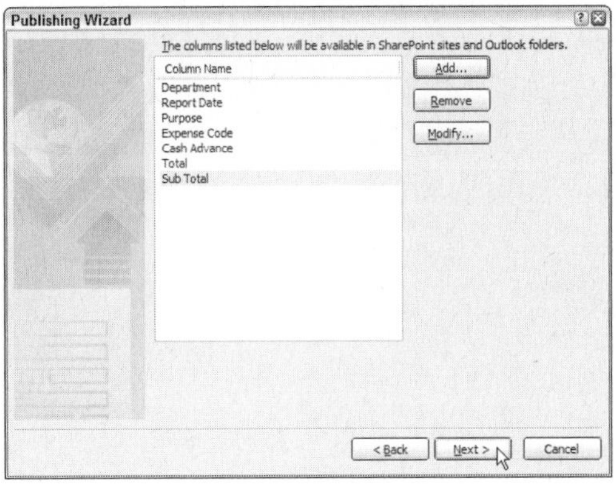

Figure 14-16:
Add the
form fields
to be used
in the new
content type
template.

5. **Click the Add button and then select the fields you want in the new content type in the Select a Field or Group dialog box. When you finish adding the fields, click the OK button to close this dialog box and then click the Next button in the Publishing Wizard.**

   InfoPath displays the dialog box of the Publishing Wizard (shown in Figure 14-17) where you verify the template information before publishing it to the SharePoint site.

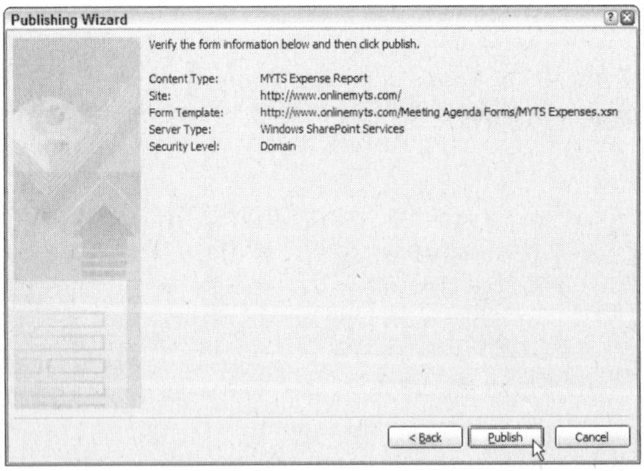

Figure 14-17:
Verify
the form
template
informa-
tion before
publishing
it to the
SharePoint
site.

6. **Verify the form content type template information and then click the Publish button.**

   InfoPath saves the template to the SharePoint site. You can then click the Manage This Content Type link that now appears in the dialog box to open the template's page on your SharePoint site (see Figure 14-18) or simply click the Close button to close the Publishing Wizard and remain in InfoPath.

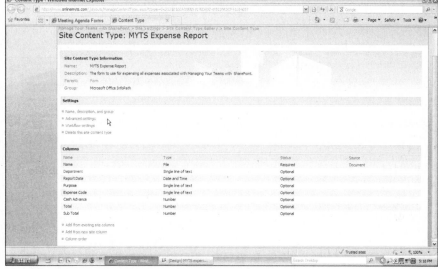

Figure 14-18:
The Site
Content
Type page
displaying
the new
form con-
tent type.

Adding a form's content type to a SharePoint form library

After defining a new form content type (as outlined in the previous section), you still need to associate this content type with the various form libraries on the SharePoint site where you want to make the form template available to your team members. To do this, follow these steps:

1. **Open the Form Library page on your SharePoint site to which you want to associate the new content type and then choose Form Library Settings from the Settings drop-down menu.**

   SharePoint opens the Customize page for your form library.

2. **Click the Advanced Settings link in the General Settings column.**

   SharePoint opens the Form Library Advanced Settings page for your form library, similar to the one shown in Figure 14-19.

3. **Select the Yes radio button under the Allow Management of Content Types question at the top right of the page and then click OK.**

   SharePoint returns you to a revised version of the Customize page for your form library, where all the content types associated with the library are now listed in a new Content Types section.

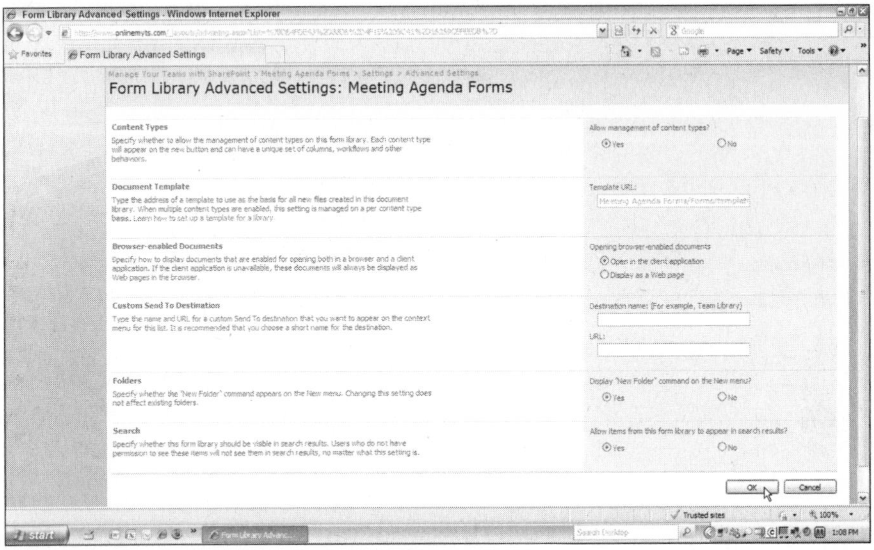

Figure 14-19:
Enable the manage-
ment of content types for the current form library.

4. **In the Content Types section of the Customize page for your form library, click the Add from Existing Content Types link.**

SharePoint opens the Add Content Types page for your form library, similar to the one shown in Figure 14-20.

Figure 14-20:
Add the content type to the current form library.

5. **Click the name of the form content type you want to add in the Available Site Content Types list box on the left side and then click the Add button to move it to the Contents Types to Add list box on the right. Then click OK.**

   SharePoint adds the selected content type to the form library and returns you to its Customize page.

6. **Click the Content Navigation Breadcrumb link with the name of your form library at the top of the Customize page.**

   SharePoint opens the Form Library page.

After you associate a custom content type with a list or document library, SharePoint adds a content type–specific option to its New drop-down menu. You and your team members can then use this menu option to add forms based on any template that you've customized in InfoPath and then defined as a SharePoint content type.

Figure 14-21 demonstrates how this works. Here, you see the MYTS Expense Report option that was added to the New drop-down menu after I associated this custom content type with the Meeting Agenda Forms library on my SharePoint site.

Figure 14-21:
The content type–specific option is added to the form library's New drop-down menu.

Creating a form library in SharePoint for your InfoPath form template

Although it's usually much more efficient to create the form library on your SharePoint site by publishing the form template from InfoPath 2007 (right after you finish customizing and saving the form template), this is not the only way to create a SharePoint form library for use with your InfoPath form templates.

You can also create the library in SharePoint as I outline in the following procedure. Just be aware that when you do create the form library in SharePoint, SharePoint links the library to a generic InfoPath form template so that when you or your team members select the New Document option from the library's New drop-down menu, SharePoint displays an Open with Form Template dialog box, where you need to designate the InfoPath form template to use. At the time you select this template, you can also select the Always Use This Form Template for This File check box if you want to make it the only form template associated with your form library.

The steps to creating a form library in SharePoint are as follows:

1. **Click the Documents link in the Quick Launch of the subsite where you want the new form library to be.**

   If you want the form library to be part of the top-level SharePoint site, open the home page.

   SharePoint opens the All Site Content page for the site using the Document Libraries filter.

2. **Click the Create button at the top of the page.**

   SharePoint opens the Create page for the current site.

3. **Click the Form Library link in the Libraries column.**

   SharePoint opens the New page similar to the one shown in Figure 14-22, where you designate the name and description of the new form library along with the Navigation, Document Version History, and Document Template settings.

4. **Type a name for the new form library in the Name text box and then press Tab.**

   SharePoint advances the cursor to the Description list box.

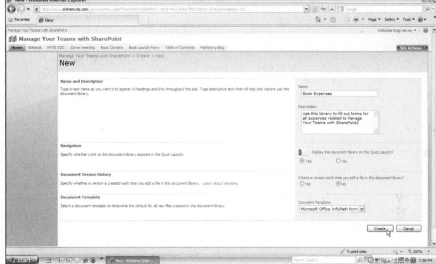

Figure 14-22:
Create a
new form
library
for your
SharePoint
site.

5. **Type a description of the new form library.**

   By default, SharePoint adds a link to the new form library on the site's
   Quick Launch but does not turn on the version history. The program
   also selects the generic Microsoft Office InfoPath Form as the default
   template for all new files added to the library.

6. **(Optional) Make any necessary changes to the Navigation, Document
   Version History, and/or Document Template settings for the new form
   library.**

7. **Click the Create button.**

   SharePoint creates the new form library and then displays its page in
   your Web browser.

After creating a new form library in your SharePoint site in this manner, if
you use InfoPath, you can then associate any form you customize with the
program with the library by publishing it to this particular library. (See
"Publishing a customized InfoPath form to a SharePoint form library," earlier
in this chapter, for details.) If you've created a content type for a form template that you want to add to the new form library, you can do so by following
the steps outlined in the immediately preceding section, "Adding a form's content type to a SharePoint form library."

Part V
The Part of Tens

The 5th Wave   By Rich Tennant

"It appears a server in Atlanta is about to go down, there's printer backup in Baltimore and an accountant in Chicago is about to make level 3 of the game 'Tomb Pirate.'"

In this part . . .

Last but never least is the Part of Tens. Here, I get the opportunity to share with you some of my tips for customizing the design of your SharePoint site to meet the particular challenges presented by your collaborative project. I also share some of my ideas on what it takes to put together top-notch teams and give them all the things they need in order to make the best use of your SharePoint site and, thus, collaborate successfully.

Chapter 15

Top Ten Tips for Designing Your SharePoint Site

In This Chapter

▶ Customizing the look and feel of your SharePoint site

▶ Creating subsites for particular teams

▶ Adding SharePoint components — including libraries, lists, and workspaces

Right out of the box (or, better yet, straight out of the IT department), a new SharePoint site is a pretty generic place. From replacing its standard Windows SharePoint Services logo on the home page and adding content to its empty default lists all the way to creating the specific SharePoint components that your teams need, you have a lot of customizing to do when dealing with a new SharePoint site.

In this Part of Tens chapter, I offer some concrete suggestions (backed up with chapter references) for tailoring a new SharePoint site to your teams' needs. This ten-part customization covers everything from tweaking the look and feel of the site to adding the SharePoint components that make team collaboration and communication possible.

Tailoring the SharePoint Site for Your Teams

The first thing you probably want to do to your new SharePoint site is to either remove the standard Windows SharePoint Services logo that graces the top of the Right Web Part zone on the home page of the site (as well as every subsite that you create based on the Team Site template) or replace it with your company's logo:

> ✔ **To remove the SharePoint Services logo:** Choose Edit Page from the Site Actions drop-down menu, click the Edit drop-down button on the Site Image Web Part containing the logo, and then choose Delete from the drop-down menu that appears.

> ✔ **To replace the SharePoint Services logo:** Choose Edit Page from the Site Actions drop-down menu, click the Edit drop-down button on the Site Image Web Part containing the logo, and then choose Modify Shared Web Part from the drop-down menu that appears. Then replace the URL for the SharePoint Services logo graphic file in the Image Link text box with the URL to the picture library (see Chapter 5) where your company's logo graphic file has already been uploaded.

In addition to tweaking the SharePoint Services logo on the home page, you may want to do the following tasks:

> ✔ **To change the site's title, description, and/or icon:** Choose Site Settings from the Site Actions drop-down menu and then click the Title, Description, and Icon link in the Look and Feel column. Edit the Title text box and Description list box as needed and enter the URL of the graphic file you want to appear at the top of the site next to the title in the URL text box.

> ✔ **To select a new color scheme:** Choose Site Settings from the Site Actions drop-down menu and then click the Site Theme link in the Look and Feel column. Click the name of the new theme you want to use (using the Preview pane to see how its color scheme looks) and then click the Apply button.

Making a Special Place for Each Team

One way to organize your new SharePoint site is to reserve the top-level site elements for information of a more general nature as well as announcements that pertain to all of the teams who have access to the site. Then create subsites for each of the particular teams (Accounting, Sales, Marketing, HR, and so forth) that contain team-specific elements and information.

To create new subsites for your teams, click the Sites link in the home page Quick Launch on the right and then click the Create button at the top of the All Site Content page. Next, click the Sites and Workspaces link in the Web Pages column. When defining the site on the New SharePoint Site page (by designating the name, description, URL, template, permissions, and navigation for the site), be sure to select the Team Site template if you want the new subsite to have Web Part zones similar to those on the home page.

Supplying Your Teams with the Documents They Need

Remember that SharePoint libraries provide the places where you make available the documents that your teams need in order to collaborate with one another. SharePoint supports three standard types of libraries where you can upload particular types of documents for general distribution to your teams:

- ✔ **Document library:** Use this type of library to store all the types of documents (other than graphic files and electronic forms) that your teams need to access. (See Chapter 5.)

- ✔ **Picture library:** Use this type of library to store the various graphic images your teams need to access. (See Chapter 5.)

- ✔ **Form library:** Use this type of library to store the various forms that your teams need to fill out as part of their collaboration. (See Chapter 14.)

Using Announcements and the Calendar to Keep on Top of Updates and Events

The Announcements list and the Calendar are the two SharePoint lists you can rely on to keep your team members informed of important changes that occur during the course of a project. They also keep everyone informed about upcoming events. (See Chapter 4.)

The Announcements list gives you a quick-and-easy way to call attention to recent additions and other changes made to the SharePoint site and to updates on the scope and duration of the collaborative project. It also helps you to rally your teams and give them the encouragement and support they need.

The Calendar provides you with an easy way to remind team members of important events in the life of the collaboration. These events can include project milestones and deadlines along with the inevitable team meetings and other more social get-togethers that are scheduled during the period of the collaboration.

Organizing and Managing Team Meetings

Formal team meetings, both physical and virtual, are the lifeblood of successful collaboration. To help you schedule and manage these meetings, I encourage you to take full advantage of your SharePoint site's meeting workspaces. (See Chapter 6.)

SharePoint 2007 makes it easy to create a meeting workspace using any one of the following three methods:

- ✔ **From scratch in SharePoint:** Using this method, you create the meeting workspace just as you would any other subsite, except for the fact that you select one of the templates on the Meetings tab of the Select a Template list box instead of one of the Site templates on the Collaboration tab.

- ✔ **From a SharePoint Calendar list:** With this method, you add a new item to the Calendar list using the New Item option from the New menu. Then, when defining the new item, be sure to select the check box labeled Use a Meeting Workspace to Organize Attendees, Agendas, Documents, Minutes, and Other Details for This Event.

- ✔ **From an Outlook 2007 meeting request:** Using this method, you fill out a new meeting request in the Calendar module of Outlook 2007 and then use the Meeting Workspace button on the Ribbon to open the Meeting Workspace pane, where you set up the workspace on the SharePoint site.

Enabling Collaborative Editing with Document Workspaces

Sometimes, the documents you make available on your SharePoint site aren't there as supporting materials for the purpose of informing and supporting your team members but rather as works-in-progress that require team member input and editing. When this is the case, instead of uploading the documents to standard document libraries, you send them to document workspaces.

A SharePoint document workspace is specifically designed to enable collaborative editing by all the team members to whom you grant access (with the appropriate permissions). Then, after you've had the opportunity to review and approve the collaborative edits, you can move the final version of the document from the document workspace to the appropriate document library for general distribution on the SharePoint site. (See Chapter 9 for details.)

Getting Feedback from Teams with Discussion Boards and Surveys

Getting timely feedback from the members of your various teams is often an essential ingredient in accomplishing collaborative projects. SharePoint facilitates this feedback process through two different components (both of which are covered in Chapter 7):

- **Surveys:** Surveys enable you to poll your team members and publicize and statistically analyze their responses. You can use surveys to get concrete feedback on any of the issues that arise as part of your collaborative process.

- **Discussion boards:** Threaded discussions enable you to provide forums for your team members to give their opinions and exchange ideas about topics that are of vital interest to the team. Through the discussion boards, you can touch upon their collaborative endeavors.

Facilitating the Exchange of Ideas with Wiki Pages and Blogs

A large part of successful team collaboration comes from the open and free exchange of ideas. SharePoint facilitates this exchange among team members in two forms (both of which are covered in detail in Chapter 8):

- **Wiki pages:** This special type of library enables the members of your teams to edit the library's content and layout and to easily link to other pages both on and off the SharePoint site.

- **Blogs:** This special type of SharePoint subsite enables you and your other team members to post responses to original comments whose general topics can be separated by category.

Assigning and Managing the Tasks Teams Need to Get Done

Monitoring the tasks that each of your teams and individual members need to complete as part of the collaboration is made easier in SharePoint with the use of its different types of task lists (all covered in Chapter 10):

- ✓ **Tasks lists:** Enables you to keep track of all the tasks that you assign various team members, including their current status, priority, and due date.

- ✓ **Project Tasks lists:** Enables you to keep track of all the tasks that you assign various team members using a Gantt chart display that graphically depicts how the assigned tasks overlap and interrelate.

- ✓ **Issue Tracking lists:** Enables you to keep track of any issues that arise and need to be resolved during the course of the collaboration.

Automating Standard Business Processes with Workflows

Workflows help automate standard business processes that your company routinely follows in completing the tasks that are part of the collaborative project. By using workflows, you automate the responses that are made when assigned tasks enter different phases, thus relieving yourself of the necessity of having to manually monitor the task from start to finish in order to stay on top of it.

If you're using only Windows SharePoint Services, you're restricted to a single three-state workflow template that tracks your business process through three distinct phases that correspond to the Active, Resolved, and Complete phases of a typical Issue Tracking list. (See Chapter 10.) If you're using MOSS 2007, you have a few more choices of document-related workflow templates.

However, if you have access to Office SharePoint Designer 2007, you can use its Workflow Designer to create as many custom workflow templates for your SharePoint site as you could ever possibly need. (See Chapter 13 for details.)

Chapter 16

The Top Ten Challenges to Successful Teamwork

In This Chapter

▶ Understanding the key characteristics of successful teams

▶ Keeping your teams motivated and on track

▶ Giving your teams what they need to collaborate successfully

SharePoint services themselves can do only so much to ensure a successful collaboration. Successful collaboration also relies upon your ability to put together winning teams and support them throughout the entire collaborative project. In this chapter, I give my top ten secrets for creating teams that work well together, along with my tips for reinforcing their success and encouraging and sustaining their continued cooperation.

Unambiguous Team Responsibilities

Teams need to clearly understand their responsibilities in order to have any chance of achieving the goals of the collaboration.

To accomplish this, you need to make sure that each and every team member knows what you expect of him. Bear in mind that it can also be quite helpful for each team and team member to clearly comprehend the purpose of the collaboration and the reasons for working together.

You may be able to do this by communicating the overall goal of the project as well as the intermediary objectives that you've set for the teams (perhaps initially using the Announcements list on the SharePoint site). Of course, you can also do this later in Tasks lists that clearly spell out the steps that each team member needs to take in order to achieve the objectives and reach your goal.

Effective Team Leadership

Behind every successful team there needs to stand an effective team leader.

The key to being an effective team leader depends much more on your ability to reach out and be there for each of your teams than on any particular skill set that you bring to the collaborative project. Keep in mind that your openness to new ideas and your willingness to find out the answers to questions that you don't immediately know can go a long way towards building rapport with the team.

Another way to establish this rapport and also show your support for your teams may be to get the teams together and take the time to introduce them to the SharePoint site they'll be using. This offers a good opportunity for you to discuss both the rationale for using SharePoint technologies as a collaborative tool and the benefits that you believe it can deliver. This is also an opportunity to express and discuss any reservations that the teams may have over using this technology (especially if the teams have never used SharePoint before or have had less than stellar experiences with collaborating on previous SharePoint sites).

By airing your hopes for using SharePoint technologies in your collaboration and relieving any qualms that your teams may have about it, you get a chance to set some of your expectations for the project in the context of demonstrating your level of support for your teams.

Easily Accessible Information

Teams have to have easy access to the information they need to make decisions and get their work done.

However, information is not just data. Data is just lots of facts and figures coming at you that all too often become a kind of din that you tend to shut out. To convert raw data into useful information, you often need to filter it, and you almost always have to organize it so that your teams can readily find it.

Fortunately, SharePoint's many lists and libraries and their ability to filter out unwanted data can go a long way in helping you transform raw data into the type of information that your teams can quickly put their fingers on and readily use in their collaboration.

Universal Team Participation

A team is only as strong as its weakest member.

Each member of every team needs to buy into the goals and objectives of the collaboration. For team members to buy into the project, each team member not only needs to understand his responsibilities but also know that his voice is being heard and his contributions appreciated.

Keep in mind that every member of the team brings to it a different point of view along with his unique skill set. Harmonizing these different perspectives and harnessing these different ways of working are the preeminent challenges of teamwork. Failure to bring about this type of concord can result in team members who give up on the team and slack off in their teamwork. This, in turn, can negatively impact the morale of the group and threaten its ability to bring the collaboration to a successful conclusion.

Competent Communication

You're never going to respond to a message you never receive.

To be successful in collaboration, team members have to communicate with one another. However, this communication has to be effective, and in order for it to be effective in today's business environment, it has to remain timely.

The first steps in terms of maintaining competent communication in a SharePoint collaboration is to use its e-mail messaging abilities and automated alerts to keep your fellow team members informed of changes, especially those that require some type of timely response on their part.

Timely Team Feedback

You can't begin to deal with issues until someone tells you that they exist.

One of the most challenging aspects of collaboration is being able to listen to the teams' concerns and learn from their experiences (both good and bad) as a group. One of the best ways to do this is by eliciting feedback from your teams during the course of the collaborative project.

SharePoint makes this easy to do through the use of its surveys and discussion boards. You can use surveys to poll your teams' opinions on any issues that arise in the course of the collaboration. You can use discussion boards to encourage your teams' members to air their concerns and share their feelings, and to learn about their group experiences.

Straightforward Issue Resolution

Issues always come up when people work closely together — it's how they're resolved that counts.

How well you're able to resolve the issues that arise during the course of completing a collaborative project may determine whether you can complete the project within budget and on time. Even when your project isn't so big and resource intensive that it requires the use of special project management software, you still need to account for the way that issues are tracked and resolved.

In SharePoint, you can make liberal use of its Issue Tracking lists to enable efficient issue tracking and ensure straightforward and timely resolution. These lists, especially when combined with SharePoint workflows, can keep you on top of the project-related issues that need to be decided, while at the same time helping your teams stay on track in bringing them to closure.

Resourceful Idea Sharing

The open give and take of ideas is often what sparks real creativity in the group.

Fresh ideas are the mainstay of successful collaborative enterprises. The old ways all too often don't stand up in the face of the new, accelerated ways of doing business. Successful collaborations promote creative problem solving by all the teams involved. In turn, creative problem solving hinges upon the open sharing of ideas. Brainstorming with your teams for new ideas and original approaches to the challenges presented by the collaborative project not only promote effective solutions but also advance team cohesiveness, making it easier to later achieve consensus when it's needed.

SharePoint helps make resourceful idea sharing possible through the use of its blogs and wikis. You can use blogs to encourage the give and take of new ideas and tactics through a series of categorized messages and responses that your teams post. You can use Wiki pages to encourage team members to respond directly to the contributions made by their fellow team members.

Sound Task Management

Tasks that don't get assigned in a timely manner don't have any chance of getting done by their due dates.

Unfortunately, things just don't get done all by themselves. Someone has to be there to assign the essential tasks to particular teams as well as monitor the teams' progress in completing them and chart when they're actually completed. In other words, it's not sufficient to simply divvy out the tasks that have to get done. You also have to stay on top of their status in order to know whether they have any chance of being completed on time.

SharePoint makes this enormous responsibility a great deal more manageable through the use of its Tasks and Project Tasks lists. You can use these lists to both assign the tasks as well as keep a watchful eye on their status.

Measuring Success

You can't measure the success of a collaboration if you can't measure your teams' performance.

When your collaboration concludes, do you have any way of measuring its success or failure? If you come up with a way of measuring your teams' performance over the course of the project, you can, at least, use that as a partial gauge of the collaboration's relative success.

Fortunately, SharePoint's Tasks lists enable you to keep track of your teams' performance on tasks. You can then export the data in such Tasks lists to a program such as Microsoft Excel and use its analytical capabilities to get the statistics you need in order to judge the areas where your teams performed like champs as well as pinpoint those areas where they could stand some improvement on the next collaboration.

Glossary

SharePoint Technical Jargon

SharePoint is great, but it does have its share (I think you get the point) of technical jargon that can be a bit off-putting when you first start to work with it. To help you get your bearings, I've assembled this list of SharePoint technical terms that you're bound to come in contact with as you and your teams start using it to collaborate.

alerts: E-mails you can have SharePoint automatically send you and your other team members who use a particular list or library on the site whenever any of its contents change. You can set up alerts so that SharePoint sends messages only when you make additions or deletions or when anyone changes the contents.

All Site Content list: The list that's displayed when you click the View All Site Content link above a site's Quick Launch area. This list shows all of the items added to the subsite, arranged by the category of the components (Document Libraries, Lists, and so forth). Note that you can have SharePoint display a filtered version of this list by clicking the name of a category (Documents, Lists, and so on) in the site's Quick Launch. *See also* Quick Launch and subsites.

ASP.NET 2.0: Microsoft's Net Pages framework (originally called Active Server Pages, thus the ASP acronym) that renders the contents of your SharePoint site in your Web browser. *See also* master page.

authenticated users: SharePoint site users who have been assigned both a username and password that enable them to access the SharePoint site. You can grant different site- and component-level permissions only to those users who are authenticated to use your SharePoint site.

blog page: SharePoint 3.0 includes special templates for blog (Web log) sites that enable you to publish an online journal as a series of posts to which your fellow team members can comment. You can also use blogs in combination with RSS feeds as a one-way communication tool that keeps your team members informed on topics of interest by automatically delivering to them any new posts that you make to the blog. *See also* RSS feeds.

Content Navigation Breadcrumbs: The sequence of links that appears immediately above the name of a SharePoint page that shows the links you followed in displaying the current page. You can use Content Navigation Breadcrumbs to move up a level or return to the home page of the SharePoint site. *See also* home page, subsites, and top-level site.

content type: A special template that SharePoint lets you create for the various lists, libraries, and other subsites you maintain on your SharePoint site. After creating a content type for a particular SharePoint component, such as a list, library, or subsite, you can then attach it to a new component of the same type. This enables you and your team members to create pages following the template by simply selecting its option from the component's New drop-down menu.

Datasheet view: A view of a standard list of data in a spreadsheet-like format that is designed for quick editing, sorting, and filtering. In a standard view, a SharePoint list displays the data in columns and rows, with a row of column headings at the top without any borders. In a Datasheet view, SharePoint adds drop-down buttons to the column headings (for sorting and filtering the data) and borders between the columns and rows that create a system of cells that you can select for copying and pasting data. *See also* filters.

discussion board: A basic component of a SharePoint site that enables you to set up a forum for online discussions in which you and your team members can post questions and comments as well as respond and reply to them. When you start a new SharePoint site, its Team Site template includes a blank discussion board called Team Discussion. You can use this default discussion board as well as add other discussion boards as needed.

document library: The general term for a basic component of a SharePoint site that enables you to store copies of the various documents that your teams need during the course of their collaboration. In SharePoint 2007, you have a choice between four different types of libraries: document library for storing standard documents with text and data; form library for storing forms based on templates created with Microsoft Office InfoPath 2007; Wiki page library for storing primarily HTML documents that teams can interactively edit; and picture library for storing graphic files and photo images. *See also* InfoPath 2007 and Wiki page library.

document workspace: A basic component of a SharePoint site that enables you and your team members to collaboratively work on a document that requires input and edits from different team members' sources before you approve the final version and move it to a more permanent document library.

filters: Controls that enable you to separate the data that you don't currently want displayed from the data that you do want displayed in a particular SharePoint list. Filters in SharePoint occur in two forms: list views that filter out all but a particular set of data and AutoFilter buttons that carry out the same task in the Datasheet view of a list. *See also* datasheet view and view.

groups: SharePoint enables you to assign authenticated users to various user groups, such as Members, Visitors, Owners, and the like, each of which would have its own set of site permissions. *See also* authenticated users and permissions.

home page: This is the initial SharePoint Web page that your Web browser renders when you enter the site's URL into the browser's address bar. This page is given the filename default.aspx and it is the master page that uses the Team Site template that determines the look and feel of all the other pages on the site. The home page also forms the apex of the top level of your site, from which all other subsites that you add hang. *See also* master page, subsites, and top-level site.

InfoPath 2007: Part of Microsoft Office 2007, this auxiliary application enables you to customize electronic forms for use on your SharePoint site. Tight integration between InfoPath 2007 and SharePoint enables you to create form libraries and form content types for your SharePoint site from within InfoPath 2007.

links: A basic navigation control for Web pages. Since SharePoint is Web-based, it makes extensive use of links. As with standard Web pages, links attached to text on a SharePoint site appear underlined. (However, on SharePoint pages, the underlining, as a rule, does not appear until you position your mouse pointer over some portion of the text.) When you click a link on a SharePoint site, the program normally jumps you to a new page on the site.

lists: The most basic component of a SharePoint site that typically displays the data it tracks in some sort of tabular format. Almost everything that's not a navigation control on a SharePoint page is some sort of list. Although some SharePoint lists (the Calendar and Project Tasks list, in particular) depict their data in a more graphical display by default, all SharePoint lists can take on views that present their data items in some sort of table.

master page: A special ASP.NET 2.0 Web page that provides the SharePoint site with its consistent look and feel and a set of navigation controls that you and your team members can use to jump from site to site. *See also* ASP. NET 2.0.

meeting workspace: A basic component of a SharePoint site designed specifically to track and manage various types of physical and virtual meetings that you have with your teams over the course of the collaboration. Note that while meeting workspaces enable you to manage meetings, they don't include any type of Web conferencing software that you can use to connect with other team members so you can conduct the meeting online.

Microsoft Office SharePoint Server 2007: SharePoint Server 2007 (also known as MOSS 2007) is built on top of the basic Windows SharePoint Services 3.0, extending its functionality considerably. Specifically, MOSS 2007 provides additional capabilities in the following six areas: Collaboration, Portal, Enterprise Search, Enterprise Content Management, Business Process and Forms, and Business Intelligence. *See also* Windows SharePoint Services 3.0.

Office SharePoint Designer 2007: The modern successor to Microsoft's FrontPage Web design software created specifically for working with SharePoint sites, this auxiliary application enables you to customize the master pages of your SharePoint site. More importantly to some, this stand-alone program contains a remarkable Workflow Designer Wizard that enables you to create custom workflows for your SharePoint site without you having to write a single line of code. *See also* workflows.

permissions: The settings that you grant to particular authenticated SharePoint site users or to user groups that determine which sites they can view and what content they can edit. *See also* authenticated users and groups.

Quick Launch: The area in the left-hand pane of many SharePoint subsites that contains a bunch of links that you can click to jump to particular components within that subsite. Links in a site's Quick Launch are divided into different categories, such as Surveys, Pictures, Documents, Lists, Discussions, Sites, and People and Groups. Note that each of these category items contains its own link that you can click to display the All Site Content page filtered to display only the items in that category. *See also* All Site Content list.

RSS feeds: Standing for Real Simple Syndication feeds, RSS feeds enable application programs such as Outlook 2007 and browsers such as Mozilla Firefox (designated as RSS readers) to subscribe to particular SharePoint sites and lists (especially those such as discussion boards, blogs, and wikis that get frequent updates) and then deliver to you the updated content. *See also* blog page, discussion board, and Wiki page library.

site collection: The entire SharePoint site, including its top-level site and its child sites (also known as subsites) and all the various types of lists and libraries that you add to them. *See also* subsites and top-level site.

site tabs: Whenever you add a new subsite to your SharePoint site, the program by default adds a site tab as a navigation control to the Top Link bar that you can then click to display the site's page. *See also* Top Link bar.

subsites: Also known as *child sites,* subsites refer to all the sites within the SharePoint site collection that you add to the preexisting top-level site. In the site collection's hierarchy, all subsites are directly beneath the top-level, parent site. *See also* site collection and top-level site.

team site: The site created from the default Team Site template that determines and formats the elements on the SharePoint site's home page as well as all subsites that you add (unless you select another site template). Team sites come with a document library, discussion board, and various types of data lists. They also contain a Quick Launch area for quick access to those elements not on the main page. *See also* discussion board, document library, lists, and Quick Launch.

Top Link bar: A bar containing the site tabs, it appears immediately beneath the name of the current SharePoint Web page. The Top Link bar provides you with controls for jumping directly to the main page of any subsite you add to the SharePoint site, whereas the Quick Launch provides you with controls for accessing individual components such as document libraries, lists, and discussion boards that you add to a particular subsite. *See also* Quick Launch.

top-level site: Also known as the *parent site,* the top-level site is the main site or collection with no site above it that appears when you open the SharePoint site's home page. All the sites that you add from the top-level, parent site become its subsites or child sites. *See also* subsites.

versioning: The process by which SharePoint keeps track of each updated version you save of a particular document that you place in a SharePoint document library or document workspace. By turning on versioning, you ensure that you have a history of the different edited versions of a document and can refer to and use an earlier version if the need arises.

view: Each SharePoint list and library that you add (including surveys, calendars, discussion boards, and the like) has its own default view that determines how its data are displayed. In most of these components, you can switch to another predefined view, customize the current view, or create a custom view of your own. The view can determine not only how the data are displayed, but also which data are displayed.

Web Part: The basic building blocks of a Web Part page, Web Parts are reusable blocks of information that enable you to display different data sets in various ways throughout your SharePoint site. When you first start work on a new SharePoint site, the program comes with a number of different types of Web Parts that you can choose from. As you create your own lists, libraries, and other SharePoint components, SharePoint creates special Web Parts for each that enable you to redisplay their data in new ways using different views. *See also* view, Web Part page, and Web Part zone.

Web Part page: A special type of Web Part–enabled Web page that already has Left and Right Web Part page zones defined for it that you can then use to add the Web Parts you need. *See also* Web Part and Web Part zone.

Web Part zone: Refers to the areas defined on a Web Part page into which you can add and move the Web Parts you add to the page. These zones determine the width of the Web Parts (and therefore how many columns of data can be displayed from their lists) and are only visible when you put the Web Part page into Edit mode. *See also* Web Part and Web Part page.

Wiki page library: A special type of SharePoint library that enables you and your team members to easily edit the content and layout of their pages as well as create links to other pages in the library, providing a convenient way for the team to share information and ideas as well as to collaborate directly on designs.

Windows SharePoint Services 3.0: The latest version of Windows SharePoint Services, the software part of Microsoft Windows Server 2003 and 2008 that provides you with all the various elements and components for collaborating and sharing information with your team members. *See also* Microsoft Office SharePoint Server 2007.

workflows: Automated parts of business processes routinely followed in approving or reviewing such things as document edits or issue resolution. Note that if you use Microsoft Office SharePoint Designer 2007, you can supplement the workflow templates supplied with your version of SharePoint with workflows of your own design. *See also* Office SharePoint Designer 2007.

Index

• *B* •

• *C* •

Notes

BUSINESS, CAREERS & PERSONAL FINANCE

Accounting For Dummies, 4th Edition*
978-0-470-24600-9

Bookkeeping Workbook For Dummies†
978-0-470-16983-4

Commodities For Dummies
978-0-470-04928-0

Doing Business in China For Dummies
978-0-470-04929-7

E-Mail Marketing For Dummies
978-0-470-19087-6

Job Interviews For Dummies, 3rd Edition*†
978-0-470-17748-8

Personal Finance Workbook For Dummies*†
978-0-470-09933-9

Real Estate License Exams For Dummies
978-0-7645-7623-2

Six Sigma For Dummies
978-0-7645-6798-8

Small Business Kit For Dummies, 2nd Edition*†
978-0-7645-5984-6

Telephone Sales For Dummies
978-0-470-16836-3

BUSINESS PRODUCTIVITY & MICROSOFT OFFICE

Access 2007 For Dummies
978-0-470-03649-5

Excel 2007 For Dummies
978-0-470-03737-9

Office 2007 For Dummies
978-0-470-00923-9

Outlook 2007 For Dummies
978-0-470-03830-7

PowerPoint 2007 For Dummies
978-0-470-04059-1

Project 2007 For Dummies
978-0-470-03651-8

QuickBooks 2008 For Dummies
978-0-470-18470-7

Quicken 2008 For Dummies
978-0-470-17473-9

Salesforce.com For Dummies, 2nd Edition
978-0-470-04893-1

Word 2007 For Dummies
978-0-470-03658-7

EDUCATION, HISTORY, REFERENCE & TEST PREPARATION

African American History For Dummies
978-0-7645-5469-8

Algebra For Dummies
978-0-7645-5325-7

Algebra Workbook For Dummies
978-0-7645-8467-1

Art History For Dummies
978-0-470-09910-0

ASVAB For Dummies, 2nd Edition
978-0-470-10671-6

British Military History For Dummies
978-0-470-03213-8

Calculus For Dummies
978-0-7645-2498-1

Canadian History For Dummies, 2nd Edition
978-0-470-83656-9

Geometry Workbook For Dummies
978-0-471-79940-5

The SAT I For Dummies, 6th Edition
978-0-7645-7193-0

Series 7 Exam For Dummies
978-0-470-09932-2

World History For Dummies
978-0-7645-5242-7

FOOD, GARDEN, HOBBIES & HOME

Bridge For Dummies, 2nd Edition
978-0-471-92426-5

Coin Collecting For Dummies, 2nd Edition
978-0-470-22275-1

Cooking Basics For Dummies, 3rd Edition
978-0-7645-7206-7

Drawing For Dummies
978-0-7645-5476-6

Etiquette For Dummies, 2nd Edition
978-0-470-10672-3

Gardening Basics For Dummies*†
978-0-470-03749-2

Knitting Patterns For Dummies
978-0-470-04556-5

Living Gluten-Free For Dummies†
978-0-471-77383-2

Painting Do-It-Yourself For Dummies
978-0-470-17533-0

HEALTH, SELF HELP, PARENTING & PETS

Anger Management For Dummies
978-0-470-03715-7

Anxiety & Depression Workbook For Dummies
978-0-7645-9793-0

Dieting For Dummies, 2nd Edition
978-0-7645-4149-0

Dog Training For Dummies, 2nd Edition
978-0-7645-8418-3

Horseback Riding For Dummies
978-0-470-09719-9

Infertility For Dummies†
978-0-470-11518-3

Meditation For Dummies with CD-ROM, 2nd Edition
978-0-471-77774-8

Post-Traumatic Stress Disorder For Dummies
978-0-470-04922-8

Puppies For Dummies, 2nd Edition
978-0-470-03717-1

Thyroid For Dummies, 2nd Edition†
978-0-471-78755-6

Type 1 Diabetes For Dummies*†
978-0-470-17811-9

* Separate Canadian edition also available
† Separate U.K. edition also available

Available wherever books are sold. For more information or to order direct: U.S. customers visit www.dummies.com or call 1-877-762-2974.
U.K. customers visit www.wileyeurope.com or call (0)1243 843291. Canadian customers visit www.wiley.ca or call 1-800-567-4797.

 **WILEY**

INTERNET & DIGITAL MEDIA

AdWords For Dummies
978-0-470-15252-2

Blogging For Dummies, 2nd Edition
978-0-470-23017-6

Digital Photography All-in-One Desk Reference For Dummies, 3rd Edition
978-0-470-03743-0

Digital Photography For Dummies, 5th Edition
978-0-7645-9802-9

Digital SLR Cameras & Photography For Dummies, 2nd Edition
978-0-470-14927-0

eBay Business All-in-One Desk Reference For Dummies
978-0-7645-8438-1

eBay For Dummies, 5th Edition*
978-0-470-04529-9

eBay Listings That Sell For Dummies
978-0-471-78912-3

Facebook For Dummies
978-0-470-26273-3

The Internet For Dummies, 11th Edition
978-0-470-12174-0

Investing Online For Dummies, 5th Edition
978-0-7645-8456-5

iPod & iTunes For Dummies, 5th Edition
978-0-470-17474-6

MySpace For Dummies
978-0-470-09529-4

Podcasting For Dummies
978-0-471-74898-4

Search Engine Optimization For Dummies, 2nd Edition
978-0-471-97998-2

Second Life For Dummies
978-0-470-18025-9

Starting an eBay Business For Dummies 3rd Edition†
978-0-470-14924-9

GRAPHICS, DESIGN & WEB DEVELOPMENT

Adobe Creative Suite 3 Design Premium All-in-One Desk Reference For Dummies
978-0-470-11724-8

Adobe Web Suite CS3 All-in-One Desk Reference For Dummies
978-0-470-12099-6

AutoCAD 2008 For Dummies
978-0-470-11650-0

Building a Web Site For Dummies, 3rd Edition
978-0-470-14928-7

Creating Web Pages All-in-One Desk Reference For Dummies, 3rd Edition
978-0-470-09629-1

Creating Web Pages For Dummies, 8th Edition
978-0-470-08030-6

Dreamweaver CS3 For Dummies
978-0-470-11490-2

Flash CS3 For Dummies
978-0-470-12100-9

Google SketchUp For Dummies
978-0-470-13744-4

InDesign CS3 For Dummies
978-0-470-11865-8

Photoshop CS3 All-in-One Desk Reference For Dummies
978-0-470-11195-6

Photoshop CS3 For Dummies
978-0-470-11193-2

Photoshop Elements 5 For Dummies
978-0-470-09810-3

SolidWorks For Dummies
978-0-7645-9555-4

Visio 2007 For Dummies
978-0-470-08983-5

Web Design For Dummies, 2nd Edition
978-0-471-78117-2

Web Sites Do-It-Yourself For Dummies
978-0-470-16903-2

Web Stores Do-It-Yourself For Dummies
978-0-470-17443-2

LANGUAGES, RELIGION & SPIRITUALITY

Arabic For Dummies
978-0-471-77270-5

Chinese For Dummies, Audio Set
978-0-470-12766-7

French For Dummies
978-0-7645-5193-2

German For Dummies
978-0-7645-5195-6

Hebrew For Dummies
978-0-7645-5489-6

Ingles Para Dummies
978-0-7645-5427-8

Italian For Dummies, Audio Set
978-0-470-09586-7

Italian Verbs For Dummies
978-0-471-77389-4

Japanese For Dummies
978-0-7645-5429-2

Latin For Dummies
978-0-7645-5431-5

Portuguese For Dummies
978-0-471-78738-9

Russian For Dummies
978-0-471-78001-4

Spanish Phrases For Dummies
978-0-7645-7204-3

Spanish For Dummies
978-0-7645-5194-9

Spanish For Dummies, Audio Set
978-0-470-09585-0

The Bible For Dummies
978-0-7645-5296-0

Catholicism For Dummies
978-0-7645-5391-2

The Historical Jesus For Dummies
978-0-470-16785-4

Islam For Dummies
978-0-7645-5503-9

Spirituality For Dummies, 2nd Edition
978-0-470-19142-2

NETWORKING AND PROGRAMMING

ASP.NET 3.5 For Dummies
978-0-470-19592-5

C# 2008 For Dummies
978-0-470-19109-5

Hacking For Dummies, 2nd Edition
978-0-470-05235-8

Home Networking For Dummies, 4th Edition
978-0-470-11806-1

Java For Dummies, 4th Edition
978-0-470-08716-9

Microsoft® SQL Server™ 2008 All-in-One Desk Reference For Dummies
978-0-470-17954-3

Networking All-in-One Desk Reference For Dummies, 2nd Edition
978-0-7645-9939-2

Networking For Dummies, 8th Edition
978-0-470-05620-2

SharePoint 2007 For Dummies
978-0-470-09941-4

Wireless Home Networking For Dummies, 2nd Edition
978-0-471-74940-0